ZACK MORRIS LIED 329 TIMES!

Reassessing every ridiculous episode of "Saved by the Bell" ... with stats

MATT PAIS

ISBN 978-1-7352504-0-3 (paperback)

ISBN 978-1-7352504-1-0 (ebook)

Cover design: Trent J. Koland

For my family

Table of Contents

Preface

Approach 100 people on the street and sing, "I'm so excited! I'm so excited!" The vast majority won't respond "About what?" or "Sweet, another Pointer Sisters fan!" They're going to do their best, caffeine pill-addicted Jessie Spano impression and cry, "I'm … so … scared!"

That episode ("Jessie's Song") is obviously a classic. Yet I bet you could make reference to Lisa Turtle dancing "The Sprain" or Zack Attack's chart-topping "Did We Ever Have a Chance?" and inspire a burst of recognition and nostalgia. "Saved by the Bell" has had an undeniably long echo despite the NBC Saturday morning teen sitcom ending more than 25 years ago. Mark-Paul Gosselaar stars in a new show and interviewers really just want to ask him about Zack Morris. Mario Lopez guests on "Brooklyn Nine-Nine" and Jake Peralta (Andy Samberg) addresses him as A.C. Slater. John Mulaney references a specific behavior by a minor "Saved by the Bell" character in his special "The Comeback Kid" and trusts that his audience remembers bad-influence actor Johnny Dakota. A pop-up restaurant modeled after The Max is one of the most difficult reservations to secure for months in Chicago.

And Jimmy Fallon doesn't do reunion shows with just *anyone.*

On a more personal level, to name only one example, I'm very aware of how the episode ("Drinking and Driving") in which the gang had one beer and felt horrible the next morning (temporarily) impacted my perception of drinking. The stuff you watch as a kid has that effect, and I know a lot of people who grew up in the '80s and '90s who feel just as strong of a connection to the show. At one point early in my 11 years as movie critic/music editor for the Chicago Tribune's RedEye, my editor told me to stop referencing "Saved by the Bell" so often. I did for a while, but not entirely.

When I thought about doing this project, I was shocked to find no books encapsulating the full run of the series (including the junior high season when it was originally called "Good Morning, Miss Bliss" as well as "The College Years," but not "The New Class" for obvious reasons). I previously had read Chuck Klosterman on "The Tori Paradox" and seen some of Funny or Die's "Zack Morris is Trash" series, and also found Vulture's ranking of all the episodes and a podcast. But that was it.

So I dove back in, starting when Zack, Lisa (Lark Voorhies), Samuel "Screech" Powers (Dustin Diamond) and Principal Richard "Mr." Belding (Dennis Haskins) lived in Indiana and went all the way to when Zack, Slater, Screech and Kelly Kapowski (Tiffani-Amber Thiessen) attended CalU and almost never spoke of their friends (including Elizabeth Berkley as Jessie) who weren't on the show anymore. (The two SBTB movies, "Hawaiian Style" and "Wedding in Las Vegas," are not part of the series' half-hour format but were included here.) The point wasn't just to revisit something I watched faithfully as a kid, and it wasn't that no one had realized that the show was silly or that its lead character was, well, trash in how he treated other people. I'm not sure anyone who loves "Saved by the Bell," myself included, actually would claim that it's good.

But I wanted to attach some numbers to the show that would help gauge how the characters did or didn't change as they got older. Beyond Zack clearly being a bad friend who the others maybe should have ditched early in the series, I wanted to go deeper: Did the self-involved king of the fourth-wall-breaking timeout ever learn anything or show even a little growth? Did he deserve what he got, for better or worse?

This isn't a thesis, though — the book is presented in numbers and categories that are meant to be fun and skimmable. Pieces of interviews with cast members and others involved with the show are also threaded throughout, and you can find the overall statistical findings and complete interviews (edited and condensed for clarity) at the end. It's all a way to fondly re-experience the show while marveling at its ridiculousness and processing what it was actually saying, whether or not 11-year-old brains had any idea of that at the time. Because some of the episodes and messages are handled really well, and others are, um, not.

Disclaimer: Numbers were tallied as best as possible while rewatching each episode once; it is certainly possible that I missed a lie or a line or something else here and there. While I apologize for anything that is not spot-on, if there's one thing we should all learn from Zack Morris it's that anyone can apologize. Not everyone can show they mean it.

Eighth Grade (1988-1989) aka the Disney Channel's "Good Morning, Miss Bliss" aka "What happened before three friends and their principal moved across the country to the same place at the same time"

A quick reminder about what is now considered Season 1 of "Saved by the Bell": No Kelly, Slater or Jessie. No episodes about going to the beach. Instead, some very muted, late-'80s Midwestern colors and opening credits containing as many educators as students, including Hayley Mills ("The Parent Trap") as titular eighth grade teacher Carrie Bliss, Joan Ryan as Tina Paladrino (a teacher who is Miss Bliss' best friend), and T.K. Carter ("The Thing") as Mylo Williams, a maintenance supervisor whose catchphrase is "The pipes have ears."

As for the kids who were left behind: Max Battimo (who grew up to be a college hockey referee) as Zack's second-in-command Mikey Gonzalez and Heather Hopper (who never again appeared on more than one episode of a show) as Lisa-adjacent Nikki Coleman. Despite growing up with the others, their connections were obviously so superficial that once Zack, Lisa and Screech moved to California they never spoke to or of Mikey and Nikki, who I think we all assume are happily married and living across the street from John F. Kennedy Junior High.

Episode 1: "Summer Love"

Aired November 30, 1988

Plot: Over the summer, Zack and Karen (Carla Gugino, who's had a better career than any of the "Saved by the Bell" stars) went together like rama lama lama ka dinga da dinga dong. When she turns up at school on the first day (her dad was just transferred, ICYMI), Zack's terrified that she will find out he lied about being in the ninth grade like she is and then not be interested anymore. At no point does Karen seem like the kind of person who would care about age that way.

Zack's lies (9):

- He is in ninth grade
- His experimental ninth grade class meets off campus
- He has a driver's license
- His license doesn't work on Wednesdays
- He's in an experimental homeroom with Miss Bliss
- He's only lied about one thing
- It won't happen again
- Pretending to be the paperboy
- When Zack indicates he wants to resign from his role as student council rep, Screech tells Mikey, "He can't resign. We spent too much money buying him votes." One of the odd abilities of "Saved by the Bell" is that it can feature a team of lackeys helping an egotistical and selfish candidate steal an election and make it seem innocent and charming. Hey, that sort of thing can't happen in real life, right?

Worth noting: In these early days, Miss Bliss served as a mentor to the students, with Zack talking to her about his relationship problems and even showing up uninvited to her house while she's on a date. Yet while counseling him on the importance of telling the truth, she lies to her date about who's in the house, causing Zack to have to lie again. Brilliant attempt to meet the kid on his level (no) or bad example (yes)?

Not a therapist, but: Zack's swagger masks his insecurity, causing him to lie to Karen immediately and later fear that being exposed will mean he's no longer desirable. He does know the difference between right and wrong, but his self-esteem is so low that he cannot be genuine and think someone could just want him for him. Even when Bliss says he has to tell the truth, Zack says, "But I like her too much to do that."

Was he awful to women? Yes, obviously. He also backs off on a plan to come clean after Karen tells him her parents will be out of town and they have her pool all to themselves, with "a special bikini I was too shy to wear at the lake." So Zack keeps up the ruse even though he has to know that the pool party and whatever happens there would only make Karen more upset when she finds out the truth.

Does Zack get what he deserves? He does. Karen dumps him not for being too young but for being dishonest, and the show ends before he has a chance to apologize to her or try to get another chance. In theory, it seems like he learned something. In theory.

Episode 2: "Love Letters"

Aired December 7, 1988

Plot: Assuming viewers haven't yet read "Cyrano de Bergerac," Zack agrees to write love letters to Lisa on Screech's behalf as long as his easily manipulated friend will write a paper about the War of 1812 for him. Naturally the letters fall into the wrong hands after Lisa gets them, causing Miss Bliss to think a studly new teacher is behind them, then believing Belding wrote them, until Belding thinks Bliss wrote them. Is it getting hot in here?

Nikki gets it: This plan couldn't be more self-serving — Zack knows Lisa hates Screech (technically the agreement is the paper for a date with Lisa, which Zack knows won't ever happen) but doesn't think anything of playing with her emotions as long as he gets what he wants. Also, when Miss Bliss talks about the war, Nikki observes, "Men. All men. There probably wouldn't be any wars at all if it wasn't for men. *Zack*."

Zack's lies (3):

- Turning in the paper Screech wrote as his own
- Swearing to Miss Bliss that he didn't promise Screech anything in return
- A past lie that Miss Bliss references: when Zack claimed he didn't have his homework done because his grandmother was reading it and she spontaneously combusted

What a guy: Zack's advice to Screech is that "Love is pain" and things are never fair "in matters of the heart." This comes not from a person who, say, learned something from his Karen-related heartbreak but just a guy stringing along his gullible friend until the poor guy writes Zack's paper. In fact, the way the lines are delivered Zack doesn't seem to attach any feeling to the sentiments, using them only as a bargaining chip. Unsettling.

Justice? Well, he gets a zero on the paper, but we don't see any impact on his friendship with Lisa, who ends the episode shrieking when Screech identifies himself as her secret admirer. Kudos to the guy for believing in himself no matter how many times the never-supportive Zack (who Miss Bliss advises, "A cute smile and apologies aren't going to get you through life") told him he had no chance.

A note on Miss Bliss: That's two consecutive episodes to begin the series in which she has had colleagues commenting on her appearance. On the plus side, the show is willing to give a widow in her early 40s a romantic life (even if she dresses like she's in her 80s), and obviously late-'80s norms were different than they are now. Still, it's not as if everyone's going around commenting on Mr. Belding's appearance.

One word, two letters, an honest day's work: Mikey's only line the entire episode? Saying "Yo" to Miss Bliss in the hallway. But what a line reading it was; I really believed that he was telling her "Yo."

Episode 3: "Wall Street"

Aired December 14, 1988

Plot: Because the trusting Miss Bliss has not yet accepted that everything Zack Morris touches turns to disaster, she allows her students to learn about financial management by making their own investment decisions. Before you can say "What self-serving scheme have you cooked up this time, Morris?" Zack has persuaded the class — well, just the people with speaking parts — to shift their investment from an airline to potatoes, which Mylo assures them are the food of the '90s.

Maybe he just wanted everyone to profit together? No. Zack's motivation stems from needing $300 to replace the video camera he broke without his dad knowing Zack was messing with it.

At least it was for a good reason? No, Zack was spying on nearby twin girls who, as Mikey identifies, live two blocks away from Zack. "It's amazing what they've done with zoom lenses," Zack raves. Sadly, this type of predatory leering was comic fodder for the show and the '80s/'90s. Fortunately that's the only example of it, and the career of Adam Sandler does not exist.

I don't want to compare to a certain president but how can you not: Besides for being a manipulative liar who's creepy toward women and constantly messing up, Zack also has very bad business sense and doesn't care at all about losing other people's money. He shrugs off the notion that potato stock plummeting would mean financial hardship for Miss Bliss.

Zack's lies (5):

- Secretly taking the video camera when his dad told him not to
- Hiding the broken camera from his dad
- Manipulating his friends for his own benefit (we'll call that one lie)
- When Miss Bliss asks if Zack knew she'd owe the difference because they bought on margin, he says "Not exactly" even though Mikey told him
- After she says this is "the most dishonest behavior I've ever encountered in 14 years of teaching," Zack again claims he didn't know things he did know

Fortunately, he gets what he deserves: No, he does not. For the lesson to really hit home, we should see how angry his friends are with him and consequences he faces at home from destroying his dad's camera and lying about it. Instead, Miss Bliss apologizes for being too hard on the class (driven by her sadness that the money she owes means she can't get a new car) and again we get the notion of Zack learning a lesson but not demonstrating behavior that reconciles real results with follow-through. Methinks this may not be his last get-rich-quick endeavor.

Ouch: When the students are dreaming about what they'd do with a windfall, Lisa, in an uncharacteristic moment of caring about Screech, asks what he'd do with his share. "I was so busy having fun in your fantasies," he says," I'm too pooped to have one of my own." That is a really sad comment for a kid to make but revealing about the character of Screech as written and also, it seems, how resentful Diamond grew to feel about him over time.

Prescient: In the opening voiceover, Miss Bliss notes, "The computer age is upon us. You can bank, shop, even invest without ever leaving home." She also tells Mr. Belding, "This is a generation raised on video games, computer games and MTV. I have to compete for their attention."

Episode 4: "Leaping to Conclusions"

Aired December 21, 1988

Plot: Because who could turn down a storyline in which an actress named Hopper fights for frog rights, Nikki protests the impending dissection in science class despite none of her friends caring about the issue in the slightest.

Real quick: Under the direction of weirdo science teacher Mr. Morton (who gets off on the smell of freshly stirred Cup of Noodles and is played by someone named Deryl Carroll), the class will be killing live frogs and then dissecting them. What?! Pretty sure that's not how it was when I was in biology. And even if the frogs always arrive live, clearly it's going to send a difficult message if the students know the frogs are still alive but about to be killed for their study.

And on that note: This is a very disturbing episode. Like, jeez. A few sample lines about how the guys — and it is the guys specifically — feel about the project:

Zack: "I've been waiting for this day my whole life."
Mikey: "We're going to slice those frogs to shreds."
Zack: "I was really looking forward to slicing and dicing those little green suckers."
Screech, to Nikki: "On the one hand there's your friendship to consider. On the other hand there's the feel of a nice, cold pancreas against your skin."

If you were a teacher you would, uh, not be thrilled to hear this type of excitement about putting a knife to an animal.

On the subject of debate: At the heart of this episode is a worthwhile moral discussion, but the show weirdly dismisses it by suggesting Nikki should respect other people's opinions and leave it at that, as if nothing is worth fighting for. Even more concerningly, there is an anti-science message that comes through when Miss Bliss says Mr. Morton can't argue with Nikki's appreciation for others' viewpoints and Morton says, "I'm a man of science. I can argue with anything."

Also problematic: For some reason this one aligns the two sides of the frog-killing conversation with talk about the Civil War, which is not exactly the most respectful parallel to draw. It also leads to Mikey saying a ruthless battle between family members "sounds like an ordinary weekend at my house."

(Curls into fetal position): In the subplot about Mr. Belding giving Miss Bliss more supplies than the school can afford because he's worried that she will be poached by another school, that school is *Trumphill* Academy. Are you kidding? Speaking of power corrupting, as soon as Miss Bliss puts Zack in charge of the class, he instantly reports his friends for minor infractions. Though I guess compared to letting all hell break loose, following rules and holding people accountable is progress.

Zack's lies (only 1!):

- (Technically not a lie, but the promotion of dishonesty) While considering the best way to approach a woman, Zack tells Lisa the answer is, "You open your heart and tell them with sincerity the biggest lie you can think of." She says, "That'll work if it's the right lie." Inspiring message!

Episode 5: "Parents and Teachers"

Aired December 28, 1988

Plot: The gang experiences varying levels of fear about what their parents will think during parent-teacher conferences (a good, relatable storyline) and complications arise when Miss Bliss discovers the charming man she met on a weekend rafting trip is actually Zack's dad (not as relatable).

Hello, innuendo: The rules of the rafting outing were no last names, no past, no present. Quite the intimate setting for a singles event which, clearly, also prevents anyone from learning valuable information about each other, such as where they live and if they have kids.

Actual poignancy: Nikki worries her parents won't be satisfied with her only living up to her potential; Lisa doesn't want her parents to learn she wears makeup to school; Screech thinks his parents will think he's "a dud" if they learn he isn't, as he told them, president of the eighth grade, editor of the paper, captain of the baseball team, lead baritone in the glee club and homecoming king. (He is later relieved to discover his parents not only support him but that his dad was also glue monitor.)

On the issue of consent: Miss Bliss feels disappointed and conflicted when finding out who Peter (Robert Pine of "CHIPs" and father of Chris Pine) is but says nothing would have started between them if she had known before. "It's already started," he says, and proceeds to kiss her even as she's saying, "No, no, Peter." That the episode makes numerous points about how Peter lacks boundaries and discipline just like his son makes this all the more troubling.

For what it's worth: Gosselaar is quite good in this episode, capturing Zack's struggles to handle walking in on his dad and teacher kissing. Of course he tries to use this for leverage, but there's genuine feeling in the scene in which he tells her, "I hated [seeing] it! I don't want you to be my father's girlfriend, is that what you want to hear?!" This is a struggling kid who, for a change, you can root for because of what he's dealing with.

Striking line: In voiceover, Miss Bliss wonders, "How do you tell parents their child is best-qualified to be a speed bump?"

Wait, this one: Trying to cheer up Screech, Zack says, "Have you heard at exactly two o'clock today a shower of asteroids is going to level Cleveland?" I know he's kidding and I guess thinks Screech would be amused by that, but that's a curious thing to be perked up by. Woohoo, annihilation!

Zack's lies (0): Whoa!

Getting off easy: It's fair, I suppose, that Zack isn't penalized for cutting class to buy concert tickets (which they then can't buy because the band got the mumps? Was the show happening that night?), but there is never actually a parent-teacher discussion between Miss Bliss and Peter, which seems needed for a kid that is constantly lying and never doing work.

Episode 6: "The Showdown"

Aired January 4, 1989

Plot: A new, instantly feared kid in school allows for yet another Freddy Krueger reference and Screech a chance to prove he's more courageous than anyone knew. Playing leather jacket- and scowl-clad Deke is Andras Jones, who appeared in "A Nightmare on Elm Street 4: The Dream Master" the year before and makes the show's Freddy Krueger joke seem not lazy but cleverly meta.

Credit where credit's due: This is easily the best episode so far in terms of presenting identifiable human behavior. Deke initially strikes terror in the students and several of the educators, what with his "I only answer one question on quizzes" attitude and fourth-place-in-a-Matt-Dillon-look-alike-contest personal style. But once Miss Bliss determines that he can't read, it's clear that Deke's behavior is a defense mechanism, attacking others before they can start bullying him for something he feels embarrassed about, which comes to a head in the scene when Deke tries to goad Screech into mocking him but Screech doesn't, saying that it isn't funny that Deke can't read. That Deke then no longer wants to beat him up and asks Miss Bliss for help is surprisingly moving, as is the teacher's persistence to help her student even as Mr. Belding wants to send him to Siberia. A solid commentary on how hard it can be to do the right thing in education but how important it is for people in positions to help to not give up on kids.

The second-consecutive zero-lie episode for Zack! Well, he does lie to tell Deke that Screech is a master of "Kung Fu, Jiu-jitsu and Mitsubishi," but he does it as a (racist) way of trying to protect his friend, so we'll give him a pass. (It's awful that he's only willing to help after Screech agrees to pay him $10, but, well, he does waive the fee once Deke says learning about Screech's martial arts skills means he won't go easy on him.)

Major conflict everywhere: The episode's subplots involve Lisa and Nikki arguing over a play that Nikki wrote (Lisa wants to wear a gown to play a forest ranger, moving the story to Manhattan) and Mylo not wanting Tina to mess up his stage (which he calls "Woody") by nailing trees into it. Forgettable stuff but also good, everyday disagreements that the characters must work out through compromise.

One more round of applause for Screech: While it's understandable that someone his age would care about appearances, it's more admirable that Screech simply doesn't want to back down from Deke and let this situation go on longer. He's willing to step up and confront the problem. Plus, "The school nurse says I have terrific clotting time."

Mikey is awful: The guy's advice to Screech? "When Deke hits you, fall on a fat kid."

Question for later: In this episode Zack refers to Screech's brother. I thought he was an only child?

*****Interview with Jones:** "I was bullied terribly. So I definitely was channeling guys that I don't particularly like. Maybe that's why those scenes have a little bit more bite because I was definitely Screech a lot more than I was Deke. Sort of between fifth grade and tenth grade ... I know how I approach playing a role, and it's a combination of not judging the character and also totally personalizing it. People think I'm joking when I tell them that my favorite work that I did as an actor on film is that, but maybe that's one of the reasons, too. I always say it's because it was pretty much live and I was working with two phenomenally talented people, in my mind. Most of my scenes are with Screech or with Hayley Mills. I call him Screech – Dustin. But on the set, I just called him Screech. Not 100% method actor-y, but that's just how we played. I think it also could be the schoolyard violence that I faced gave that an extra level of intensity that wouldn't be there for someone that was pretending more." *(Read more from Jones on page 283.)*

Episode 7: "Save the Last Dance for Me"

Aired January 25, 1989

Plot: Needing a place for their feet to get loose, the gang successfully argues that the school policy banning dances (after two guys brawled over a girl at the last one six years ago) shouldn't apply to them. Commence two guys fighting over a girl once again.

This is actually a nice use of the show: Conflicts like this are part of adolescent friendship, and "Save the Last Dance for Me" surprisingly handles it pretty well. Mikey asks Zack for help in asking out a girl but doesn't specify his interest in Shana (Alexondra Lee of "Party of Five"), so Zack asking her out is relatively innocent — aside from his motivation being entirely driven by her mention of a leather miniskirt. That Zack ultimately apologizes when confronted and seems sincere in telling Mikey that losing him as a friend would hurt more than being punched is refreshing.

However: I realize these are 14-year-old boys, but this is still a disturbing exchange:

Zack: "First of all, girls like to be called women. Second of all, when you're talking to them look deep into their eyes. And last and most important, let her know that you think she's awesome."
Mikey: "I can't do this; it isn't me."
Zack: "Hey, it isn't anyone, but it works!"

As if that weren't bad enough, the guys then fondly remember when Mikey stood on Zack's shoulders trying to spy into a girls' slumber party. Because karma is real, they accidentally watched someone's grandma soak her teeth. And because they used the word "watched" and not "saw," that suggests they stayed once they realized what they stumbled onto, which is a different kind of wrong.

Zack's lies (2):

- Advising Mikey to manipulate women with something he doesn't mean counts as a lie
- Telling Mr. Belding he and Mikey were only in the locked bathroom to clean off graffiti

Jeez, great advice: Lisa repeatedly advises Nikki not to accept any invitations to the dance because someone better could come along. She then winds up inviting something like 10 guys to the dance, and this leads to no problems whatsoever. Mandatory reminder that Voorhies later appeared in the Bill Bellamy-starring "How to Be a Player."

Too many subplots: While all this is going on, Miss Bliss and Tina also repeatedly bash a teacher named Sherman (Original Mouseketeer Lonnie Burr), who Miss Bliss is forced to associate herself with because of a Save the Whales benefit. They repeatedly call him a dork, sending another lousy message to young viewers about tolerance and kindness as adults. Though I guess Sherman gets the last laugh when the episode ends with a surprisingly long dance sequence of him busting loose on the dance floor with Miss Bliss.

Yikes there's a lot of sad stuff in this one: Mylo says his eighth-grade dance was the best time he ever had and that "We partied all night!" Great, but "best time ever"?

But funny stuff too: When Mikey walks into the dance, Screech, having a blast as the DJ, cuts the music to maximize the tension between the friends even further. Maybe not the best move as their pal but pretty savvy as the guy reading the room. He also plays a song called "Vaporize My Love" and its flipside, "Love My Vaporizer," which may not look funny on paper but (throws pride off a cliff) the comic timing of teenage Dustin Diamond makes it work.

Episode 8: "The Boy Who Cried Rat"

Aired February 11, 1989

Plot: Contrary to what the title implies, Zack really does persuade Screech (promising a double date with the continually referenced, never-seen Zeffirelli twins) to release his rats in school to delay the midterm history exam. That way Zack will get to go on the ski trip his dad promised him without having to earn it through a good grade, but will it cost Miss Bliss the Indiana Teacher of the Year award she desperately wants?

A lot of this just does not make sense: The school was going to be closed for a week, but as soon as Zack and Screech confess then the school is somehow able to reopen. Also, the doctorate-possessing representative from School Days magazine, Dr. Atwater (Martina Finch), takes her job extremely seriously but scheduled her visit to observe Miss Bliss at the last possible moment before the editors vote for the winner.

Kudos, Miss Bliss: Her "Challenge of the Eighth Grade Stars" activity, which is mostly her dressing up as people like Teddy Roosevelt for a game show as the class is divided into two teams, does look pretty fun. She really shows that Joseph McMillan! (Because obviously she and Mr. Belding are very familiar with the second-best teacher in Indiana.)

Zack's lies (1):

- Telling Miss Bliss that in Sweden students receive grades before the test to ease the pressure

Consequences? Zack and Screech initially receive two weeks of detention but get that cut in half by working to help Miss Bliss win the award. He's able to get the grade he needs and assumedly goes skiing. Overall, his scheme worked.

Oddly enough: The episode's focus is less on penalties for Zack's actions than identifying him as a predator. When Dr. Atwater sits down at a desk next to him, she instantly scoots in the opposite direction. He taps her hand and she flinches, telling him, "Never touch me again." When Zack later tells Nikki he has a way with women, she replies, "Yeah, you have a way to make them sick." Is the show acknowledging how slimy Zack is to women here?

Episode 9: "Let's Get Together"

Aired February 18, 1989

Plot: Cross-referencing their longtime friendship with the fact that she seems to hate him for good reason, Nikki and Zack must work together on a project to convince Miss Bliss to buy one of several iconic 19th century American inventions (they're assigned the telephone). Meanwhile, Tina is simultaneously dumped and evicted by her landlord boyfriend (this deserves more exploration than it gets) and crashes with Miss Bliss, whose strict habits and deadlines for Good Earth magazine (doesn't sound made-up at all) clash with Tina's fondness for dancing like Elaine Benes and breaking family heirlooms.

Remember what I said about the last episode calling out Zack for how he treats women? Yeah, never mind. This episode has more awful behavior but mostly as bad attempts at humor, as Zack physically assaults Nikki, pushing her out of her seat on the bus to make room for another girl. (Disputing Nikki's assessment of the girl's appearance, he says, "I wouldn't knock you on the floor for a 3; she was a 5 with potential!") Also, Screech, who spends the episode inappropriately gawking at his partner Jennifer (they're assigned the camera), sneakily steals a kiss on the cheek while snapping a photo of them during their presentation, to Jennifer's horror. Mikey applauds Screech while the latter nods to Zack, who takes credit for the stunt. "Never doubt the master!" Gross.

Plus: The dynamic between Zack and Nikki is terrible, with her working hard and him mansplaining how the presentation should go. Ultimately she flounders and he saves the day, and the show can't seem to figure out if it wants to create romantic tension between them or not.

Zack's lies (1):

- When Nikki accuses him of pushing her off the seat, he says the bus lurched; she reminds him they were at a red light

Blehhhh I give up: This episode is exhausting and hardly illuminating in its lessons about compromise. Bad.

Episode 10: "Practical Jokes"

Aired February 25, 1989

Plot: Miss Bliss' certainty that no one can fool her during the annual Happy Harvest Week prankapalooza crumbles in the face of a mysteriously painted chair, landing Screech on trial for the crime and the class on the hook to show they've learned something about the judicial system.

And now Zack isn't so bad: The only continuity in this series is the total absence of it, meaning that in this episode Zack is a team player who knows what he's doing in class and isn't horrible to everyone.

Actually: During the trial, after Mikey (as the bailiff) swears in Lisa and asks if curly hair turns her on, Zack asks Miss Bliss (as the judge) if the bailiff (whom the judge already told to stop hitting on Lisa) can restrain the witness "for her own protection." Sleazy.

Zack's lies (0): Nice!

For what it's worth: This episode shows the students applying their knowledge in an engaging way and ends with the simultaneous double whammy of Miss Bliss (who pulled the prank on herself to teach the kids a lesson) pulling one over on the students and Screech having the last laugh by getting Miss Bliss to open his booby-trapped locker. Overall, this is about 25 times better than the previous episode.

Episode 11: "Stevie"

Aired March 4, 1989

Plot: As Zack is a totally stable person who knows how to appropriately handle new people in his life (especially women), he bets Nikki a year of gym clothes-washing that he can kiss 17-year-old pop star Stevie (Suzanne Tara), who went to JFK and looks way older than 17. While Zack inevitably pretends to be dying so Stevie will choose him as the lucky student on stage while she performs at her alma mater, Stevie, whose real name is Colleen Morton, crashes with her old teacher Miss Bliss and decides she'd rather go to Notre Dame than be the international sensation behind epic jams like "Hotline to Your Heart."

The good: To an extent, this episode serves as a good reminder to kids that celebrities are people too. Nikki initially acts too cool to care about Lisa's upcoming interview with Stevie, but in the moment it's Lisa who asks valid questions (before the expected line of questioning about nail-breaking) and Nikki who gets starstruck. If this took place in the social media era, would the students be more or less in awe of this singer who was learning in the same classrooms that they do just a few years before?

The bad: This is quintessential Zack Morris dishonesty, doing whatever he has to do to get what he wants. Miss Bliss explains how many people he hurt by claiming he was dying, but Zack never really bears much blame for this, and the fact that Stevie ultimately kisses him tends to wipe out what Zack did wrong. Just because she does so as Colleen and Zack doesn't even realize he's kissing Stevie (and ultimately loses the bet) doesn't matter when Zack so frequently forgets what he's learned even when it's straightforward, much less when there's any ambiguity or distraction.

The ugly: Zack's confidence that he can kiss Stevie while on stage comes from pretty sinister logic: "She won't be able to say no while the cameras are rolling."

Zack's lies (6):

- Sending the letter that he's dying to Stevie's manager so Stevie will choose him
- Perpetuating the lie separately to Mylo, Mr. Belding and Miss Bliss (3)
- Telling Miss Bliss he has deskarosis and that it affects one in 12 billion people (2)

Hard line to hear now, as Lisa describes Stevie's taste in guys: "She goes out for older guys like River Phoenix."

Hard line for a different reason: "My manager says I'm only supposed to be adorable to people under 21." Again, Stevie is only 17. Ick.

Episode 12: "Clubs and Cliques"

Aired March 11, 1989

Plot: Older dudes Rick (Christopher Carter of "Hangin' with Mr. Cooper") and Trevor (J. Trevor Edmond of "Pacific Palisades") invite Zack into their elite, red jacket-wearing club called the Rigmas, which involves a fraternity-style pledgeship process that eventually forces Zack to embarrass his friends. It would be a big mess for Mr. Belding to handle except this week he and Miss Bliss switch places and discover neither educator's job is as easy as it seems. (Actually, Bliss nails the role of principal, she just doesn't know she has to call the Board of Education about stuff.)

To clarify: Rigmas is an ancient acronym for Ritual Initiation of Gentleman Making a Stand. No, it isn't. The first Google result for the seemingly meaningless word "Rigma" is the Urban Dictionary definition about this episode.

Otherwise: This is a good episode, in which Zack at first tries to stick up for his pals ("You guys know my friends?" he initially asks Rick and Trevor, trying to include Mikey and Screech), decides to sell them out for dreams of wild parties and beautiful women and ultimately discovers that he was never actually pledging, only acting as a pawn for Rick and Trevor's initiation. It's an important lesson for kids to learn about friendship and social climbing, reinforced by the large quantity of forgiveness that Zack's real friends show by taking him back after ensuring that Zack sees that he now feels as betrayed as he made them feel.

Plus: No lies!

In case you forget what year this is: Trying to be cool after telling the students "Let's rap," Belding lets out a "Cowabunga."

A lesson I assume kids won't care about but still: This one shows that teaching and school administration are both difficult, with many decisions that may be out of people's hands and a lot of unexpected challenges. PAY TEACHERS MORE, SOCIETY. (Those words aren't on screen but should be.)

Episode 13: "The Mentor"

Aired March 18, 1989

The plot: Miss Bliss questions what kind of teacher she wants to be when her favorite teacher Mr. Lyman (Robert Donner of "Mork & Mindy") returns and ruffles feathers by taking the class outside. Meanwhile, star pitcher Nikki replaces her cap and mitt with earrings and makeup after Lisa assures her that guys don't want to go out with girls who play sports. (Or, more specifically, "who spit," which now that I think about it is totally different advice and let's just move on.)

For the second episode in a row: "The Mentor," like "Clubs and Cliques," showcases challenges faced by people who work in the school system. For the most part, this approach did not stick around once the gang went to high school and the show moved from Disney to NBC and Indiana to California.

On top of that: There's a great dose of hope that comes through as Bliss doubts Lyman's techniques, Lyman admits he's been fired and doesn't want to fight bureaucratic battles anymore, and in the end inspires Miss Bliss to remember why she was so excited about Lyman's fondness for dressing up like historical figures and finding any way possible for history to come alive. (Never mind that Bliss just did that herself a few episodes ago.) Even Zack likes Lyman's approach, which, while not explored in enough detail to make a huge statement about educational strategies, does reinforce teachers' need to engage with material and their students, not just do the bare minimum and expect kids to care.

And also! Another **zero-lie** episode for Zack, suggesting that by the end of eighth grade he was learning how to be a better, more honest person, which also includes how he treats women. This would surely last forever.

I wish: Nikki's subplot sets a strong example for being yourself, and while by no means should the show suggest she needs a guy to be happy, it would have been nice if a guy was interested in her after seeing her pitch really well, reinforcing her decision to do what she wants to do for herself and not to impress others. Sadly, Nikki was never heard from again.

Stats/Looking Back on Eighth Grade

Eighteen of Zack's 28 lies occur in the first four episodes, and he ends the year with two consecutive episodes in which he neither lies nor treats women badly, something he hasn't done since episodes 5 and 6. So it's both notable that he closes out his time in junior high on a better note than he went in (the first episode was his largest lie total by far) and also that when he lies, it results in him treating women badly (in 62 percent of the episodes overall!), even though he isn't only lying to women.

Outside of Zack, Screech has more of a backbone than I remember, and Mikey and Nikki factor into the plot more than I thought. Lisa, outside of demonstrating poise while interviewing Stevie, doesn't get to do much beyond the superficial, though Voorhies shines enough in small moments (like when she and Mikey team up on a presentation about the typewriter) that I hope that's the reason producers kept a relatively peripheral character around for the West Coast reboot.

As for Miss Bliss, I'm not sure this style of show could have lasted much longer, giving time to so many adults as well as the students. The problems of teenagers will always (and should) be of higher interest to young viewers. Still, the show really missed a chance for a strange bonus episode explaining how the Morris, Powers, Turtle and Belding families suddenly moved in unison, and how coldly they seem to have severed ties with Mikey, Nikki, Miss Bliss, Tina and Mylo. As everyone experiences in one way or another: Junior high is nothing if not a time of change and heartbreak.

High School Season 1 (1989) aka "Saved by the Bell" proper aka "Forget some but not all of what you knew about these people while welcoming new/old friends?"

A lot can change between junior high and high school. For Zack, Lisa and Screech, it meant starting over in Southern California but, for our purposes, acting as if they've been there all along, with well-established relationships with Kelly, Jessie and Slater and no discussion at all about the 2,000-mile move from Indiana. In case they feel any cognitive dizziness there (this seems more like sci-fi material, not comedy), at least they have the stability of the same principal, as Belding also made the trek and clearly has signed the same waiver to pretend he's a lifelong West Coaster. In sitcom world, if you refuse to acknowledge it, it never happened, and while I get Chuck Klosterman's "Tori Paradox" point that adolescence can be a blur and in hindsight certain people may as well have vanished, it remains notable that the folks behind "Saved by the Bell" elected to assume any existing viewers wouldn't care if the transition from Disney to NBC and Indiana to California meant slamming the door not just on characters but the idea that the continuing characters ever had any relationship with them in the first place. Assuming that the vision wasn't just "Eh, who cares," is the idea that for the kids to move on they really had to start fresh and it would have been too much of a downer to confront the hard stuff? Sure, let's go with that.

Episode 1: "Dancing to the Max"

Aired August 20, 1989

Plot: Because every season premiere has to bite pieces of "Grease," Bayside High gets its own high-profile dance contest, hosted by teen heartthrob Casey Kasem (nearly 60 at the time and an astounding choice for a high-school comedy season-premiere celebrity cameo). First, though, Kelly must wait around to identify her partner after Slater flashes impressively balletic moves and Zack vapidly claims to be way better than that, leading to dance lessons with Jessie and a lot of stalling.

Zack's lies (2):

- He's a great dancer
- Instead of playing baseball over the summer he's always gone to dance camp (after which he asks, "Why did I say that?" as soon as Kelly's out of earshot)

Quality subplots: Watching "Dancing to the Max" for the first time in years, it's actually sort of surprising how well a lot of it works as an exploration of freshman-year feelings. Jessie feels too tall for all of the later-developing dudes around her ("I've grown an inch since lunch!" she cries) and thus is reluctant to dance in public, while Lisa dismisses Screech's affections as usual but has fun dancing with him — and, of course, wins the dance contest by creating a new, mostly hopping dance called "The Sprain" — when her date bails after she sprains her ankle (checks notes) *kicking the TV because of a Revlon commercial.*

Not as quality: In addition to the passive behavior it inspires in Kelly, Zack and Slater's battle over who gets to be her dance partner makes it awfully hard to discern the relationships among their friend group. It's absolutely not confusing or even rare for two guys in a group to be interested in the same girl, but the first episode simultaneously suggests the six of them are all tight and have been for a while but Zack not-so-silently resents Slater and wants him gone. Had we seen their earlier bonds and felt for how that changed once new girls and hormones took hold in high school, that might have been a worthwhile conflict instead of just vaguely defined frenemies (a stupid word but applicable).

Encouraging: Continuing his trend of improved behavior toward the end of last season, in this episode Zack ultimately sets aside his feelings for Kelly to be a good friend and enter the dance contest with Jessie, who's far more comfortable with her longtime pal than any of the others vying to gaze up at her chin.

Real quick: Also in the opening credits is magician Ed Alonzo as Max, owner of the Max and mostly around to display his flair for illusions. He receives a telegram from Casey Kasem, and that is a really old-sounding sentence.

After running the numbers: Jessie claims Zack has never entered her room through the door (as opposed to climbing in her window) in their last 11 years of friendship, suggesting that as a 4-year-old Zack was scaling a tree and entering a second-floor bedroom. Even for Zack, this seems like a stretch.

*****Interview with Alonzo on Max's life outside the Max:** "I always just assumed that Max was out doing shows. Doing charity events or whatever because he's a magician and put this restaurant together to have a platform to do his show. I always assumed that the Max character would be out doing what the Ed Alonzo character was doing. I never really looked that far into it [regarding a spouse or kids]. I always kind of considered him like a Pee-wee Herman type of character to where he didn't really think about that too much. Like Mr. Rogers – you just watch and learn from his teaching and his examples. Max was an extension of that kind of a character. I also think that's part of the same reason that the Max character didn't have the longevity of the other characters because they saw this was better for a younger audience, where the original show was meant to be for a younger audience on Saturday morning, and then it just blossomed into something that was more for teenagers and college students. And that's when they decided, 'Well, we really don't need Max around for that; he's the trickster.' So then they would just bring me in for an episode here or there to try and tie the loose ends together to make it make sense." *(Read more from Alonzo on page 227.)*

Episode 2: "The Lisa Card"

Aired August 28, 1989

Plot: When Lisa goes overboard ("like the crew of the Titanic," Zack says tactfully) by charging $386 on her dad's credit card, the gang bands together to raise the money, even if it means pimping her out.

Wait, what? Yep, Zack's first effort to raise funds involves selling tickets to guys to kiss Lisa on the cheek during class as she yells, "Get away, creeps!" This is hard to watch, though otherwise it's another good episode about a relatable teenage problem (responsible spending, not involuntary prostitution).

Zack's lies (2):

- Advising that Lisa copy his methods when he does something wrong: "Enjoy it, then deny it" (suggesting dishonesty counts as a lie here)
- He also suggests confessing to her mom but paying her to keep things quiet from her dad

Watching this all again: As kids I'm sure we all registered Jessie constantly calling Slater a pig and being the show's loudest feminist voice. But it naturally plays a lot differently now as Slater and Screech refer to girls as "fox" and "chick" and Jessie says, "May I remind you both that we are girls; we are not foxes nor chicks nor any other cute animal you boys like." If these exchanges were played for lessons and not laughs, more young people watching might have learned something.

Also deserving analysis for a very different reason: During a class discussion about reproduction in the animal kingdom, Slater asks, "How come birds aren't attracted to horses?" and the best part of that question is he doesn't appear to be joking.

Continuity: Not only does Zack address Lisa's dad as "Mr. Turtleay" (oops), Slater refers to changing schools frequently, suggesting that he is a new kid and further muddying the idea that he is so bonded to all of these people. Why not actually use new additions as a way to establish storylines instead of simultaneously pretending they're not new?

SMH: Belding says that he never had a date until he was in the army, and "even she was with the enemy." After the war he was dateless again because "That Vietcong girl dumped me." Oh my god.

Episode 3: "The Gift"

Aired September 8, 1989

Plot: Screech getting hit by lightning might be the best thing that's ever happened to Zack, now that his friend can predict the future and the blond prince of manipulation can win back the radio he lost to Slater in a rigged bet. With the entire gang stressed about the impending midterm from fast-talking Mr. Testaverde (John Moschitta Jr., best known as the guy from the "Micro Machines" commercial), Zack also finagles a study date with Kelly in which he does nothing but stare at her and attempt to kiss her while her eyes are closed.

Jeez, the kid doesn't quit: Once again, "Saved by the Bell" either uses Zack's antics to expose predatory behavior or shrugs off a kid's uncomfortable definition of consent in hopes that he can be charming. Debate away.

On the other hand: "Saved by the Bell" is often thought of as nonsense, but a lot of these early episodes tap into worthwhile experiences. This is particularly true for Jessie, who feels like being smart and having exclusively straight As is part of her identity, making her the most anxious about the test.

On the other, other hand: Zack and Slater making a bet where the loser has to be the other's slave for a week? Really?

Zack's lies (2):

- Calling Mr. Testaverde pretending to be Mr. Belding and saying that the school's pipes burst and midterms are postponed
- Calling Belding as Mr. Testaverde to say that he's sick and Belding must administer the test with three specific questions
- Note: Giving Zack a pass here for the lies involved in using Screech's powers (oh, hey, I just got that) to win bets against Slater because Slater started the battle of dishonest gambling

Must be said: Diamond is funny here again as Screech's abilities start to short-circuit: "Zack, did you know that Lincoln freed the Japanese?"

Justice: Zack gets what he deserves, failing the test and losing the bet to Slater, though seeing him perform the tasks assigned to him might help viewers actually feel like Zack is suffering the consequences.

Episode 4: "Fatal Distraction"

Aired September 9, 1989

Plot: A teenage play on "Fatal Attraction" that also references Michael Jackson, River Phoenix and Dennis Quaid (I'm really not making this up), this episode features Zack and Screech secretly bugging Jessie's slumber party to find out who Kelly's taking to the dance (she still hasn't decided but probably Zack OMGGGG) and what Lisa really thinks of Screech (pffffff).

Zack's lies (1):

- Just the bugging

It's like they're deliberately trying to have zero continuity: Just a couple episodes after Belding told Slater he couldn't get a date, he now tells Zack that he was a big ladies' man and not in a way that seems like he's lying, just completely rewriting what was said like five minutes ago. Come onnnnnn.

Also: Four episodes in and we're already back to wondering if Kelly will take Zack or Slater to a dance? Try a little harder. Same goes for the weird demonization of Rhonda (Kirsten Holmquist), an aggressive tomboy who scares Zack, though not as much as his fear of Kelly once she, Lisa, Jessie and Slater conspire to get revenge on Zack's eavesdropping and make him think Kelly physically injures any guy she likes. It's good to see Zack get as good as he gives as well as provide a showcase for Thiessen, who pulls off something challenging in establishing layers and strength under Kelly's perkiness (which some shows might not have expanded beyond).

Once you see it you can't unsee it: After overhearing that Lisa's attracted to Michael Jackson, Screech comes to school in his best Jackson outfit and, in falsetto, tells Lisa, "I'm not like other boys." Though I did laugh when Belding tells "Michael" he's coming to the principal's office for violating the Bayside dress code and the kid responds, "Mr. Belding, it's me, Screech!"

One million bonus points: If you can identify the two other girls who attend Jessie's party without looking them up (I cannot).

Episode 5: "Screech's Woman"

Aired September 16, 1989

Plot: With Screech seeing little success from ace lines like, "Did you know that worms are a source of protein?" Zack attempts to find his pal a woman. This, of course, leads to Zack inventing a fictional person named Bambi and eventually dressing up to become her, sparking, among other things, an obligatory reference to Thumper.

Zack's lies (1):

- Calling the creation of Bambi one all-encompassing lie here, and his deception (which involves a wig, blue dress, red-tinged glasses, high heels and shaved legs) might be debatably forgivable if Zack's motivation weren't driven by wanting Screech to focus on doing their science project instead of feeling lonely

"Bambi's rules of livin' and lovin'," which prompt great responses from Screech:

- "Straighten your hair and dye it blond." (Screech: "Consider me Billy Idol.")
- "I'm allergic to all types of animals." (Screech: "Done. I'll shave my birds.")
- "I'm very possessive. I must have you all to myself. Now get rid of your friend Zack Morris." (Screech: "Well, Zack is awfully cocky, and he's always taking advantage of me, and sometimes I think he underestimates my intelligence. But he is my friend, and I'm sorry, I won't trade him for anything else in the world. Not even you, Bambi.")

Sort of good? In many ways this episode calls out the folly of Zack's arrogance and sleaziness toward women. He assures Screech that he needs top-notch pickup lines (granted, Screech botches the cheesy Miss Universe line Zack feeds him), says transparently stupid things ("Love and science don't mix. Did you ever see Einstein with a chick?") and is ultimately revealed to be far less in control than he'd like to admit. When he tells Jessie he has a problem, she quips, "I know that, Zack, but we've all learned to live with it." And when Kelly thinks Bambi is a girl and asks if she wants to come to the bathroom with her, Jessie's there to stop Zack from, you know, flagrantly violating the privacy of the person he claims to have deep feelings for.

Huh? At one point Slater is seen talking on the school pay phone (ha) to his girlfriend in Italy. What? Not only does this idea not set up an ongoing storyline, it makes Slater look shady for his previous interest in Kelly. He does, however, give Screech good advice ("Don't try to impress anyone. Be proud of what you are, whatever that is"), the last line of which had me considering to what degree Screech is inspired by Gonzo. (Verdict: Moderate.)

Episode 6: "Aloha Slater"

Aired September 23, 1989

Plot: Losing Kelly-related ground to muscular wrestling champ Slater, Zack discovers that the guy's military dad (Gerald Castillo of "General Hospital") might move him to Hawaii and determines that claiming Slater is dying can only help the cause, considering how well Zack's fake-dying scheme worked with Stevie.

Zack's lies (12), a new record for most in an episode:

- Claiming that he bugged Belding's office when it was just Screech scrunched in the file cabinet (either way, it's deceitful)
- Slater is dying
- Slater has mumbioquadrilationosis, which affects the brain
- That one last burst of strength is symptomatic of the disease, hence Slater's wrestling success
- Only a clinic in Hawaii can treat it
- Slater wants to live out his remaining days with friends, but they have to make him want to leave by treating him terribly
- Zack read a medical book
- The book said Slater is in immediate danger only if symptoms start to appear such as sneezing, itching and loss of memory
- Slater was supposed to meet him in the weight room last period
- Slater forgot about that
- The girls are crying because it's peel-an-onion day in home ec
- Slater's trophy was stolen by vandals and melted down

The continuity of no continuity: Again, it's very hard to tell how long Slater has been there and known everyone. This episode suggests he's new, but the show did nothing to acknowledge anyone arriving/acclimating to established groups.

Family communication? While it's pretty weird that Major Slater talks to Belding before talking to his son, it's reassuring that he listens and respects Slater telling him that, unlike in Iceland apparently, Slater has made real friends at Bayside and would miss them if they moved. Major Slater's also quite good at messing with Zack with the help of non-active grenades.

Big deal! This episode features Zack's first use of "Timeout," in which he freezes everyone and everything while addressing the camera. Amusingly, after a quick check shows that Slater can't move after the timeout is called, Zack talks to us without any concern that Slater can still hear him (which he can't, but still).

Foreshadowing? Kelly referring to having family in Hawaii actually makes that aspect of "Saved by the Bell: Hawaiian Style" less random, but during the movie no way did I remember that she said that previously.

The show in a nutshell: After learning that Slater's staying and he was just scheming to get back at Zack (who never puts any stock in what Kelly wants), the girls are mad at both of them, with Lisa even telling Screech he looks good by comparison. It prompts this:

Screech (to Zack and Slater): Thanks for being slimeballs.
Zack (to Slater): They'll get over it. I've been putting them through this since the first grade, and I'm still here.

Episode 7: "The Substitute"

Aired September 30, 1989

Plot: As teenage girls are "suckers for the great poets" like Jon Bon Jovi, Axl Rose and Jazzy Jeff (Zack really says this), studying "Romeo and Juliet" seems to be a major chance to woo Kelly with words like "yonder." That's until the girls decide they prefer men to boys when handsome substitute Tony Crane (Hank Stratton of "The Unit") takes over after hearing-impaired English teacher Miss Simpson (Pamela Kosh of "The King of Queens") throws out her back (an old hockey injury).

Zack's lies (1):

- Telling Kelly there's a spider on her chair so she'll stand up and accidentally volunteer to play Juliet while he plays Romeo

Teenagers certainly do develop crushes on educators, but: Watching it now, "The Substitute," which FWIW aired seven years before the Mary Kay Letourneau scandal broke, often feels icky, like when Mr. Crane plays Romeo to 15-year-old Kelly's Juliet and Kelly introduces herself in class simply with, "I'm yours." Again, kids absolutely do fantasize about teachers, and the world has changed a lot since this episode was made. But.

That said: This episode has a few hilarious, Shakespeare-inspired lines, like Zack getting Kelly to swoon with, "Oh to be that straw sitting in my lady's cup. Gladly would I be made of plastic and risk drowning in a sea of cola for the chance to touch fair Kelly's lips." This inspires Screech to attempt, "Fair Lisa. Would that I were that blob of ketchup lying in your plate, so that you may dip your French fries in my face," which, obviously, she does. This is also a solid "Romeo and Juliet" reference from Zack: "Something's rotten in the Max, and for once it's not the chili."

Plus: Considering how often the guys of "Saved by the Bell" fight over women, it's a welcome reversal to see the girls competing, including a vision in which they all declare in unison, "It's him, it's Tony, he's come for his bride!" When they all realize Mr. Crane — er, Tony — won't be around forever, Lisa declares, "Well, you never think when you're in love."

Sitcom nonsense at its finest: When the guys hire an actress (previously the third pepperoni in a dancing pizza commercial) to pretend to be Mr. Crane's fiancé, she accidentally clings to Belding while gushing, "I could not wait until June! I took the first plane from Rome, let's get married today." Observes Screech, "We should have hired an actress with hallway experience."

Episode 8: "Cream for a Day"

Aired October 7, 1989

Plot: In one of the series' best episodes, Screech's chemistry accident not only zaps away his first and proudly puberty-indicating blemish (named Murray) but drives Zack to market the pimple-busting Zit-Off to any teenagers in need. This includes Kelly, whose reddened nose could prevent her from winning homecoming queen versus rivals Susie Van Fike (sure, that could be a name) and Muffin Sangria (nope, nothing weird about that).

Zack's lies: None!

Refreshing: For a change, "Cream for a Day" not only features consistently relatable and reasonably sensible situations but endearing reactions and honest emotions. Kelly's not normally as shallow as Lisa but longs to look her best and win a crown because of how rarely anyone stands out in the seven-child Kapowski clan; Zack intelligently utilizes the sadly nicknamed Crater-Face Coburn (Scott Fults) as a guinea pig to prove Zit-Off works and brilliantly gets other students to paint their faces red to show school spirit and make Kelly feel better about the maroon rash left by the cream; and, most importantly, Zack tells Kelly the truth about the flaws in Zit-Off and does his best to support her in a way that doesn't hurt anyone!

Define irony: A show that has already had multiple dances revolves an episode around homecoming … and does not mention the homecoming dance at all.

Like, gnarly, dude: Bayside students' impressions of the kids at rival high school Valley are right in line with SNL's "The Californians."

Not quite as enduring: Excited about the cream's skin-healing potential, Screech exclaims, "It could work wonders for Gorbachev!"

Episode 9: "Pinned to the Mat"

Aired October 14, 1989

Plot: The gang contemplates their futures during Career Week, with Zack admitting he wants the most money for the least work and Slater feeling uneasy when everyone seems to have more sophisticated goals than "professional wrestler." That doesn't bode well for his upcoming match with Valley star Marvin Nedick (Gino De Mauro) or Zack's bet on his pal, wagering his nonexistent dirt bike against Nedick's real one.

Then and now: It's stunning how different Zack seems when watching this as an adult. Most of the time he's not a charismatic smooth talker but just a scared kid, even if the source of his anxiety is rarely explored in depth. Here, he's not excited for Career Week because "It's the first sign our parents aren't going to support us forever." That isn't really the fear of growing up or finding direction, though, just someone who's always looking for the easy way out, which is not endearing.

Zack's lies (3):

- He owns a dirt bike
- He heard Nedick has been threatening to tie Slater's tongue to his toes and use him as a hula hoop (it's not entirely clear if this is a lie but it seems more like Zack trying to rile up Slater than sharing real information)
- Calling Slater's dad and pretending to be Slater's guidance counselor Mr. Frank Furter (Zack is holding a hot dog at the time)

All objectification all the time: What is the nature of Zack and Kelly's relationship at this point? She knows he's interested and is still deciding if she is? Anyway, when Kelly asks him if she'd be a good actress he says "Every night you star in my dreams" (not an appropriate way to address her career goals) and when she says she wants a lot of kids he says he'd love to help her with that (one of the more sexual innuendos the show ever offered).

Masculinity: This episode challenges perceptions of manhood, sort of, by having male characters mock women in aprons (Max even says his dad became a cabdriver simply because Max's mom expected him to cook if he was going to stay home, an uncomfortable moment) only for Slater to discover he's a natural baker. Of course, he only joined the class because Kelly was in it and inevitably goes back to wrestling because his quiche blew up and he didn't care, so half-credit at best.

Best line: After the group marvels at Slater's cake and Kelly says she loves sensitive guys, Screech tells Lisa, "A bologna sandwich turns me into an emotional dishrag."

Wow: This episode features references to Vanna White and Pat Sajak, who are both still on "Wheel of Fortune." Crazy.

Not as timeless: In the futuristic vision, game show host Zack announces a brand-new, 19" cable-ready TV. Ooh, cable-ready!

Episode 10: "Beauty and the Screech"

Aired October 21, 1989

Plot: Combining the sex appeal of George Michael with the unbridled passion of a high school science class, Screech tutors Kelly for a huge test taking place just before she attends a concert by the "Faith" singer, with the other ticket not yet spoken for. Guess who desperately thinks she should take him and isn't quite thrilled at the emergence of nicknames like "Screechie" and "Kel-Kel."

The epitome of a bad friend: As you'd expect, Zack does not celebrate good things in his friends' lives and can only see through the lens of how he's impacted. Granted, he's made his interest in Kelly abundantly clear, but his reaction to the sudden flirtation between the two study buddies reflects how much Zack does not consider his friend to be a full person with wants and needs of his own. Meanwhile, Zack has no concern for what Kelly wants, only how he can connive to guarantee that it's him.

Although: This episode does a surprisingly good job of removing physical perceptions from the concept of chemistry as Kelly raves about a guy who's intelligent, has a great sense of humor and is really fun to be with. Cue Lisa's spit-take when Kelly attaches the praise to Screech, and the ultimate comedown when Screech and Kelly realize that they aren't as compatible as they thought, what with him hating George Michael and her disinterest in the International Insects Expo. "We'll always have science," says Screech, Bayside's answer to Bogart.

Zack's lies (1):

- Telling Belding that Screech and Kelly are getting married in hopes that the principal will break them up, leading to the classic exchange of "Screech, you can't elope!" "Who are you calling a cantaloupe, you melonhead!"

Surreal: After Slater observes "Screechmania" taking over Bayside because of Kelly's clear influence on the minds of all other girls, the inevitable dream sequence shows Zack and Slater dressed like nerds (this was long before being a nerd for something was accepted) and showing off to Jessie and Lisa by pulling their cheeks in and out very quickly. Kelly has a pizza on her head, Screech does a James Bond impression, it's a whole thing.

Illustrious debut: "Beauty and the Screech" marks the arrival of Kevin, a talking robot programmed by Screech who delivers one-liners like claiming to be Hunk of the Month in "Robot Illustrated" and, regarding Kelly, "She's cuuuuuuute." As he obviously didn't make it to the end of the series, the question is WHAT DID SCREECH DO WITH/TO HIM.

Episode 11: "The Friendship Business"

Aired November 4, 1989

Plot: An unofficial sequel to the junior high episode about investing as the gang aims to revolutionize the friendship bracelet market only to tragically split into rival companies: bracelet-focused Friends Forever and headband-centric Buddy Bands.

Ugh, the presidential comparison has to be reiterated: In a leadership role, Zack doesn't just have narrow business sense and awful people skills (he wrestles the title of president away from Jessie because "I don't want Jessie to blow it") but he doesn't even want to pay the people doing the work. When Lisa says the Fashion Club can make 60 bracelets a day or 80 if they're paid, Zack says, "Sixty's fine."

Parting of ways: While Kelly, Jessie and Slater leave Zack quickly, it takes Lisa and Screech longer to remember who they're dealing with. Of course Zack eventually enlists Screech to be a free friend that comes with purchase of bracelet, resulting in carrying people's books and, oddly, having to dance all day with a girl who seems to have loaded up on bracelets in order to rent a partner. On his way out of Zack's room and the business, Screech says, "Sorry, Zack; being your friend's too exhausting." Preach.

Also chilling: During a "Lifestyles of the Rich and Famous" parody, Zack goes from being the fifth richest man (not person but man) in America to the fourth because "I just bought Bill Cosby." This was made a long time ago.

Another time stamp: It is now very noticeable how frequently "Saved by the Bell" referred to political figures of the era like Gorbachev and Quayle. Like, a lot.

Zack's lies (1):

- Telling Belding that wearing his Buddy Band would mean a lot to him, which is just a ploy to make Buddy Bands look uncool and put his friends out of business

The message: Regardless of execution, "The Friendship Business" does teach young viewers how quickly business can drive friends apart and let greed and power grabs take priority over relationships. You could argue this episode was the foundation for much of "The Social Network." (No, you could not.)

Episode 12: "The Mamas and the Papas"

Aired November 11, 1989

Plot: It's apparently essential that freshmen in high school consider marital challenges as early as possible, hence a social science project that pairs up students for a week to see how they handle spousal relationships and raising children. Alphabetical pairings include Zack and Kelly, Slater and Jessie, and Screech and Lisa, with the rest of the class asked to watch in silence.

Oh dear god: This is easily one of the worst episodes in terms of shrugging off toxic masculinity under the guise of humor. Slater asks, "Why did Preppie wind up with my Kelly?" to which Kelly just smiles. When Jessie reminds Slater no woman is his possession, Zack asserts, "She's right. Kelly's mine." Jessie calls Slater a macho pig after he notes that great legs are important for a marriage, to which he replies, "Oink oink, baby." Slater says he isn't fixing anything for dinner because he's a guy (despite proving himself an expert baker a few episodes ago) and claims to think the women's movement means Jessie will "put on something cute and move it into the kitchen." Belding says Slater (who pulls a Zack in later manipulating Screech's affections for Lisa) wanting a maid, not a wife is a problem they'll have to work out, and the couple ultimately failing to make their marriage work feels like too much joint responsibility and not enough "Slater is being the worst." Meanwhile, Zack spends every role-playing opportunity trying to kiss Kelly, and though she does call him out and reject his selfishness while Belding asserts that affection can't solve all problems, it's hard to believe Zack has done enough to deserve Kelly taking him back.

On that note: The show just cannot decide what kind of agency to give Kelly in terms of how she feels about Zack and Slater and what role she will play in directing her relationship status. It's a major issue in many episodes and just never seems clear, which is why there's no continuity from one to the next. Also, Screech saying "What a hot mommy" after he becomes Zack and Kelly's child adds yet another moment for Kelly to be objectified without opportunity to react.

If only: As Zack turns to the camera and says, "If I can't stay married to Kelly, she'll never go out with me," it's hard not to wonder (if you haven't already) why he's even the main character. It would be great if the show followed Kelly throughout this ordeal, not him.

Zack's lies (0): An extremely rare instance of not lying at all while being absolutely horrible to women.

Worst moment: Slater holding up his fist and saying, "Jessie, you're a great girl, but I think we should break up before I send you to the moon." Seriously. Threatening violence, even as a "joke." This is marital humor taken from the '50s, and it's terrible.

Best moment: Jessie telling Slater, who says he should be the man and order for them, "If the husband's a real man he wouldn't be threatened by a woman who knows what she wants."

Episode 13: "The Election"

Aired November 18, 1989

Plot: In a scenario that could never, ever happen in real life, an arrogant jackass with no experience (Zack) soars to the top of the polls because the far more dedicated and qualified (and female) candidate (Jessie) is deemed not likable enough.

AHHHHHHHHHHHHHHHHHHHHHHHHHHHHHHHHH: I'm really not trying to go overboard on these connections. I wish they weren't there. But wow is this episode hard to stomach now. Zack specifically says he doesn't care about the school constitution and only runs to try to win a secret free trip to Washington, not because he wants to help anyone. (He initially says he only runs for buses, blonds and brunettes.) He comments, "What would the world be like if a woman ran it?" (Slater answers: "Less violent and color-coordinated?"), and Belding notes, "Zack Morris is like a vacuum cleaner. He'll suck you in if he can." Zack even has comments like "Me? Run? That's like asking Roseanne Barr to skip a meal," which isn't that far off from what Trump said about Rosie O'Donnell. So disturbing.

Back to the Kelly issue: After Zack suggests hers is the only student body he cares about (insert vomit emoji), Kelly says, "And that's one campaign you're never going to win." This after she just ended an episode in which she was married to him, seemingly forgiving everything he's ever done and wanting to be with him. Now she can't decide who she wants to vote for and ultimately says she voted for Zack because she felt bad for him (and then says she actually voted for Gilligan). Whiplash-inducing narrative randomness.

Sheesh, again: Another Gorbachev mention! And another pointless continuity error, with Jessie saying Zack has been coming in her window for the past 10 years, even though she previously said 11. Why not keep this the same?

Zack's lies (2):

- Running for president with an ulterior motive
- After believing the trip is canceled, enlisting Screech to persuade people to vote for Jessie (who is ashamed after playing stupid to appeal to voters following Slater's insistence she needs to lighten up) by telling them things like, "Zack takes ballet lessons, pass it on"

What a slogan: Zack's mantra is, "Whenever there's trouble, that's where I'll be," which is very similar to a line in the fantastically creepy "Nightcrawler": "If you're seeing me, you're having the worst day of your life."

Episode 14: "The Zack Tapes"

Aired December 2, 1989

Plot: As it's been like five minutes since Bayside had a dance, Zack and Slater are back to jockeying for Kelly's affections, this time to go with them to the Sweetheart dance. Because it would be total lunacy to just let her decide based on what she feels, Zack takes a lesson from Miss Wentworth (Carol Lawrence of "Valley of the Dolls") and fills Kelly's new Bo Revere tape with subliminal messages, which as a kid led me to believe were commonly found in generic pop songs.

Zack's lies (2):

- Using tapes with hidden messages to brainwash Kelly (who suddenly believes Zack is "a blond Tom Cruise") and Belding, the latter of whom needs to meet with Zack and his mom after Zack dumps tea bags in the pool and uses a teacher's toupee to erase the blackboard (2)

I think I need a shower: That makes two consecutive, deeply unpleasant episodes. "The Zack Tapes" is a patriarchal fantasy land of female mind control, including helping nerds attract their "dream girls" who sometimes ask, "What can I get you, master?" Meanwhile, Screech ruthlessly pursues Lisa and causes her to scream, "I'm not safe anywhere!"

As usual: Even though Zack's horrendous behavior is exposed (Miss Wentworth leads the female students, as well as Slater and Belding, in a prank in which they all fall in love with him) and he doesn't get what he wants, the episode ends before he has any real, lasting consequences. Tomorrow he and his mom will have their much-delayed meeting with Belding, but that's clearly material for another episode (by which I mean never).

How nice: In junior high it seemed Zack's parents were divorced, but I guess now they're back together. That couldn't possibly be a continuity error, just love finding a way.

Episode 15: "King of the Hill"

Aired December 9, 1989

Plot: Wait. Wait. Wait. This is the season premiere, set on the first day of school as Slater (an Army brat who's been at 14 schools in three years) arrives at Bayside and duels with Zack for Kelly's affections and status as, well, look at the episode title.

So much I don't understand: Why was this aired out of order (with an opening voiceover from Zack saying "I'll never forget the day Slater showed up," which was like a few weeks earlier at this point?), depriving any context for Slater's relationships with the group? With four high school seasons, isn't this freshman year, in which case there's no explanation for how Mr. Belding knows everyone already (and obviously they're pretending the junior high season didn't happen, so …)? Why is Zack so shy around Kelly here ("This is the year that I make my move," he says, later claiming to have waited out two years and six boyfriends, which doesn't seem like something he would do) when in later episodes he's very outspoken? And why does this episode set up an ongoing rivalry between Zack and Slater only to integrate him into the core group and have them be close friends but also at war and also treating every conflict and fight over Kelly like it's the first time?

On a somewhat lesser note: Does Lisa really want her locker as close as possible to the boys' bathroom? And Kelly reacting to Slater putting an onion ring on her finger with "I think I'm going to cry" is … something.

Unsettling from the start: In the opening scene Zack presses a button and a life-size photo of Kelly in her volleyball uniform descends from his ceiling. Teenage crushes are one thing, but that is, uh, pretty extreme, especially when we find out how long he's been pining for her. When Jessie asks if he's asked her out yet, he says, "Technically not yet, but in my mind we already have children." Yikes.

Zack's lies (5):

- Telling Slater that Kelly has leprosy
- Offering Slater a hall pass containing Belding's signature (it's not really his signature)
- Claiming Lisa asked to switch seats with him
- Getting Screech to pretend he's choking so Kelly will be late to class and get detention
- A reference to Zack previously telling Belding that aliens took over his body (he now says the aliens are home for the holidays)

Irony: In a moving moment, Belding says that he doesn't just want to punish Zack but instead wants to try to help: "There are no bad boys, only boys who haven't been reached." He is then easily outsmarted by the teenager, who wants to be sent to detention and is rarely counseled again.

Deadpan champ: No one kicks off a year like monotone math teacher Mr. Dewey (Patrick Thomas O'Brien): "How was everyone's summer? Mine stunk."

Episode 16: "Save That Tiger"

Aired December 16, 1989

Plot: Another unofficial sequel (following "Practical Jokes" in junior high) as Zack and Slater compete in a prank war against Valley while Kelly and Lisa (and eventually Jessie) prepare for the city cheerleading finals, which includes a whopping three schools.

Zack's lies (0): Nicely ending the season on a positive note, including not being awful to women.

Par for the course: This is a typical example of the guys getting all the nonsense and the girls having to be productive. Since they win both the prank war and cheerleading contest, it seems like a wash, although the guys' prank gets Screech kidnapped and the girls band together for an impressive cheerleading routine that attempts to elevate their words even a little bit. (Though Kelly and Lisa shut down Jessie's proposed line of "Winning's not important because our minds are sound.")

Good kind of reminder: Confusion over who's in a mascot outfit (as Valley's Dan Clegg, played by C.W. Hemingway, performs in Bayside's tiger outfit instead of Screech) recalls a "Freaks and Geeks" episode about Neal (Samm Levine) wanting to be the mascot. Anything that brings to mind one of the all-time best shows about high school can't be a bad thing.

Fun fact: On Anna Faris' "Unqualified" podcast, Gosselaar said that at one point in his life he almost went to Valley Community College!

Fun fact related to this episode: Mark Clayman, who plays Valley goon Stan Clegg, plays a different student (at Bayside) named Moose in two later episodes. Imagine how many letters from confused fans the producers must have received!

Stats/Looking Back on the First High School Season

Despite the major changes to the show since junior high, Zack remains the main character — while proving to be an objectionable human being a high percentage of the time. In junior high he was bad to women in 62 percent of the episodes, and in season one of the high school years he is bad to women in 56 percent of the episodes. While in junior high he lied zero times in five out of 13 episodes, in high school so far he only has two episodes out of 16 without a lie, and one in which he lies 12 times. His rate per episode remains at 2.2 (35 lies in 16 episodes).

On the plus side, in no other episode does he lie more than five times, and that is only in the premiere (which aired as No. 15). And he once again closes out the season with a zero-lie episode in which he is not bad to women, which is either a clever/unearned attempt to show growth or just a hope that viewers will forget all of the awfulness that came before.

Massive continuity errors occur in more than half of the episodes, and I started tracking if Kelly was being objectified but stopped because she always was. The more intriguing storylines would be how Slater's acclimating to the new environment (which is briefly addressed but mostly muddled), Jessie navigating a world in which being a tall, smart, confident woman is far more challenging than it should be (an exploration that's far less upsetting in "Dancing to the Max" than "The Election") and Screech remaining loyal to Zack while recognizing the troubling aspects of his character (that is, most of it). Lisa is far too often used simply as the girl Screech loves, and same with Kelly's inconsistent motivations and agency on the receiving end of attention from Zack and Slater.

More often than not, "Saved by the Bell" simply focuses on Zack doing bad things and not getting away with it but also not learning anything that lasts and suppressing big ideas below humor. Sometimes it entertains with a light touch. Other times Slater raises a fist to threaten Jessie (!!!!!).

High School Season 2 (1990)

The only context to note here is that you'd think the seasons would start at the beginning of the school year and finish at the end, but that isn't the case. That would require a basic interest in continuity that the show just doesn't have, as evidenced by this season opening with "The Prom," which normally would happen at the end of a school year, which this can't be a continuation of because of how much older everyone looks. So, um, welcome back, students, even though you never left?

Episode 1: "The Prom"

Aired September 8, 1990

Plot: Kelly goes from excited to devastated when her dad loses his job and accepts the money (?) when she returns the cash he gave her for her dress. Obviously this would be helpful information to share with her date, but Zack's far too pumped to notice that Kelly has more going on in her life than him.

Important: When Zack and Slater open the episode bursting into Kelly's room to ask who she's going with to the dance, it suggests they drove over there together. Odd.

Same old Zack: In junior high he supposedly learned that his friendship with Mikey was more important than a crush. While clearly his feelings for Kelly are way more than that and his friendship with Slater is newer and rockier than things with Mikey, Zack telling Kelly "If you want to hurt Slater, that's OK" seems awfully blunt considering the way the two have bonded, or at least settled into being in the same friend group.

Or maybe not: Starting off the season with a **zero-lie** episode seems to bode well. Zack spends much of "The Prom" focused on himself but winds up being sincere and supportive to Kelly, who finally has a chance to be a person, not an object.

Unfortunately, there's another Zack in training: Screech is just horrible to Lisa here, persisting and persisting (including shouting at her, "You're weakening!") and withholding her drink at the movie she agrees to see with him until he can put his arm around her. When he ultimately loses interest because of how much she talks during the movie, he tells her date at the prom "Now you know why I dumped the babe" after he complains about her talking too much. Lisa is given no voice here, just used as the butt of the jokes.

Disturbing once again: The show continues its increased aggression toward Jessie in a vision in which Screech plays Geraldo, hosting a show about women who love two men as Kelly debates between Zack and Slater. After Jessie says she doesn't like the "reverse macho pig-ism" of the show, Geraldo tells her, "And I don't like you." Though Geraldo previously says, "It's trashy, it's tacky, it's tasteless. It's Geraldo," so at least it's clear that his perspective is moronic anyway.

Best line: Belding telling Slater and Jessie (who are arguing about the planned prom music), "I'm sure there must be a compromise between 'Dirty Dancing' and 'The Best of Nelson Mandela'!"

Episode 2: "Zack's War"

Aired September 15, 1990

Plot: As Bayside hosts the pilot program for the California Cadet Corps, Lieutenant Adams (Cylk Cozart) attempts to whip Zack into shape while Screech competes with Butch (Dylan Tucker) for the uncredited Molly, who isn't given anything to do except hang on the arm of whoever proves to be the toughest suitor.

Underdog story: It's hard not to get a kick out of this episode as Zack, who wants to quit but sticks around after making a deal with Adams, tries to stack his team for the red vs. blue competition but winds up selecting the team led by Slater, leaving Zack with the far less-athletic group he wanted to compete against. It leads to a David vs. Goliath showdown in events like tug-of-war, joust and an obstacle course that gives Screech a chance to improbably take down Butch and less improbably not care about how Molly makes her decisions.

Zack's lies (4):

- Telling food-obsessed Alan (Dion Zamora) that the Army serves cake at every meal
- Telling Butch that in the Army he can beat up anyone he wants
- Telling Screech that Molly will be interested in him if he's "a real man" and she sees him in a uniform
- Telling Adams that the teams Zack chose for the competition are fair

Giving Jessie a voice: When Slater says women aren't allowed on the front line "Because we need cooks!" Adams quickly asserts that in the Army women are second to none in intelligence, stamina and courage. (Feel free to debate if that was actually the military's policy at the time.) Later, Jessie, who wants to be called Ms. instead of Miss, only has to say, "Excuse me?" to get Adams to change "separate the men from the boys" to "the persons from the persons." For a change, the show gets laughs out of the situation without undermining the message.

Also rare: There's actually evidence of deliberate direction as Screech, standing in Zack's room while his awful friend sits in a beanbag chair, tells him, "Ever since we were little I looked up to you. You had everything. I always wanted to be like you; now I'm glad I'm not." Even though the spatial alignment is simple, it's nice to see a choice like that made here.

Unexpectedly political: Trying to show he's not intimidated by Adams, Zack says, "Lighten up, Lieutenant, there's no war. Haven't you heard? Peace broke out all over the world." This comes after the previous episode in which Kelly's dad lost his job because of how world peace impacted his role at a defense plant. 1. Was the world really at peace for long enough to mention once much less multiple times? 2. Why emphasize this so much on a show like this? 3. Come on, this is really getting in the way of all those Gorbachev references!

*****Interview with Zamora:** "The way they wrote shows back then and the way they write shows now are completely different. Zack was kind of a bully in the show; he bullied people into things, and he was a wisecracker and trying to make things happen. If you watch shows now, the people who do things like that are viewed as more of a negative connotation, whereas when I was a kid and you were filming shows like 'Saved by the Bell,' playing the nerd was the bad thing. Being the sly, cool kid was the good thing, and those roles have definitely reversed over the last 30 years … the nerds, obviously, they're definitely being laughed at. It wasn't a laughed-with situation. You really don't stop when you're filming it as a kid. It's all make-believe. Because you're wrapped up in it, and you know that this isn't what they're really like. When you're on set you have to have school three to three-and-a-half hours a day, so I was in a classroom with Mark-Paul and Mario and Tiffani and Elizabeth and Dustin. We sat very close together, we were sharing tapes and earphones, and it was a really nice experience. These are super nice people that I had a chance to work with, and I had a really good time working with all of them. So when the shows aired and I saw the shows, it never really hit home as to what the public was seeing. It wasn't until later on, in my 30s, and someone was like, 'Oh, you were that nerd,' and they kept telling me, 'You were that nerd,' 'You were that nerd,' and it started setting in: 'Wait a minute: Maybe the character I played was made fun of a lot.' But it didn't really affect me. I have nothing but positive things to say about 'Saved by the Bell.' It was a really good experience." *(Read more from Zamora on page 261.)*

Episode 3: "Save the Max"

Aired September 22, 1990

Plot: In a very 1980s storyline, the gang fights to revive the newly rediscovered Bayside radio station (KKTY 98.6) and use it for a fundraiser to help their favorite restaurateur/magician come up with the $10,000 in back rent he owes the school board.

Zack's lies (1):

- Making an announcement as Mr. Belding (who earlier in the episode refers to him as "Pinocchio Morris") and saying that school is out

Young at heart: Before this episode Belding has always been trying to recapture something from his youth but just seemed like an out-of-touch dad. "Save the Max" does a nice job tracking him from his rebellious days as the Zack Morris of the '60s to the rare time when he wants to be a little more like the Zack Morris of the '90s.

Truth among friends: This one also really works in the way the gang embraces the radio station, with Wolfman Zack on music, Jessie on news, Kelly Desire on romance, Lisa on gossip, Screech hosting Screeeeeech's Meeestery Theeeeaater and Slater being the only weak link as the world's worst sports reporter. No one knows how to handle this problem, and Slater's ability to show his character and motivate callers during the dwindling telethon is an act of Jason Heyward-esque last-minute redemption. Made all the better because Slater has a Cubs poster in his room!

Dammit, Zack: His response to Jessie telling him she's found what he's looking for is, "A peephole in the girls' locker room?" Yes, he's an immature teenage boy, and yes, it was a different time. But this invasion of privacy is still played for a laugh.

Episode 4: "Driver's Education"

Aired September 29, 1990

Plot: Putting the "possessive" in "I can't wait to possess my license," Zack schemes to keep Kelly away from Slater, whose 16th birthday comes first and therefore (in Zack's mind) will swoop in and steal away his not-even-exclusive non-girlfriend. Naturally, the plan to get Slater in trouble leads to a head injury for Kelly, who later fakes more severe damage to make Zack feel guilty.

Zack's lies (5):

- Telling Slater he could have bought a car if he hadn't bought a ring for Kelly (no way that ring is expensive)
- Telling Mr. Tuttle that he's going to take driver's ed seriously from now on
- Telling Tuttle that Slater is being cocky
- Adding that Slater is telling everyone he should teach the class
- Enlisting Screech to pretend to be Tuttle to call Belding

Accurate: This episode certainly captures the way that many kids think about cars, figuring that anyone who has one has infinite opportunity and power and anyone without one has fallen behind to a life of disappointment and sadness. It's crystallized in Zack's vision in which he and Screech watch a drive-in movie on his bike while next to them Slater and Kelly sit in Slater's car, Kelly cooing, "You know, Slater, I never realized how much fun movies could be until I watched them in your beautiful car."

Welcome presence: Jack Angeles (seen previously in "The Friendship Business") continues to be hilarious as Mr. Tuttle, minimizing Zack's heckling and refusing to accept any perceived arrogance from Slater. Most memorable line: "Pushy, pushy. Move your tushy."

Here we go again: As usual, the Slater/Jessie banter involves her saying she is not a babe and him responding with (in this case), "And I respect that, sugar lips." Later, after she asks, "Why don't you be a man and confess?" he responds, "Why don't you be a woman and cook?" Rarely are we ever meant to see Slater negatively for this commentary, only to laugh at his comebacks and Jessie's frustration.

And as you'd expect: Zack suffers consequences in the sense that he flunks driver's ed and will have to wait another year to get his license, but Kelly instantly forgives him and, despite insisting she's not ready to go steady (a term many young viewers will likely need to look up/only understand through context), shrugs off him ending the episode still trying to control what she does: "Wait for me, Kelly … but not in Slater's car."

Episode 5: "House Party"

Aired October 6, 1990

Plot: A classic! Years before the King was popularized for a new generation in "Forrest Gump," Screech's Elvis-obsessed mom (and his never-seen dad) head out for four days in Graceland, leaving the guys to lip-sync The Beach Boys' "Barbara Ann" in their bathing suits and fail to prevent Screech's admirer Violet Bickerstaff (Tori Spelling!) from accidentally smashing his mom's prized Elvis ceramic. Naturally, the only way to fix all this is to swindle and embarrass Violet's sleazy ex-boyfriend, a pompous rich dude with the unfortunate yet fitting name of Maxwell Nerdstrom (Jeff Asch).

No hypocrisy here: One of the traits that the gang finds most sickening about Maxwell is how controlling he is toward women. Boy, good thing that's not something Zack ever demonstrates.

Though, to be fair: Maxwell says and does many legitimately awful things, including, after Jessie defends Violet, telling her "I know exactly what you need," then dipping and kissing her. Boy, good thing Zack has never done any creepy, sexually aggressive things like that.

Zack's lies (2):

- Saying it wasn't his fault he lost Screech's dog Hound Dog in a poker game to Maxwell
- Pretending to be Hound Dog on the phone while "talking" to Screech's mom

What a group dynamic: After Zack says Maxwell will regret the day he met Zack Morris, Slater quips, "Most of us already do."

On that note: When Maxwell says he'll return Screech's dog if he can go on a date with Jessie, Zack and Slater delight in how much Jessie will hate that. I get that Slater's relationship with Jessie is built on messing with her, but Zack's really isn't, and it's weird how excited he is to enable something he knows his longtime close friend really, really does not want to do.

Personal reflection: Watching this again, I'm struck by how status-obsessed "Saved by the Bell" always was, establishing firm distinctions between cliques with no room for nuance. While that wasn't out of the ordinary for shows/movies of the era, I also register how that caused me to unwisely categorize people in real life at that time. These messages can have that effect on young viewers.

Episode 6: "Blind Dates"

Aired October 13, 1990

Plot: Zack can avoid suspension if he takes out Belding's niece Penny (Jodi Peterson) on, whaddayaknow, the same night he's supposed to be Kelly's date for her birthday party! Jessie has a similarly on-brand problem, struggling with the height difference between her and Brett (Timothy Williams), a nice guy recommended by Lisa.

Textbook storyline: Zack could very easily just explain the situation to Kelly, who is a remarkably understanding person. Instead he never once considers the simplest, most honest solution, eventually causing Zack to train Screech to walk like him (which apparently includes snapping all of a sudden) and Screech wearing a blond wig to increase his "Zackocity." Sounds about right.

Zack's lies (4):

- Claiming that he had a skateboard accident (represented by a fake cast and crutches) and can't go out with Penny
- Belding referring to Zack pulling the skateboard-based stunt already at midterms
- Getting Screech to pretend he's Zack and go out with Penny
- Asking "Would you believe we're on 'Totally Hidden Videos'?" when cornered by Kelly

One good message, one not as good: Kelly and Lisa effectively show Jessie the error of her ways to get her to date Brett, and she gradually eases up with him on the dance floor. (In other words, he calls her Beanpole, she calls him Shorty, they have chemistry and we never see him again.). Zack, however, suffers no consequences for his deception, and Kelly for some reason is just touched that he'd do so much to make her happy. It's nonsense and a cop out.

This exchange right here: After Lisa says she doesn't go anywhere without a date, this happens:

Jessie: "This is the '90s; men and women can go to parties alone, and it's perfectly acceptable."

Slater: "Yeah, of course when a guy goes alone it's because he wants to. Now, when a girl goes alone, it's because she can't get a guy to take her."

Jessie: "Please, I just ate."

Slater: "When you do that feminist thing, your nose scrunches up and it's so cute."

In this episode Slater still wants Kelly back, but the way his mentality is endorsed and Jessie's is smothered is less than empowering.

More of that: Belding tries to get some of Bayside's "nerds" to go out with Penny, who are too busy with chess training and M&M sorting to accept and also ask "Is she an oinker or what?" Screech is more agreeable, what with his policy of "I'll date anything." Are any dudes in this school not awful?

OHMYGODOHMYGODOHMYGOD: In Jessie's vision of a dating game show, her three suitors are Teddy Krueger, Mason Voorhies, and, played by Screech, Donald Chump. In other words, the person who became the president is effortlessly included on a list of two fictional murderers, from whom a blown kiss is meant to be equally objectionable. Accurate.

Wise words: Catching Zack's plan and wanting his scheme to be exposed, Slater notes, "It's incredible what you can hear standing on a toilet."

Episode 7: "Rent-a-Pop"

Aired October 20, 1990

Plot: Weirdly copying from the junior high episode "The Boy Who Cried Rat," Zack again wants to go on the ski trip and again doesn't want to let his dad's annoying belief in good grades get in the way. Cue new Max waiter James (Mark Blankfield, hilarious) using his (over)acting talents to both impersonate Zack's dad with Belding and impersonate Belding with Zack's actual dad Derek (John Sanderford).

A tad familiar: The subplot about Zack being frustrated that his computer-salesman dad worked too much has been seen in so many shows and movies, including "Liar, Liar" (which of course arrived a few years later; that's just what jumps to mind first). In "Saved by the Bell," it means Derek carrying around a giant cell phone and answering it in the middle of every conversation with his son, which I guess is the reason Zack, who misses the ski trip but gets to go on a fishing trip with his dad, suffers no consequences for his deception.

Zack's lies (4):

- Utilizing James' skills to misrepresent his identity twice (2)
- Telling his dad he has "a friend" whose grades are a little below average to test the waters about if he could still go on the ski trip
- Getting the chess team to pretend to be poisoned as a distraction for Belding

In non-Zack news: At the carnival meant to raise funds for the ski trip (where they get the money for the carnival itself is unclear), Slater of course insults Jessie, daring her to knock him into the dunk tank the only (sexist) way he knows how. The two do have chemistry, though, and credit the show for building their rapport instead of just suddenly having them be together.

A personal note: In eighth grade science class I played an old man in an exercise video. We received an A- but had points taken off for being insulting to the elderly. For this I blame the vision in this episode in which the gang is all very old, visiting Zack in his room after he's been grounded for decades. When he questions Slater and Kelly being together, she explains that Zack wasn't around for 60 years and "After 60, I got frisky!"

Episode 8: "Miss Bayside"

Aired October 27, 1990

Plot: A reworking of "Pygmalion" more than eight years before "She's All That" as Zack bets Slater he can make anyone win the school's upcoming pageant, prompting Slater to choose Screech. While Zack's less than thrilled, Jessie's relieved when the event becomes more than just a chance to ogle girls in swimsuits.

Empowerment: For obvious reasons, "Miss Bayside" offers a chance for Jessie to bring her beliefs literally front and center, including wearing a trench coat for the swimsuit component of the competition (she only agrees to enter after Screech's involvement suggests men and women will be treated equally) and briefly describing the bathing suit she's wearing underneath. She isn't one of the finalists, but she gets to speak out, and her courage and conviction are stirring.

Talent competition: Apparently Lisa is proficient on the violin? Why does Kelly sing "Blue Moon" if she has a lousy voice? Though it's no worse than Jessie's interpretive dance about a caterpillar emerging from a cocoon.

Drama minimized: After they've all entered the pageant, Jessie, Lisa and Kelly argue in the locker room, with Kelly calling Jessie a hypocrite and Lisa feeling like Kelly always tries to upstage her. If this were a different show, the exchange might offer some ongoing insight into the dynamics of their friendship. Instead, they all remember that they're competing against Screech, laugh and forget they were upset.

Zack's lies (3):

- Telling Jessie he can get 20 men to join her picket line by lunchtime
- Starting a rumor that Slater beat up Screech
- Telling the pageant crowd not to listen to Screech because he's on medication

Weak answer: Lisa's defense of why pageants aren't out of step with modern womanhood is that there are a lot of things to be upset about, so "Why not have a pageant that makes you feel good?"

Better: When Belding asks an (uncredited) competitor named Jeanie Tyler if she's ready for her question, she says, "Yes! That was an easy question." Clever, concise, to the point.

Episode 9: "Jessie's Song"

Aired November 3, 1990

Plot: Remarkably combining a sobering portrait of adolescent stress and a nonsensical music industry fantasy, Jessie gets hooked on caffeine pills so she can study longer for Mr. Dewey's geometry midterm ... while also taking time to sing and dance with Kelly and Lisa in the suddenly existing/blossoming girl group Hot Sundae.

The good: The storyline is a great match for Jessie, who's terrified that one bad grade will derail her chance to go to Stanford and lead the life that she wants. That she learns she should go easier on herself and neither overschedule nor feel compelled to be the best at everything is an important lesson for stressed-out kids, and her classic scene with Zack (who initially refuses to believe Jessie has a problem but then sees she needs help) remains searing.

The ... not-so-good: Everything related to Hot Sundae is completely, hysterically absurd. That Kelly (who just had a terrible voice in *the previous episode*) is now a good singer; that Zack has such a strong connection to a record producer through his dad that he can fast-track an amateurishly recorded tape of three high school girls singing "I'm So Excited" and get them close to a deal within days; that they've somehow written and recorded a song off-camera, with full instrumentation, and are ready to choreograph and shoot a music video without any preparation; that the video is mostly them hopping around trampolines while wearing thong bathing suits over leggings; and that the song, like all the great music of the last several decades, opens with "1, 2, 3, bend! 1, 2, 3, stretch!"

Relationship building: Jessie kisses Slater after he helps her study (and worries that the "Keep Alert" pills will be, as the bottle indicates, habit-forming), prompting him to gush, "I'll never wash these lips again." Which is kind of a weird comment without a flashback to demonstrate how Slater washes his lips. Actually, no, it's weird no matter what, nobody has ever washed their lips ever.

Zack's lies (1):

- Getting Screech to sneak into the girls' locker room (dressed as a woman named Sinead O'Connor, not at all the same as becoming new student Barbara Bush in "The Zack Tapes") and secretly record them singing counts as a lie

More ridiculousness: Zack tells Slater "My girls are singing tonight" in reference to Hot Sundae; when Jessie can no longer participate Screech fills in, when obviously it would be better to get no one; and Jessie's addiction is apparently beaten within minutes simply by her getting under a blanket in bed.

A personal note: In junior high a close friend and I decided we were very determined to go to Stanford. Looking back I have no idea what put that in our minds, so it's very possible it was this episode.

*****Interview with O'Brien on the episode becoming legendary:** "The most famous – or infamous, as the case may be, depending on your point of view. I don't know that much about the whole series, but wasn't it their first attempt at the 'very special episode' where a comedy takes on a serious subject? I think it was the first try at that, so I think that's why it probably sticks out quite a bit. And I don't know if it was successful or not. [Laughs] I'm sure it probably went a little too far, a little too melodramatic, in the 'I'm so excited!' scene. I assume that's why it's the most memorable." *["Did Jessie's addiction say more about her as a student or Mr. Dewey as a teacher?"]* "[Laughs] I think considering the level of the backlash, I'd have to put it on Jessie as more of a reflection of her obsession than Mr. Dewey's cracking the whip. I don't think he was too much of an overbearing teacher." *["Would Jessie have made different decisions if Mr. Dewey were more emotionally available?"]* "[Laughs] Analyzing this as if it were Shakespeare. If I had been more open to having my classroom door open to after-hours tutoring … that just didn't come up in the script. I don't know if that backstory would be essential for consideration. [Laughs] Very possible though." *["Is the episode a more accurate portrait of addiction or the music industry?"]* "Well, I'd have to think neither. [Laughs] And another thing about the episode would be that they chose caffeine pills – probably the most innocuous thing to get addicted to – is in and of itself kind of humorous. They wanted to tread gently in their first attempt at tackling a serious subject." *(Read more from O'Brien on page 270.)*

Episode 10: "Model Students"

Aired November 10, 1990

Plot: Being the honorable businessman and trustworthy friend that he is, Zack revitalizes the struggling school store by once again using his henchman (Screech) to secretly gather footage of his female friends and use it against their will. In this case, it's calendars of them in their bathing suits, with photos captured during swimming practice.

Pretty startling: The series followed up Jessie's impassioned rhetoric in "Miss Bayside" with an episode that featured them leaping in tight clothing for completely nonsensical reasons and now an episode that hinges on exploiting their sexuality. And Zack, as usual, suffering no serious consequences in terms of his friendships or otherwise.

Plus: Jessie seems like the last person who'd make a comment like this, about the idea of filling Kelly's place on the swim team with a student who weighs 200 pounds: "She can't swim anchor; she is an anchor." So much for her comment in "Miss Bayside" about not being judged by measurements.

Also uncomfortable: After Adam Trask (Greg Kean) of Teen Fashion magazine decides to use Kelly, Jessie and Lisa as models for his spread on high school fashion, he gives them weird prompts during the shoot (to Jessie: "School's out; glasses off, hair down," which will remind many of Kitty and Gob hooking up on "Arrested Development") and walks into the Max with the magazine soon after proclaiming, "Check out these hot-looking girls!" Dude, they're in high school.

Sorry, one more thing: Zack's mission to stop Kelly from going to Paris for a month after she's chosen to be on the cover of the magazine's anniversary issue is just more insecure, controlling garbage, and for a second it seems like he'll get what he deserves when Adam acknowledges how much he sucks. But ultimately Kelly's not mad at all and Zack's scheming is brushed off as always.

Zack's lies (7):

- Getting Screech to secretly take the photos (again, we're counting deception like this as a lie)
- Telling Kelly that Screech is crying because Zack just told him she'd miss his birthday
- Telling Kelly he'll invite the gang to her photoshoot
- Telling the gang Kelly said not to invite them because it's very unprofessional

- Telling Kelly the girls were mad and Slater is bummed about her not being there to help with science and Screech is going to skip his birthday this year (3)

Calling a spade a spade: Screech, to Zack: "Let me say it's an honor working with a slimeball like you."

Somewhat less clear: Zack uses Belding's head on Jessie's body for Miss December in the calendar, and Belding's first reaction to the image is that Miss December is kinda cute. HE DOES NOT RECOGNIZE HIS OWN FACE HE HAS FACE BLINDNESS WHY AREN'T THERE MORE EPISODES ABOUT THIS.

Back to the idea of status: Zack takes over the school store from three "dweebs" who sell things that no "normal person" would want to buy. Yes, fluorescent pocket protectors and an autographed picture of Mr. Rogers don't sound like high sellers for most high-school students, and again this took place long before it became more acceptable to care deeply about things or be a "nerd" for something. But "Saved by the Bell" is remarkably unsympathetic to characters regarded as different, an awful message for young viewers.

*****Interview with Kean on if Adam still should have done the shoot after learning the calendar was taken without the girls' permission:** "Probably not. Certainly now one would say, oh my goodness, the kid should be punished, the guy should walk away. And say, 'Listen, I'm so sorry to have bothered you; I did not understand that these were taken surreptitiously. I thought that everybody was on board, and now that I've discovered that this has happened this way, this is not something I can be party to,' and walk away. And then of course there would be no episode. [Laughs] But I think you're absolutely right. If you think about it in context of what we know now or perhaps what we should have known then, moral behavior, then this guy should not in any way have ever been party to that." *(Read more from Kean on page 291.)*

Episode 11: "1-900-Crushed"

Aired November 17, 1990

Plot: Because the show's never done an episode about a get-rich-quick scheme gone wrong, Zack masterminds a teen line (mostly featuring advice from Lisa, Bayside's answer to Dear Donna) that quickly goes from endearing student resource to a way for him to, you know, cruelly manipulate his friends' lives and take their money. Meanwhile, Kelly's 13-year-old sister Nicki (Laura Mooney) falls in love with Zack, and his inability to tell the truth creates one (easily avoidable) misunderstanding after another.

Unexpected inspiration? The effort to distribute advice to high schoolers is a tame version of the very good Netflix series "Sex Education," and Lisa counseling Moose (Mark Clayman, who previously played Valley goon Stan Clegg) on love poems is not entirely dissimilar to the blue-collar understanding of poetry found in "Green Book." Plus, Zack trying to turn away Nicki with a tarantula is pretty much replicated in the holiday armadillo episode of "Friends."

Zack's lies (2):

- Telling Louise that Moose plagiarized the poem "The birds and the bees and the trees don't compare to your knees Louise"
- Pretending he's a dorky oddball who loves insects to try to turn off Nicki

Whoa, continuity! Slater and Jessie discuss how they both had fun at prom and wonder why they haven't gone out again. The show is continuing a previous narrative between the characters. What a concept!

That being said: This episode features yet another exchange in which Slater calls a woman a babe (and an "oinker"), and Jessie calls him a pig. Yet this apparently doesn't impact her desire to date him?

Emotion! Gotta love art teacher Mr. Manfredi (Michael McManus), who encourages argument ("Art is emotion!") and the silly-string fight that ensues.

Calling it like it is: After Zack finally comes clean, Nicki tells Zack she understands … well, "I understand you're a dork who couldn't tell a 13-year-old girl the truth. That is soooo immature." You'd think Kelly, who had been so excited that her sister had a crush, would want to comfort Nicki, but no, she's too busy pretending to be someone else (thanks to a blond wig and very shiny pink coat) and hitting on Zack.

Teen Line alter egos for trivia purposes: Zack is Australian bro Nitro; Screech is the Ant-Man; Lisa is Southern belle Princess, an accent seen again later in "Screech's Birthday."

From the "I Love the '90s" vault: In Nicki's vision, a twist on "Cinderella," she's cleaning the floors of the Max, and Zack, Slater and Screech walk in wearing giant gold chains while beatboxing and/or rapping. "Sorry, Prince Zack, time to retreat," Slater says after a gold sneaker doesn't fit Kelly, Jessie or Lisa. "All of these ladies have fat feet!"

Episode 12: "Close Encounters of the Nerd Kind"

Aired November 23, 1990

Plot: In another episode about raising money to replace a broken video camera (after Season 1's "Love Letters"), the gang conspires to trick a tabloid into believing that Screech is an alien. At $1,500 for a picture and $10,000 for a meeting, the temptation (to commit fraud) is undeniable, especially after the makeup work (including several extra eyes on his forehead) was already done for the Zack-directed student film "Alien Invasion of Bayside."

Pretty weird: This episode was a holdover from the first high school season, which is why everyone suddenly looks much younger and the episode is included as part of the intended season on the box set (but is being written about here in the order it ran).

Zack's lies (2):

- Submitting a photo of Screech as an alien to the National Babbler
- Telling Belding that Jessie (in disguise as very respectfully named Mexican woman Maria Tortilla) played not Batman but "Batmamacita"

The aggression returns: When Zack says the best thing to do about the broken camera is to blame Jessie and she says Zack is irresponsible and disloyal, Kelly tells Jessie to "Stop being a stiff pickle." Who cares that Jessie's right, right?

Comic relief: Somehow the decision was made to make Lt. Thompson (Sean Masterson), who the students believe is from the Babbler but is actually in the Air Force's UFO investigation unit, a total klutz, and it's oddly hilarious every time he knocks over the pencils in Belding's office or botches even the most basic interaction by stumbling. Sadly, the recurring role-turned-spinoff series never came.

Can't argue with that logic: When Belding asks Thompson if he really thinks there are beings here from another planet, he responds, "Well, they have to be somewhere." The gag of Screech taking off his face and pretending to be Zorch (prompting Thompson to claim, "Even when I thought it was real and sensed it was a prank, I still knew it was real") is clever, and we'll just move past wondering how they got such a good Screech mask.

Continuity: Running out of order must have confused people when the episode ends with Belding and Zack saying this is the first time they've ever worked together on something (after joining forces to get Thompson off their backs), seeing as they just did that in "Save the Max."

Sometimes this show doesn't feel that old, and other times: Max references "Mork and Mindy." Enough said.

*****Interview with Masterson:** "Why is [Zack] the leader? Everything's positioned from his point of view. And things all work out on a certain level for Zack. They didn't so much attack white male privilege, but they certainly questioned it, and they certainly exposed the arrogance, and how many get-out-of-jail-free cards did he get? I don't think in the writers' room they were trying to pull back the onion on white male privilege, and white male privilege is what we call it now, but it's really about the mechanics of growing up, being cool and 'Where do I fit in?' That whole show is about 'Where do I fit in?' And everybody's always trying to figure out how to fit in. He's not; he's kind of been given Elvis status." *(Read more from Masterson on page 327.)*

Episode 13: "Running Zack"

Aired November 24, 1990

Plot: Ugh, I've been dreading this one. When everyone must do a presentation on their ancestors, Zack at first perpetuates several offensive Native American stereotypes before befriending the benevolent Chief Henry (Dehl Berti), who has many stories about Zack's ancestors available on cue. Meanwhile, Jessie begs Lisa, whose great-great-great-grandfather was a slave who escaped and returned to help other slaves do the same, to forgive her for descending from slave traders, demanding, "Unleash those centuries of repressed anger!"

Hmm, how to say this: "Running Zack" is ambitious, I guess, attempting to nod toward heritage and uncomfortable U.S. history in a way that still fits within a 21-minute Saturday morning teen sitcom. But Zack's stuff is the "I Now Pronounce You Chuck and Larry" of Native American understanding, trying to generate laughs out of prejudice only to wag a finger at it later. Meanwhile, Henry comes off more like a magical, imaginary presence than an actual person with a life of his own, and him dying does not help that. He also offers this very helpful explanation when Zack asks him "Why couldn't the white man and the Indians get along?": "Why can't get the lion get along with the zebra? Why can't the *A-rabs* get along with the Israelis? And why can't I get along with my ex-wife?"

Zack's lies (2):

- Claiming his tribe was Cherokee when he has no idea who they were
- Adding that they lived in Burbank, past the freeway

Very confusing version of continuity: After the opening, never-seen track meet it's noted that Zack hasn't run so fast since he stole Cindy Zeffirelli's bathing suit, a reference to a character in the junior high season. Zack claims this was before Kelly, which does not quite line up with how at the start of the first high school season it's suggested Zack has pined for Kelly for years. A good reminder of the undeniable fact that Zack spent his childhood in both Indiana and California and — wait. Is it possible there are two Zacks who lived in different places at the same time, and then trade off after one moved to the same place, resulting in such inconsistent behavior? (This is the kind of extremely rational thinking that a show without continuity inspires.)

Controversial idea for a new competition: Slater defends his great-grandfather's bullfighting experience, claiming it's not barbaric but a sport. Says Jessie: "It would only be a sport if the bull had a sword too." For better or worse, there are many people out there who would watch that.

Hearing what you want to hear: Screech is psyched when Jessie refers to her forefathers, marveling that having four fathers means four allowances. In other words, Screech is Amelia Bedelia.

Episode 14: "The Babysitters"

Aired December 1, 1990

Plot: Even though there's never been any mention of Kelly having a new baby brother, suddenly little Billy needs someone to watch him while Kelly takes cheerleading photos (obviously an all-day requirement) because her parents are snowed in at a ski lodge (a very normal trip to take after just having your seventh kid). Somewhat moving forward from the parenting and cooperative lessons of "The Mamas and the Papas," Zack now takes charge (everyone else has excuses) and, for starters, brings Billy to French class in a duffel bag. "Whatever you do," he says, "Don't go wee-wee."

Once again: This was a holdover from high school Season 1, meaning everyone looks younger and Max is there and (oh, whatever).

Is this the same guy? On caring for Billy, Zack says, "You do what you have to do, but I'm not going to shirk my responsibility," which is pretty much the opposite of his policy on everything. Also it seems he's on the track team (and needs to take photos with them) despite how that requires the kind of commitment he rarely displays. And we never, ever see him running track despite how many episodes depict Slater wrestling.

Also: Because the episode aired out of order, we're back to Kelly turning down Zack when he asks her out, just saying she's happy she can count on him.

Different kind of continuity error: After noting an especially pungent dirty diaper, Zack and Slater tear the last unused diaper and Slater bolts, leaving Zack to solve the problem using Slater's T-shirt. BUT HE DOESN'T WIPE BILLY AT ALL.

Zack's lies (1):

- Telling Kelly they only said they were worried because they were worried Mr. Belding wasn't getting any work done while watching Billy

Self-awareness: It's absurd that Screech, attempting to retrieve Billy in a class full of fake babies, accidentally takes a doll instead of a live baby. It's a relief when Lisa speaks for viewers and says, "You absolutely have to be some kind of major doofus."

Episode 15: "The Fabulous Belding Boys"

Aired December 9, 1990

Plot: It doesn't matter that no one's passed the history midterm in three years when Mr. Belding's long-haired, easygoing brother Rod (Edward Blatchford) takes over for evil Mr. Dickerson (Raf Mauro) and instructs everyone to tear up the test. Cue Zack thinking this guy is the coolest and the elder Belding butting heads with the astonishingly casual fill-in he for some reason trusted with his students.

In Rod they trust: Rod Belding has to be one of the low-key most ridiculous characters in the history of the show, instantly abusing his brother's already limited faith in him by not just blowing off the midterm he's supposed to administer but watching the Dodgers game in the principal's office with Zack and Screech. He also encourages the trip to change from his brother's choice of Yosemite National Park to whitewater rafting in Colorado, which Rod would then chaperone instead, something I'm sure is a common thing for substitute teachers to do.

Unforgettable: Of all the "Saved by the Bell" lines I've quoted over the years, this is definitely in the top 5, courtesy of Screech: "Wow, a building with two Beldings, one of whom is balding!"

Sometimes this show is just not nice to people: When Milton, a heavier student defined only by his size, says he wants to go to the Hershey's factory, Zack says "Fat chance" and pokes his belly. Stop endorsing cruel behavior, dammit.

Real quick: Pretty sure this is now the third episode hinging on kids' need to get good grades or they can't go on a class trip. That's a lot of repetition that doesn't really register until you watch it all like this.

On the other hand: "The Fabulous Belding Boys" teaches an important lesson about getting too swept up in a new person as Rod ultimately flakes on the trip because of a stewardess named Inga ("She's a 10!" he explains, not convincing his brother why it's OK to disappoint kids). Belding telling him "Get out of my school, Rod" is a memorable, impactful moment, as is Zack recognizing that Rod being more exciting doesn't necessarily mean he's better.

Zack's lies: None!

In a different kind of show: They'd actually go on the trip and we'd see them encounter a new set of challenges, feelings, experiences, conflicts. Alas.

*****Interview with Blatchford on why Rod Belding and this episode struck such a chord with people:** "I think the biggest thing is a guy who you really enjoy watching lets everybody down. How somebody you like so much can let you down; that's what I got out of it. That's what his lesson is. 'Cause Zack loves Rod, as I recall. And he let him down. So that's a big thing: How could someone you like so much and put so much faith in just blow you off like you're nothing? I think that resonated with people. And people put too much on certain people as heroes. 'Cause really Rod didn't give a shit about the kids; he just wanted to go get laid. Which is a normal thing for a guy like him. He didn't care about being a substitute teacher, he was just doing a favor for a weekend. He didn't care about the kids. And Zack [thought that he did]. So it was a misconception." *(Read more from Blatchford on page 243.)*

Episode 16: "From Nurse to Worse"

Aired December 15, 1990

Plot: Zack isn't as concerned about whether or not Kelly will agree to go steady with him once he sets eyes on Jennifer (Nancy Valen), the new school nurse who wears skirts shorter than the students do and almost instantly tells him he's cute. Meanwhile, normally tough Slater reveals a fear of needles.

Worth reiterating: Once again, Zack's definition for how he feels about Kelly leads back to her appearance, explaining that his cheerfulness is because "I expect to be going with the most beautiful girl in school by the end of the day."

On the subject of Nurse Jennifer: She should not be shamed for her wardrobe, as we have no idea what Bayside rules indicate for dress code. However, telling the obviously smitten Zack "I wonder what's going on in that body of yours" is not exactly justified simply because she ultimately helps the gang teach Zack a lesson (a totally professional thing for a new school nurse to do) by pretending to be in love with him and asking him to run away with her.

Zack's lies (4):

- Faking illness to get out of class
- Telling Jennifer his head feels hot
- Pretending to be Slater to take his flu shot for him
- Telling Kelly "There's not another student I'm interested in," which counts as a lie because of the manipulative word choice

A nerd by any other name: Fun to see the show challenge its usual "Give nerdy characters nerdy names" approach when the hunky Melvin Nerdly turns out to be a long way from Maxwell Nerdstrom, instead proving to be a chess champion who also plays football, baseball and hockey and also models. Zack regrets thinking it would be OK for Kelly to go out with him, and in theory learned a lesson about not judging a book by its cover. Again, in theory.

That continuity thing: Despite frequently carrying the banner for inner beauty, Jessie's reaction to being told she needs glasses is, "Do you want me to look like a four-eyed frog face?"

Valuable comic relief: Miss Simpson continues to be a hoot, including mistaking Lisa's poem about the mall for an ode to the Rocky Mountains and, when Belding shrieks on the intercom (after receiving a flu shot), noting, "Personally, I like the old school cheer better."

*****Interview with Valen on the show's affinity for sexy nurses:** "The creators and writers did an incredible job bringing to life a fantasy that a young kid would have. So that is from the mind of that character. I think there's something to be said about our perceptions. If it's a 16-year-old kid, maybe he's seeing everything sexually. Maybe the way that they did the show, the characters came to life through his perception. Could they get away with it now? Maybe not. However, I think they did a great job because it's true today. Sixteen-years-old, a boy is going to have those type of fantasies, and he is going to be feeling like he's the man if a pretty girl is flirting with him. [It ends the way it does] because he really wants to be with somebody his own age. That's what he shows; it may sound great, but he's not ready for all that yet. I think that's actually good to make that 15-, 16-year-old boy that's thinking he's ready for all that back up a minute. And say, 'Oh, OK, I may be thinking these things and feeling these things, but I'm not really going to act on these things because I'm not ready for it.' Just like he's not." *(Read more from Valen on page 248.)*

Episode 17: "Breaking Up is Hard to Undo"

Aired December 16, 1990

Plot: Completely erasing the previous episode (or just fast-forwarding more than two months and a lot of relevant events later?), now apparently Zack and Kelly have been going steady for, according to Zack, "68 days, 14 hours and 37 minutes." But Bayside relationships hit major bumps when Zack tries to tell Kelly she can't get dinner with her ex and Jessie's romantic-dinner-and-ballet date idea does not quite sync with Slater's acquisition of Raiders tickets. (For the rare Saturday-night game?) In other words, big fight, sexist pig, oink oink, etc.

As it turns out, though: This episode might have one of the best resolutions of the series, in which Zack and Slater sincerely take accountability for their idiocy, staging the "What I Should Have Said" theater at the Max in which Lisa plays Jessie, Screech plays Kelly and the guys redo how they should have reacted to their significant other's ideas. "Saved by the Bell" didn't often do realistic storylines about relationships, but in "Breaking Up is Hard to Undo" the couples fight, wonder how they can move forward and ultimately resolve things thanks to humility, apologies and perspective. Good lessons all around.

Zack's lies (0): Wow! That's twice in the last three episodes. Keep it up, preppie.

Because Belding has to do something: Yet again the principal is involved in the lives of (a few very select) students in a ridiculous and over-the-top way. In this case Belding is on the outs with his wife because of differing feelings about her mother staying with them, leading to Belding bonding with Zack and Slater and providing terrible advice that just seems like he wants the guys to hang with him instead of making up with their girlfriends. So praise for this episode comes with an asterisk for the utter ridiculousness of Belding existing as part of this misguided bro trio.

Once more about Jessie's sudden superficiality: When Lisa asks why Jessie can't just forgive and forget, she says she'd rather be "short and fat with bad hair." What?

Once more about Zack's perpetual superficiality: When Kelly appears in his vision, Zack's only response is, "Gosh, she's pretty." Dude, is that all she is to you?

Trivia: One of Slater's nicknames for Jessie is apparently Honey Lips.

Episode 18: "Glee Club"

Aired December 23, 1990

Plot: Just like when Zack ran for student council president simply to win a trip to D.C., he joins the glee club in hopes of going to the finals in Hawaii. To do that he and the rest of the equally deceitful club will have to fake their way through singing and hinge their chances on the legitimate pipes of the less than spotlight-seeking Violet.

The elephant in the room: Scott Wolf plays a waiter at the Max who is also in the Glee Club! You'd think there would be more sightings like this of people who got their start in the background of "Saved by the Bell," but it's surprisingly rare.

Zack's lies (3):

- Recording a different glee club and playing the tape for Belding as if the Bayside glee club was singing
- Using the tape again during competition
- Claiming that the ridiculous performance, in which the tape plays very fast and then very slow, is their impression of a glee club tuning up

Quick question: If you were in a room in which people were pretending to sing while a tape of other singers played, you'd know, right? It is possible Mr. Belding is not the smartest.

This line: After Zack supposedly learned a lesson in the last episode about how to treat women, it is not awesome when he tells Screech, "She's your woman. Take her out into the hall and talk her into it."

Why even bother mentioning but: Kelly still can't sing, despite her brush with stardom in Hot Sundae.

Continued emphasis on status: Even when encouraging his girlfriend Violet, Screech refers to himself deprecatingly, and not in a way that seems lighthearted. Calling himself her "nerd in shining armor" just seems like the show going out of its way to categorize people who don't look like Zack, Kelly, Slater, Jessie and Lisa. (Reminder that Violet is just future "90210" star Tori Spelling in glasses.)

More classic Screech: Advised to compliment Violet's mom by comparing her to a movie star (he's trying to impress Violet's rich parents, as his relationship with her obviously served as an inspiration for the class differences in Nicholas Sparks novels), he absurdly says she looks like Arnold Schwarzenegger. Then he asks if he'll get warts from frog legs and accidentally yanks the tablecloth and everything on it onto the floor. Look, mom, you don't date Screech for the charisma. You date him for the … um …

Stats/Looking Back on the Second High School Season

Well, that didn't last. Despite opening the season with a zero-lie episode and a one-lie outing in episode three, Zack still accumulates 47 lies this season, increasing his rate from 2.2 to 2.6 lies per episode. Where he ended the previous two seasons with zero-lie episodes, this time he closes with three lies, offering less suggestion of growth. Which is fitting, I suppose, considering the season-long increases.

And also considering another troubling consistency: Zack has now gone from treating women badly in 62 percent of episodes to 56 percent to, in this season, 56 percent again. As he's getting older Zack is lying more and still being very bad to women, and in return he has progressively earned Kelly's affection.

While major continuity errors occur in closer to a quarter rather than half of the episodes, in 28 percent of the episodes the show was particularly aggressive toward Jessie beyond just her usual banter with Slater. It continues to be odd, to say the least, to see how Jessie is sometimes used as a mouthpiece for important issues but her point is often laughed off or minimized by Slater, whose "pigheaded" behavior rarely causes him any problems.

Overall, Kelly is probably treated the most fondly, and it's hard not to feel like she deserves a lot better than Zack. Which makes the next set of episodes arrive at just the right time.

High School Season 3 (1991)

The next season is the first of two whopping 26-episode seasons, and it's pretty all over the place, incorporating the Malibu Sands Beach Club episodes as well as the two-part arc about Jessie's evil stepbrother, the two-part trip for Jessie's dad's wedding and another two-part storyline about Zack falling for a girl who is homeless. That's a lot.

Episode 1: "The Last Dance"

Aired September 14, 1991

Plot: This is the third consecutive high school season that opens with a dance! As in "The Prom," Kelly's worried about her finances, this time to go to the costume ball with Zack as Romeo and Juliet. What's new is that she suddenly can't stop thinking about Jeff Hunter (Patrick Muldoon of "Starship Troopers"), the new manager of the Max who's a sophomore at UCLA and, spoiler alert, important enough to last more than one episode.

Zack's lies (3):

- Telling Jeff that Kelly is an only child and it would break her dad's heart if she didn't have Saturday off to celebrate with him (2)
- Adding that he thought Kelly's siblings were just very short aunts and uncles

That can't be encouraged: It doesn't take Jeff long to hit on Kelly, who's assumedly 16 or 17 to his 20. Still, it's worth noting that Jeff tells her that she's terrific, which is not a specific compliment but more than Zack has ever said to her.

And overall: This is a strong episode featuring real conflict that young (and not as young) viewers can relate to, as Thiessen effectively plays Kelly's discomfort while trying to figure out what to do about this new person and new feelings. It's clear that her relationship with Zack isn't strong, and that she can't stop talking to Lisa and Jessie about Jeff is revealing. She loves Zack but it's over, and sharing one more dance outside the school, the same place they had their first kiss at the start of the previous season, is a nice touch.

Setting precedent: This is the first appearance of the Zack Attack, as the gang's band practices after school and later plays at the ball. Any time the show makes any effort to establish an idea rather than just making it up nonsensically we need to feel grateful. Of course, in the previous episode Zack couldn't sing at all and now he's singing just fine in the band, so who knows what to think about anything. (Also, Screech tells Belding they're better than MC Hammer. I'm not counting the MC Hammer references, but they're approaching Freddy Krueger levels of frequency.)

Meant for each other: It's been established Belding may not be especially intelligent. It appears to be a unifier for him and his wife, as he tells students they can't dress up as him this year because "Mrs. Belding gets confused easily."

Mind blown: When Zack and Kelly are named king and queen and he says she's the most beautiful one he's ever seen, she replies, "Thanks, Jeff." Just like saying Rachel instead of Emily at the altar! "Friends" should have had to pay royalties or something, right?

Episode 2: "Zack's Birthday Party"

Aired September 14, 1991

Plot: Wait, so all of a sudden it's the summer? Who decided this should air like this? OK, sure, now the whole gang's working at the Malibu Sands Beach Club, where exes Zack and Kelly have no tension between them, boss man Leon Carosi (Ernie Sabella, aka Pumbaa in "The Lion King") is a huge jerk and his tough-tawkin' New Yawk daughta Stacey (Leah Remini of "The King of Queens") becomes the requisite love interest for Zack.

Zack's lies: None! Perhaps Zack's behavior is seasonal.

Slater just does not quit: When Carosi notes that Jessie "likes to throw your two cents in," Slater adds, "You have no idea." Later, when Stacey takes over managing the staff, he mutters, "Great, we're working for a woman." This after the guys ask the girls to breakfast and Slater tells Jessie they intend to eat at Lisa's parents' beach house, adding, "Get in that kitchen and make me some French toast!" Again, this is portrayed as charming.

More awful mocking of the other: Dressed in a hot dog costume, Screech needs Zack's help to get out of the suit because "There's a herd of fat kids trying to barbecue me!"

But organic storylines! In the past the show might have done nothing with the idea that Kelly and Jessie were living with Lisa in her parents' house over the summer. Thankfully it's used to drive at least a little conflict as some of their habits get on each other's nerves, such as Kelly waking up early to run and Jessie being messy.

Continuity! In many, many episodes Screech has failed to keep a secret, so here the others deliberately don't tell him specifics about Zack's surprise party in advance. They're learning!

Episode 3: "The Aftermath"

Aired September 21, 1991

Plot: And now back to our regularly scheduled breakup. And yet another birthday party! Kelly wants to bring Jeff to Lisa's Sweet 16 while the gang tries to figure out how to feel about the new couple moving forward, and Zack gets set up on a series of dates by some very deliberately chosen candidates.

More on that: Lisa's pick is a superficial romance novel obsessive who talks through the whole movie (just like Lisa did with Screech that time!); Jessie's has a "great personality and insatiable hunger for life," leading to the show mocking a larger girl who pours popcorn in her own mouth and craves a big bowl of spaghetti and meatballs after the movie; more up Zack's one-dimensional alley is Screech's cousin Kimberly, an attractive blond (she's adopted) who ultimately and wisely storms off when realizing Zack is only using her to make Kelly jealous.

First, though: A moment that I assume all young viewers saw and thought was the coolest when it comes to dating: Zack ordering one shake and Kimberly fluttering her fingers as he adds "with two straws." To my surprise, this is not a common move in reality.

Zack's lies (1):

- Telling Kimberly that Kelly only slapped him because he said he wanted a strawberry shake instead

Say this for Jeff: He's going into the tough situation of a friend group that could be inclined to hate him, but at Lisa's party he does a nice job of connecting with Slater and Jessie. He doesn't really try with Screech, but he's probably picked up that such treatment is normal.

In case you missed what Slater thinks of women: "Like my Uncle Charlie used to say, women are like vines: If you fall off one, hey, you can swing with another." Replies Jessie: "You're not just a pig, you're a gorilla pig," which I Googled and is a thing on Urban Dictionary.

Still aggression toward Jessie: When she apologizes to Kelly for being "narrow-minded, judgmental and pigheaded," Kelly says, "You were just being yourself." Yikes. On that note, though, Thiessen is again really good here as Kelly becomes frustrated with how her friends treat her now that she's with Jeff. Gosselaar also has a strong moment as he confesses "I guess I was more hurt than I thought, and I didn't know how to deal with it." Good on the show for addressing the issue this way.

Less effective: "Treat her right" is such a cliché. Besides, Zack doesn't know what it means and shouldn't be advising it to anyone.

Conspiracy theory: Lisa's house looks similar to Screech's house; are they secretly living together? It can't possibly just be the same set!

OK I guess we should mention it every time now: Another MC Hammer reference! Lisa wants him to play her party. He doesn't.

Episode 4: "The Game"

Aired September 21, 1991

Plot: Haha now we're back to the beach, nothing means anything and time is imaginary. Also, Zack and company try to win a volleyball match so he can get a good deal on Carosi's '66 Mustang.

Was so excited to mention this: The really tall ringer named Gary (who charms Kelly and gets hurt before the big game) is played by a guy named Dark Sevier, which might be the coolest name ever. According to IMDB, this is his only acting credit. Because you just have nowhere to go but down after playing a guy like Gary.

Great sequence: Screech finds a group of possible replacements for Gary, which includes a girl who's the best athlete in her school (a preschool), a former Olympian (in 1936) and "Big Pete," who they all should already know from school but don't seem to recognize at all. Pete (Bryan Cooper) doesn't quite blow them away, considering Zack hits him on the back to welcome him to the team and Pete whines, "I'm telling!"

Zack's lies (3):

- Telling Carosi the gang is awesome at volleyball (hard to say what is and is not true, we'll just call it one lie here)
- Claiming their pose that's meant to hide Gary's injured foot is actually them practicing inner volleyball
- Sending a telegram himself and claiming it's from the guys at rival North Beach

The kind of misunderstanding sitcoms were made for? Lisa and Jessie definitely do not think Screech is talking about Zack's desired car when he notes, "Even with her top down I wasn't thrilled."

Star of the future! Eric Dane, otherwise known as McSteamy, plays Tad Pogue, a guy from North Beach with unrequited interest in Stacey. And Tad's brother is played by Patrick Dempsey! (Not true.)

Episode 5: "Operation Zack"

Aired September 28, 1991

Plot: Aaaaaand now it's not summer anymore, with Zack hurting his knee before a big basketball game after Belding bumps into him and then fearing the worst when he has to have surgery. In other words, the second consecutive episode that's in some way about a sports injury.

Zack's lies (6):

- Sending Screech in a blond wig to pretend to be him for a test
- Telling Mr. Dewey his house burned down
- Having Belding take his take-home math test for him (this obviously makes zero sense)
- Dressing up to impersonate a doctor
- Claiming he's about to perform a "neckteroctomy"
- Falsely deepening his voice (because of Elizabeth Holmes this must count as a lie)

Warped depiction of nurses: We've already seen the highly sexualized Nurse Jennifer in "From Nurse to Worse." Now they're presented as airheaded objects who wear skimpy outfits and give Zack the all-fingers flirty wave as they walk by. Also, a nurse named Monique who offers neck rubs by request tells Zack, "You're not sick, you're dangerous." Kids' shows aren't really supposed to seem like they're building up to something so porny.

Speaking of which: It hasn't been that long since Zack and Kelly broke up, but she doesn't seem uncomfortable in the slightest as Zack flirts with everyone he can. Continuity, hooray!

Character study: Is Lisa, tasked with being a candy striper at the hospital where her parents work, kind of terrible? Yes, she eventually learns a lesson about caring for others, but before that she's very self-involved and says, "I don't do wheelchairs." In "Zack's Birthday" she punted responsibility for not asking her parents if they could have the party at their place simply because she's attractive and fashionable. She certainly has redeeming qualities and moments too, but eek. (Note: Voorhies does have nice chemistry with Susan Beaubian, who plays her mom, Dr. Turtle.)

Aggression toward Jessie: While it is rude of her to mock Kelly's drawing on Zack's cast, Kelly threatening to punch Jessie seems just a bit out of character.

Sobering metaphor: Bayside loses the big basketball game by one point after Belding shouts, "Shoot your hopes and dreams!" and by the time Slater realizes Belding meant the ball, it's too late. As they say, you miss 100 percent of the shots your principal distracts.

*****Interview with Beaubian on the shallow, superficial Lisa still having a lot to learn from her far more selfless parents:** "Oh, she's a little princess, yeah. I chalk it up to high school. I chalk it up to her age. I chalk it up to her privilege. I can't tell you in real life how many – because now, as a matter of fact, in the last 20 years or so, I've taught voice to high school kids, and I've had a lot of kids who have come through my lessons who are beautiful young high school girls with talent that, you know, may be a little bit shallow. [Laughs] And they want what they want, and I would just chalk it up to her being immature. As Lisa's mom, I would say that I would have faith in her that as she grows up, as she matures, that all those qualities that we tried to instill in her will come to the front. But right now, she's a little bit selfish, a little bit shallow, a little bit spoiled." *(Read more from Beaubian on page 278.)*

Episode 6: "Fourth of July"

Aired September 28, 1991

Plot: You know the drill, it's summer again. Echoing "Miss Bayside," Kelly, Lisa and Jessie compete in a pageant (winner gets a $500 savings bond!) while Carosi pressures judge Zack to vote for Stacey, showing that the man in charge might have even less integrity than the guy he's bossing around.

Zack's lies: None! That's three summer episodes and only three lies!

He's still Zack, though: He suggests changing the obstacle course game of barrel jumping to "bikini jumping," which perhaps overestimates the enjoyment for the people actually in the bikinis.

The pageant: Kelly's answer is definitely the best, and kudos to Zack for having the guts to vote for her despite Carosi's threats. Of course, the event also provides a chance to yank the mic away from Jessie as she starts reflecting on America's violent past.

For what it's worth: This is a fun episode, between Slater and Lisa's sudden rivalry in the staff vs. member competition and Jessie and Kelly pulling Carosi into the water after the tug-of-war is over. Plus, Stacey proves to be a strong person when she starts to make excuses for her behavior to Zack (she foolishly let Screech convince her that Zack voted for Kelly because of their romantic history) and then stops herself: "No excuses; I apologize." Similarly, the way Kelly calms down Stacey before she apologizes shows Kelly to be patient and level-headed as well. What are these two doing hanging around with Zack?

Summer lovin': Besides for containing the first kiss for Zack and Stacey, this episode also includes Slater and Lisa going to a dance together, an extension of the fun they had during the competition. Nothing ever comes of this, of course, which we can only assume falls under the same umbrella as the brief flirtation/ultimate nothing of Rachel and Joey.

Screech being Screech: Tasked with dressing up as Uncle Sam, he instead dons the apparel of *his* Uncle Sam, including an old-looking brown suit and fake mustache. "As my Uncle Sam would say: Have fun, enjoy, when do we eat?"

Episode 7: "Check Your Mate"

Aired October 5, 1991

Plot: Thanks to the lucky red beret that Violet gave him, Screech is unstoppable on the chess field/court/whatever. But can he beat Valley's new hotshot exchange student Peter Breschnev (Matt Kaminsky), who, according to one of the goons Zack and Slater bets against, is not only from Russia but also the Soviet Union?

The part she was born to play: Hillary Hayes is a riot as Allison, who claims to be a reporter from Chess Boy Magazine but is actually a spy from Valley attempting to break up Screech and Violet so he'll be too sad to compete. The adjustments in her voice are impressive as she moves from polished reporter to, say, "Hi, sweet lips. Like, the dweeb totally fell for it."

Whose idea was this? Allison says she wants to make Screech the magazine's centerfold/checkmate of the month and invites him to the Chess Boy Mansion and its pawn-shaped pool. Had Screech gone to the party, the bizarre Playboy allusions really could have spun out of control.

Zack's lies (4):

- Giving Screech a fake beret to boost his confidence
- Telling Peter it's an American custom to take a pregame photo so if you lose there's an image of you smiling
- Labeling the janitor's closet as the press room
- Dressing up as Peter and taking his spot in the match

Status check: Doing radio play-by-play of one of Screech's matches, Jessie calls something exciting, to which Zack responds, "Oh yeah, there's nothing more thrilling than geek-to-geek combat." So, so many unchecked efforts to categorize and disrespect people. Oh yeah, and his and Slater's whole kidnapping/fraud scheme is pretty much shrugged off.

Line to use in everyday conversation, courtesy of Allison, cooing to her boyfriend on the phone: "I'll see ya. At the galleria."

Trivia: Peter impresses Screech by citing the Spaski Bishop Block, an intimidating chess move named after Peter's uncle. "Although Aunt Sophia has thicker mustache," he notes.

Episode 8: "My Boyfriend's Back"

Aired October 5, 1991

Plot: Back at the beach club, Zack puts a hold on his plan to tell Stacey he loves her after her sophomore-at-Yale boyfriend Craig Strand (Benjamin King of "Liv & Maddie") turns up unannounced, very jazzed to give Stacey his fraternity pin (hahahahahahahahaha). This sounds like something that can only be settled with an ATV race!

Zack's lies: None! Summer continues to mean better behavior.

Surprisingly valid relationship lessons: Craig's a controlling jackass who just wants to possess Stacey and boss her around. (His version of a fist pump, utilized after pinning Stacey and saying she's now his girl forever, is weird on its own and especially in the situation.) Zack's initially threatened, of course, but Stacey sees how much more relaxed and happy she is with him, ultimately putting Craig and his pin ("I hope he sits on it," she says) on a plane back to the other side of the country. In this episode, Zack demonstrates actual vulnerability and feeling, and their opposites-attract chemistry actually makes sense in terms of why Stacey's interested in him. Nice.

Before that, though: Zack very smoothly covers for his first failed attempt to say I love you, stammering, "I want you to know that I love … I love the way that you butter bread." Points to the writers for Stacey's response: "This is margarine, but thanks anyway."

And one more thing on Craig: I know the show isn't going for nuance, but this love triangle would be much more engrossing if Craig wasn't such a self-involved doofus, who also cheats "Ben-Hur"-style during the charity race. The highlight of this subplot is Kelly smacking the gong twice during the pinning ceremony. "Sorry, it just felt right!" Her positivity is a salve in a show that sometimes feels mean-spirited. Speaking of which:

More undermining Jessie: After Slater excitedly describes details of the ATV that Carosi rides, Jessie elbows him and explains she doesn't know why she did that, but what Slater said "sounds sexist." In other words, the show suggests Jessie's on her soapbox even when she doesn't have a good reason for it, thus challenging her perspective overall. The episode also includes a running joke about what a lousy driver Jessie is (culminating in her driving an ATV into the ocean), and later, when Jessie holds a baseball bat to ward off a possible intruder, Lisa quips, "You're not going to need the bat, honey; just nag him to death like you do everyone else." Bad.

Missed opportunity: This episode features a funny sequence when Screech — seeing how Kelly gets club members to sponsor her in the ATV charity race after bringing back their child who was playing too close to the water — drags a kid 10 feet to people who aren't even his parents. The boy says, "Let go of me, dweeb, I'm not lost!" and kicks Screech, but when Lisa sees Screech hopping on one foot, why doesn't she reference when they danced The Sprain together?! Clearly "What are you doing, the Mexican dork dance?" was deemed a stronger one-liner.

Episode 9: "Fake IDs"

Aired October 19, 1991

Plot: Dating college girl Danielle (Julie St. Claire of "Lincoln Heights") means 16-year-old Zack and co. need a way to get into 18-and-over dance club The Attic, which looked a lot cooler when I was a kid than it does now. Fortunately their photo class provides the perfect opportunity for Screech to falsify their ages; unfortunately they spot Jeff at the club, getting cozy with someone who is not Kelly.

Zack's lies (11), the second-most ever in one episode:

- Telling Danielle that he just started at USC and majors in photojournalism (2)
- Getting a fake ID (that says he's 54 years old)
- Telling his mom (Melody Rogers) that he, Slater and Screech are really tired
- Using inflatables, obviously inspired by Ferris Bueller, to fill space in their beds while the guys sneak out
- Utilizing a fake voice to sound older for the bouncer at the Attic
- Claiming he can't go to lunch tomorrow because he'll be in the darkroom all day
- Telling his mom he promised Slater he'd stay at his house and Slater's heart would be broken if Zack didn't (2)
- Explaining that Danielle never sees him on campus because as a photojournalism major he always has to be out capturing life as it happens (?)
- Telling Danielle that's not his mom, just his beautiful, intelligent, young-looking older sister (we'll count that as one)

Disturbingly light-hearted joke: When Slater compliments the bouncer's scar, the guy thanks him and adds, "It's a gift from my girl." Yeesh.

Did I imagine this or: When Zack tells Kelly about Jeff, of course she doesn't believe him. But I could've sworn she said, "You maggot-mouthed liar!" Whoa. That is an interesting choice of words. The scene that follows, though, as Kelly asks Jeff about the following Saturday night and he's avoiding something, is well played between Thiessen and Muldoon, as Kelly recognizes Zack might have been telling the truth about Jeff, who ultimately explains (just before Kelly ends things at the Attic) that he's not ready for a commitment. Alas, she does not call him a maggot-mouthed liar.

Unexpected connection: When Slater introduces himself to Danielle's friends, he says that the A.C. stands for "absolutely charmed." This is not that far from Gil Faizon's (Nick Kroll) "Charmed, I'm sure" catchphrase in "Oh, Hello."

Very different concept for a club: When first hearing about the Attic, Screech is psyched. "That sounds like fun; there could be bats up there!"

Another great Screech line: When Kelly asks if the guys really saw Jeff at the Attic, Screech starts crying, and has no answer after she wonders why Jeff would cheat on her. "I don't know, Kelly! Men are such fools! I hope I never become one."

*****Interview with St. Claire:** "For the time, [Zack's behavior] seemed like a typical teenage boy. [Danielle] is also young, so I don't think she put too much thought into [Zack's lie about never being seen on campus]. I don't recall his exact response, but I assume it made sense to her. Doesn't surprise me at all [that he lied 11 times in this episode]. That was his character. There have been many characters who have been/done the same. He's a tad scheme-y, like Eddie Haskell in 'Leave it to Beaver' or Jason Bateman's Derek from NBC's 'Silver Spoons.' [The message of this episode is] don't lie to your parents. They are smart and they will figure it out. Or, like the phone call [Zack's mom] intercepted, karma will get you!" *(Read more from St. Claire on page 289.)*

Episode 10: "Boss Lady"

Aired October 19, 1991

Plot: With Carosi gone and Stacey in charge, everything at the club should be lighthearted and easy ... until Zack and Stacey realize her dad double-booked the club and they have to find a way to simultaneously host both a 50th anniversary party and a Sweet 16.

Zack's lies (3):

- Telling Carosi he was just trying to loosen up the employees when he was really doing a negative impersonation of him
- Claiming that the older partiers are chaperones for the younger party and the younger people are there to remind the older ones to stay forever young (2)

Knocking Jessie off a soapbox again: When she stands up for the kitchen staff (they're mad they haven't received the raise Carosi promised them), it just turns into the show mocking her mediocre Spanish, followed by Jessie telling Zack he doesn't understand oppression because he lives in a world of privilege. His response: "Yeah, and you live next door to me." He's right, but that doesn't make it wrong for her to want to help others.

Well, that's literal: It's not new that Lisa cares about money. But when Screech finds a gold coin in the sand and Lisa starts kissing up to him in hopes of finding more, she becomes a literal and figurative gold digger at the same time. Impressive!

The message: Even though both parties wind up occupying the same space, everyone has a good time and appreciates how Stacey and Zack worked to solve the problem while also standing up for the kitchen staff. Ignoring how rude it is to cut short the speeches/dances/everything at the anniversary party while they're still trying to end it before the other one has to start, it all turns out pretty well and feels relatively benign. Progress?

Another reason I blame this show for my eighth-grade science class incident: When Zack asks the Thornhills if they can push back their anniversary celebration, Herbert says, "Son, at my age one day could be everything. I could kick off tomorrow during my tango lesson!" Yep, definitely a respectful version of the way older people talk.

Debate if this is more accurate: Persuaded by Zack that her birthday party should be outside, 15-year-old Jenny whines to her dad, "I want, I want, I want!" Isn't there a chocolate factory she should be trapped in?

Episode 11: "Pipe Dreams"

Aired October 26, 1991

Plot: A memorable one in which oil is found on the Bayside football field, leading to both big dreams of massive funding and an accident that kills the animals which the students had recently cared for and returned to the pond near the school.

Continuity? This episode pretty much features the exact opposite approach toward Jessie, which is a good thing but notable in the degree to which the show does a 180. At first the others dismiss Jessie's concerns about oil, thinking she just needs to lighten up. But the environmental cost overpowers greed, leading to Zack's memorable presentation in which he notes how oil bigwig Mr. Grayson (Gary Lahti) left off all the oil derricks from his model of the future school. Zack eventually squirts oil on Grayson, who Belding then sends away despite having previously made this intriguing point: "People died in the space program; does that mean we should stop exploring the universe?"

Zack's lies (1):

- A discussion of when he and Screech secretly put a periscope in the girls' locker room (his sleazy comment, a very deliberate double entendre when she's trying to get them to sign a petition to stop the drilling: "Jessie, you look great in a towel. Now drop it.")

More creepiness: With additional funding, Zack dreams of the school having a bigger gym and "a cheerleader in every locker." What?!

Even more creepiness: Franklin (Michael Warwick) admits that he only wanted to protest with Jessie and Kelly so he could be chained to the student council president and head cheerleader. "Ever try nerd love?" he asks, uncomfortably. After they finish a chant, he declares, "Stop the shouting, give me a kiss!" Gag.

Money equals British? The vision of a hypothetical, richer Bayside is very snooty and pretty British, finding the students drinking tea out of tiny mugs and Zack sitting in a fancy chair while reading and wearing glasses. Belding is the butler, Kelly now owns the Max (changed to Chez Kelly) and is married to Screech (?), who bought Saudi Arabia and unveils by far one of the worst cultural interpretations ever used on this show. And that's saying something.

Thing I should have started counting: There are so many Kevin Costner references being made. So many. And he wasn't even some young heartthrob, he was in his mid-30s at the time!

Episode 12: "The Last Weekend"

Aired October 26, 1991

Plot: The end of the summer means the annual luau, Zack and Stacey having to say goodbye and Kelly sweetly navigating a crush from Billy (Jordan Michael of "Full House"), who says he's "a mature 11."

Zack's lies: None! Giving Zack a pass about lying to Stacey and Carosi in order to get them in the same place for the staff photo as a way of helping them reconcile. (And Stacey pretending that Zack sold a member mayonnaise while claiming it was suntan lotion paints him as a liar, but it didn't happen so we can forget that as well.) Out of six Malibu Sands Beach Club episodes, Zack had zero lies in four of them! That's stunning and worth exploring further at the end of the season.

Unexpectedly moving: Watching this for the first time in years, I was surprised at how much these relationships crest to something impactful. There's actually a feeling of loss between Zack and Stacey, and, as stupid as it sounds, I kind of got choked up when Carosi tells Zack that he particularly hopes that he comes back to work for him again next summer. When he says "You earned it" and shakes his hand after covering all the tips he previously stiffed Zack on, the connection and warmth are palpable. And same with the gang coming to cheer up Zack on the beach after he and Stacey say they love each other and she leaves (which, of course, means we never see her again). A really nice ending to this mini season.

Lu-ow (sorry): After Slater suggests "Bodacious Bikini Babes" as the luau theme, Jessie says they should just put an apple in his mouth and he can be the roast pig. In fairness, while discussing a luau it would have been weird not to have this sort of exchange.

Funnier and more surprising: The older lady with a crush on Slater is named Mrs. Robinson! Fun fact: Dustin Hoffman was at one point attached to play Screech. (Not true at all.)

Real appearance of famous person: Denise Richards plays Cynthia, who was too afraid to talk to "hunk-o-rama" Slater all summer but sends him notes from a secret admirer and then fakes drowning so he can save her. When Jessie asks her if she's OK being called babe and chick, Cynthia says, "With dimples like those, he can say whatever he wants." And great news, she's going to Bayside! In other words, we never see her again either.

Episode 13: "The Wicked Stepbrother (Part 1)"

Aired November 2, 1991

Plot: Jessie's "mother's husband's son" Eric (Josh Hoffman) torments the gang, from annexing Jessie's room to aggressively pursuing Lisa to blackmailing Zack after the blond liar claims he's Jewish to get out of school for Rosh Hashanah (but really to spend it at the Dodgers playoff game). Only the remarkably nice Kelly feels bad for the guy, who did leave his home and friends back in New York but also specializes in manipulation and extortion.

Zack's lies (11 yet again):

- Thinking that he could say his house burned down, he has measles or that his grandmother died to get out of school (3)
- Claiming his grandmother died four times last year (4)
- Another unused idea that still counts: That the Pope invited him to the Vatican
- Raising his hand in class to indicate that he's Jewish
- Wearing a yarmulke at the Dodgers game to maintain the ruse
- Letting Eric drive the car Belding bought for his wife (Eric thinks it's Slater's) with the intention of getting him in trouble

Eric's version of a pickup line: "Let's dump these two and go to the beach; we'll make nice in the sand." Seems … unpromising.

Aggression toward Jessie: This episode contains a weird running joke about girls falling in the toilet, which Jessie eventually does. That the show so frequently undermines or embarrasses the person who's the most outspoken about ideas and values doesn't sit super well.

Because it's been like five minutes: Another Freddy Krueger reference! And a whole subplot involving MC Hammer! (Well, he's not there or anything; Zack just gives Lisa tickets to the concert to bribe her to go out with Eric.)

Actually kind of sweet: Lisa and Eric hit it off on their date, which involves seeing "Casablanca" and (shocking) going to the Max. His Bogart impression is not the worst?

Episode 14: "The Wicked Stepbrother (Part 2)"

Aired November 2, 1991

Plot: With Mrs. Belding's car wrecked (Lisa, driving it rather than Eric, crashed when Screech took a picture, flash and all) and Eric holding all the leverage, Zack tries to figure out how to repair $600 in damage and still not get caught for his Rosh Hashanah-based deception. Also, Lisa likes Eric now but may have to pay for having been bribed by Zack in ways that he is never held accountable.

Speaking of which (4):

- Holding a fixed lottery to raise money that Screech is guaranteed to win and give to him
- Lying to Belding about his car, which leads to the invention of the word "Yamasushiyakatorispeakaleaker"
- Claiming Screech said "I won" when he meant to say that math teacher Mr. Sachs (Bernard Hiller) is wonderful
- Telling Belding a hurricane hit the area last night

Hooray for math: The sequence in which Mr. Sachs solves a problem and everyone in class hoots and hollers is hilarious, since Sachs has never seen such math-related enthusiasm and the students are really hoping that the answer will match up with their lottery ticket. A clever and funny visual gag.

Hooray for writing: Eh, maybe not. This, from Lisa, is rough: "When I took the tickets I didn't like him. And now I don't like me!"

The show in a nutshell: Frustrated with the pressure to fix the car (which Eric has the shop class take apart), Slater wonders why being the captain of the football and wrestling teams, having the biggest muscles in school and having great dimples and teeth aren't enough for his friends. Why would his friends care about stuff like that rather than the person he is? Weird focus on appearance, again.

Fun with continuity: The two-part episode comes to a nice close as Jessie punches some perspective into Eric, he fixes the car and the gang successfully convinces him not to go back to New York. Which is then reinforced by us never seeing him on the show ever again!

Trivia: The CD Belding can't wait to play in the car is "Bo Jackson Sings the Blues"; also, Screech once came in third in a Wile E. Coyote look-alike contest.

Episode 15: "Date Auction"

Aired November 9, 1991

Plot: Clearly the only logical way to raise funds for new cheerleading uniforms is auctioning off dates to a dance with Bayside's bachelors, whether they're in relationships or not. That means Jessie threatening any girl who bids on Slater (Kelly does, though, because she feels badly for him and is very nice) and Zack being a shallow jerk who tries to blow off Wendy (the late Judy Carmen) because she's not as petite as the other girls lusting after someone you'd think they would by now know is not a good dude.

Zack's lies (5):

- Telling Wendy he can't go to lunch today because of an old track injury that he never knows when it's going to hit (2)
- He can recover with intensive acupuncture, needle therapy, deep tissue massage and vitamin B shots but can't dance (let's call that 2)
- When Wendy called his house and his mom said he was out surfing it's because he was body surfing

For something new and different, undermining Jessie! After she calls a date auction "sexist flesh-peddling" and says it should be forbidden, the student council takes a vote and everyone else wants to do it. Once again, a social issue is established, Jessie speaks up, and, more often than not, the show strives to minimize her opinion. Nikki from the junior high years may be gone, but parts of her live on in Jessie.

Although: Jessie's mad after she accidentally bids on Screech, later moaning, "Aw, he's such a geek. What's everyone going to think when they see us at the dance?" She's really a hypocrite when it comes to standing up for people vs. caring what others think.

As for Wendy: It's good to see her be strong and show that she doesn't want to go out with Zack if he doesn't want to be with her. Yet the episode unsurprisingly punts on developing any real connection between them, with him finally being sincere enough to convince her that he wants to hang out at the dance and go to the Max afterwards. She's excited, but we don't see the rest of the date, and, needless to say, we never see her again.

Heartbreaking: It's painful to see Herbert, one of Bayside's most awkward guys, alone on stage and waiting for someone, anyone to bid on him. It's sweet that a girl who seems to like him eventually wins the date with him for 15 cents, but A. That meager amount suggests he has no value, which is awful and B. He then says, "I didn't even expect that," which suggests he thinks he has no value, which is worse. And later Herbert's date ditches him! Brutal.

Better message: Lisa overhauls her personality to appeal to snooty Brian (Patrick Dancy), who reads classic books and practically barfs anytime someone mentions the mall. Ultimately Lisa recognizes that he's pretentious and controlling (he'd get along well with Craig, Stacey's ex) and that she shouldn't have to change who she is for a partner. Memorable kiss-off: "Au revoir, creep."

Really makes you think: While trying to impress Brian, Lisa poses some excellently pompous questions, such as: "What is art? Are we art? Is art art?"

Episode 16: "All in the Mall"

Aired November 9, 1991

Plot: Guess Jessie's not a U2 fan, as she's not around while the other five pursue concert tickets, complicated by Screech leaving the line for ridiculous reasons (he can't decide between mezzanine or orchestra level) and the gang finding a bag with $5,000 in it, leading to them being chased around the mall by two goons with a secret of their own (which is that they're all on "Candid Video").

Zack's lies (3):

- Telling an old lady in line that this is Screech's first day out of the basement in a year
- Calling his parents and telling them he's sleeping at someone's house
- Claiming to be shoe store security to check someone's shoebox

These guys are just (rolls eyes out of head): Looking at mannequins in a display for a store selling wedding attire, Zack asks, "Why can't we meet girls like that, huh?" Slater responds, "Yeah. Great figure, doesn't talk back." Archie Bunker would be proud. No one should be.

The highlight: After the first U2 show sells out and another one is announced, Zack and co. stay overnight in the mall, which always looked really fun (and the strategy of hiding out in a store's tent recently appeared again on "Arrested Development").

The message: This episode is a zany mess, and the group never gets in trouble for any deceptions or thievery and suffers no embarrassment or consequences from being on "Candid Video" either. They win U2 tickets and everything's fine. OK!

Trivia: Screech plans to use a shoehorn as a slide for his pet turtle.

Wow: Another Kevin Costner reference, which is approaching Freddy Krueger and MC Hammer levels of frequency. Quite the trio.

Episode 17: "SATs"

Aired November 16, 1991

Plot: In one of the series' most absurd episodes, Zack scores a 1502 on his SAT exam, inspiring awe from Belding and the visiting recruiter from fictional Stansbury University and jealousy from Jessie, who got a 1205 and thinks her life is over. James, the waiter at the Max who is also an actor best known for impersonating both Belding and Zack's dad, is back and more than happy to help in any scheme that allows him to wildly, hilariously overact.

Future famous co-star: Zack's score is even more absurd considering he spends part of the test just staring at Heather, played by Christine Taylor ("Zoolander," "Arrested Development").

Zack's lies (6):

- Telling Heather the mood lighting in his room is because it's the best for studying
- Claiming Kelly's arrival in his bedroom was just an aggressive girl scout
- Adding that he'll be getting peanut butter cookies in about a month
- Getting James to pretend to be a Harvard rep and start some buzz about Jessie (which reminded me of creating hype for Tobias Funke on, once again, "Arrested Development"); he later pretends to be the chairman of the SAT board to tell Belding to ease up on Zack (2)
- Telling Belding he loves school

Alert the NCAA: Stansbury rep Mrs. Billingham (Susan Osborn) offers Slater a football scholarship, which infuriates Jessie, who only wants people to succeed for their academic performance. Adds Slater after Jessie storms off, "I guess it's a good thing I didn't tell her they offered me a car!" That type of illegal bribe is just astonishing coming from Stansbury, which claims to be the Harvard of the West!

Good, brief source of conflict: Jessie, feeling very insecure, says she shouldn't feel so badly because, after all, she did better than Kelly and Lisa, then stammering to explain it's not that much better considering they're cheerleaders, then just putting her foot in her mouth. It speaks to the compelling, suppressed opinions these high school friends sometimes reveal about each other, glimpsing relationships that could be a lot more layered than they really are.

The takeaways: Fortunately Heather has a boyfriend and Zack's pursuit goes nowhere, but it's still unsettling how this episode seems to enable this lazy, lying bozo and suggest he can succeed more than anyone without even trying. Meanwhile, there are no consequences for the ridiculous deceptions, which at the least should mean James, one of the series' best supporting characters, is around more frequently. But no.

Important point of comparison at the time: Marveling at Zack's score, Screech observes, "Wow, Zack's even smarter than Doogie Howser!"

Episode 18: "Palm Springs Weekend (Part 1)"

Aired November 16, 1991

Plot: As Jessie's recently remarried mom just got her own two-part episode — no she didn't, it was her cruel new stepson, moving on — it's time to focus on Jessie's dad David (George McDaniel of "All My Children"), who's hosting his daughter and her friends at the hotel he manages as he ties the knot. Though he might not have anticipated Zack hitting on his bride-to-be Leslie (Barbra Brighton) and Jessie freaking out after learning that Leslie's a much-younger aerobics instructor.

Zack's lies (1):

- Telling Leslie he's captain of the school aerobics team

And before you can say "Don't try to pick up your friend's new stepmom": Zack suffers no consequences for pursuing Leslie and suddenly things are clicking again with Kelly, who tells him he's "so cute" for making a "Love Boat" reference. Eventually she rubs his shoulders, he helps her with his jacket and a towel (not at the same time) and they kiss. She also tells him, "You're still a gentleman, just like when we were going together," which suggests she doesn't remember their relationship that vividly.

Better: Kelly tries to help Jessie recognize that age doesn't matter, only what a person is like. Jessie isn't hearing it, though to be fair Leslie isn't being 100 percent considerate and should know that Jessie doesn't want to hear Leslie tell her dad, "I think older men are very sexy." Jessie plans to stop the wedding, and that's where part one ends.

Rather problematic: With only words like "babe" and "chick" at his disposal, Slater literally needs help (from Zack, of all people) remembering the word "women." And the show then follows this with Slater's sweet romance with Christina (Eva Loseth), the princess of Lichtenburg, which in reality is a kind of electrical charge and not a country.

More treatment of women: Screech reads "Everything You Need to Know About Girls" because apparently working without a guidebook has been ineffective. This leads to lines like, "You know, love kitten, I don't need to see the specials; you're the catch of the day." Believe it or not, girls don't go for that either, which is good that the show depicts how awful this behavior is but debatable if we're meant to laugh at Screech's ineptitude or find him sheepishly likable.

Trivia: Screech's attempt at following the book's advice and "talking cool" is telling Slater, "I hear you, blood."

*****Interview with McDaniel, who at the time was married to a woman 13 years his junior, on handling large age differences in relationships:** "Just listen to one another, and understand that these things can be potential problems, and work hard to meet them head-on. At the time, because Elizabeth and I were getting to know one another and we were talking quite a bit, I let her know early on. I said, 'Look, I know something about this because my wife is considerably younger than I. So I know there can be problems, but they're all surmountable problems.' I let it go at that, and a few days later Elizabeth came to me and said, 'I've been thinking about what you said, and I have a boyfriend who's considerably older than I am. Is it OK if I tell my mom and dad about your experience with your wife?' I said, 'Please do. If it'll help you, if it'll relax things. But you're young; you may make other choices in the next year or so.' So we really had kind of a father/daughter relationship during that period." *(Read more from McDaniel on page 275.)*

Episode 19: "Palm Springs Weekend (Part 2)"

Aired November 23, 1991

Plot: Zack and Kelly try to figure out what's happening between them, Slater tries to get comfortable dating Princess Christina of Lichtenburg and Jessie engages in several acts of light sabotage (including faking a letter from her dad to Leslie and *pushing Leslie's head underwater* during a race in the pool) in protest of her father's upcoming marriage to a woman she identifies as a "gold-digging bimbo" simply because she's younger and teaches aerobics.

Legitimate teenage response: It becomes clear that Jessie is just projecting, and she and Zack have a good, heated discussion about why she shouldn't storm off and miss the wedding. Zack displays unusually sound emotional intelligence, and Jessie makes it back just in time for Leslie to be very mature about the whole thing (though I guess any other response while standing at the altar wouldn't be a good look) and make up with her dad.

Good line: When Jessie questions how Leslie will feel in 20 years when her dad's pants are up to his neck and Leslie's still wrinkle-free, she responds, "I'm not as bad as you'd like me to be."

Nice advice: Slater's still uneasy about being so close to royalty, but Lisa advises that he be proud of his own background and who he is and let that lead the way. It's simple but effective, and fortunately Christina telling him how dumb he'd be to dump her (after he says things can't work out because she's caviar and he's hot dogs) prompts Slater to kiss her and ask her to the wedding. Of course, that's what led to the whole spinoff series in which Slater spent every weekend flying back and forth between California and Lichtenburg but ultimately became king himself after Christina's father's unexplained disappearance. (Didn't realize how fun that would be to conceive, please someone make this.)

Zack's lies: None!

But taking a page from his book: Before things improve with Christina, Slater lies his face off at dinner with her and her father, claiming his dad is a major colonel general (not a thing) and his grandfather owned most of California.

Stronger behavior: Kelly frets what Zack will think when she says she just wants to be friends (prompted by making eyes at a very inappropriate waiter), but Zack agrees and they have no problems whatsoever. It's not anticlimactic but a quality moment of two people being on the same page and able to have a spark but recognize what's best for them.

But speaking on behalf of the audience: As Lisa comments obsessively on Zack and Kelly, Slater tells her to "Get a boyfriend." Harsh but appropriate considering it's not super great to be an unrelenting gossip with your best friends too.

*****Interview with Loseth on what was her first TV role:** "I got coaching from my friend's stepdad, who was Michael Gross from 'Family Ties.' I went over to his house, and he helped coach me on the audition. I worked on the accent and just being a princess and preparing. I worked really hard on it and ended up getting the job. [Laughs] Peter Engel, the executive producer, told me after I got on set that, 'You did one thing, and I said, 'That's our girl; you've got the job." Something like that. He said, 'Do you want to know what it was?' I said, 'Yeah, what was it?' He said, 'It's the way you curtsied.' [Laughs] I remember they said after the first [audition] that my accent was too authentic. And so they wanted it to be a little more bland, where you wouldn't know exactly what country she was from, but you knew she was from somewhere. So I played around with a couple different dialects in the callback session, and then there was one he just kept wanting me to do over and over again, and that ended up being the one that they used … I think I just experimented with a couple different ways to make it not specific. So you knew she was from somewhere and probably an Eastern European country, but you weren't really sure where." *(Read more from Loseth on page 321.)*

Episode 20: "Hold Me Tight"

Aired November 23, 1991

Plot: Gender politics and jealousy collide as Zack and Jessie fight for Kristy's (Krystee Clark) right to compete on the traditionally men's wrestling team … until Jessie mistakenly believes Kristy is getting cozy with Slater and then reverses everything she said about sexism.

The message: While I guess this episode recognizes the folly of getting worked up when you don't have all the information (Jessie interprets Lisa's radio announcement linking Kristy to a school hunk as confirmation that Slater's cheating), it seems more like another opportunity to undermine Jessie's belief system. She passionately stands up for Kristy (including leading a protest in the gym) only to betray her when the cause affects her negatively. It's a non-issue because Kristy's actually dating Zack, but what if Jessie was right? Would she still have defended Kristy's right to wrestle or continued going on the radio to say "The poor dears could get hurt" and "Keep your hands off our men"?

More aggression against Jessie: When the wrestling coach discriminates against Kristy and Jessie says he can't do that, Screech responds, "He did it, momma, what's your big mouth going to do about it?" When Jessie apologizes to Slater, he still throws in a dig: "It's OK, momma, I'm used to you by now." No other character is treated this way.

Clearer: For a change the show makes a good statement about masculinity as Zack initially feels emasculated when Kristy has to defend him from a Valley bully at the Max but later explains that he was embarrassed and Kristy shouldn't let that impact her. Zack eventually feels good about dating her again, which would be useful if the show allowed anyone to appear for more than one episode at a time.

Meanwhile, on femininity: Zack makes the ignorant statement "You look so much like a girl" when Kristy wears a dress, which Kristy does correct but pretty lightly. But points for the episode leaving room for a girl to be athletic and have sexuality of her own as well, which was not the case for Nikki in the final junior high episode.

Of course: When Kristy first walks into the gym she says, "Excuse me," to which Zack says, "Hey, you're perfect. You don't need any excuses." Charming (shakes head) or sleazy (nods)?

Zack's lies (1):

- Telling Kristy he can't go to the movies tonight because he has to study

Continuity! Not only does the late Monty Hoffman return as Coach Sonski (he previously appeared as the shop teacher) but Kristy references a move Slater used while wrestling Nedick, a real character we've seen in a previous episode ("Pinned to the Mat")!

Episode 21: "No Hope with Dope"

Aired November 30, 1991

Plot: Megastar actor Johnny Dakota (Eddie Garcia, who apparently played "Hot Traxx Dancer" in "Boogie Nights"!) chooses Bayside as the place to shoot an anti-drug commercial mostly because he wants Kelly. (Nevermind that he's in his early 20s and she's 17. Moving on.) He also becomes fast friends with Zack but risks ruining everything when the gang (at a party with no alcohol) realizes he's — gasp! — a pot-smoking hypocrite.

For what it's worth: This is standard after-school special material and very era-appropriate in terms of anti-drug messaging. The gang is absolutely shocked and horrified to see Johnny so casually doing drugs, previously believing a dude named Scud (Troy Fromin) was responsible for the weed found in the boys' bathroom. Setting aside any marijuana-related politics, this is another episode that reinforces the theme of not buying too strongly into someone you don't know that well. Maybe Johnny Dakota and Rod Belding can hang out?

Zack's lies (2):

- Introducing Johnny to Belding as his close friend
- Introducing Slater to girls at Johnny's party as his driver

Clever credibility disclaimer: While it might seem like a stretch for Johnny to pick Bayside of all places, he and his producer (who mostly just says "Yo") note that this was merely the first high school they saw when they got off the freeway. Did they not plan where they were visiting in advance?

Sobering: The students discuss how basketball phenom Len Bias and comedy sensation John Belushi both died because of drugs, though those situations were a lot more than pot. The episode-ending commercial that says "Drugs will hurt your mind, your body and your life" obviously applies a lot more to deadlier, more addictive drugs than weed but, again, this is meant to be broad brushstrokes for high schoolers in the early '90s.

Subtle callback to junior high: Lisa was pretty starstruck around Stevie as well. So while part of her shakiness around Johnny is because she says he's her favorite Hollywood hunk, she does have a history of being giggly around celebrities.

This is why they always eat at the Max instead: Johnny claims to be full from Bayside's Salisbury steak. Belding says it was actually tapioca pudding. Oddly the students don't film an ad opposing those dishes too.

*****Interview with Garcia on the episode's title:** "I don't think it's effective messaging for kids because I think any time you tell a kid not to do something, they're going to try to do it first so they can experience it. I think you have to educate them and let them understand consequences that can happen by doing something. And then through those things, they can make decisions that will be good instead of being told not to do something. It's just inherently in us that if we're told not to do something, we're going to want to try to do it because we want to know why we shouldn't do it … I think the whole idea of 'There's no hope with dope' is if you get caught up in a lifestyle and it damages you and your brain cells, you're not going to come out OK, regardless of how rich or popular you are. And we've seen that over and over. We've seen people spiral, regardless of how famous they are … I think with kids you have to let them have a voice. You have to let them speak to you, and you can't speak at them. If you speak at them, it doesn't turn out well. I learned that from teaching. I can offer advice, but if I tell kids stuff that I know, they don't want to know. Whereas if I encourage them to seek out the knowledge, they feel empowered when they find it." *(Read more from Garcia on page 254.)*

*****Interview with Fromin:** "When I was Scud and said, 'I'm not stupid; I don't smoke pot,' I went home and did bong hits with my wife. We smoked pot a lot back then." *(Read more from Fromin on page 241.)*

Episode 22: "Rockumentary"

Aired November 23, 1991

Plot: An absolutely ridiculous classic in which Zack Attack becomes the biggest band on the planet thanks to the popularity of a ballad called "Did We Ever Have a Chance?" which could probably be popular with Adele's voice but instead it's a duet between Zack and Kelly.

On that note, one of the series' most stunning continuity errors: WHEN ZACK ATTACK FORMED KELLY WAS NOT IN THE BAND, AND MANY EPISODES HAVE CLAIMED SHE CAN'T SING. JESSIE WAS THE LEAD SINGER OF ZACK ATTACK, YET SHE IS NOT IN THIS EPISODE AT ALL. Granted, the episode all turns out to be a dream of Zack's, but even when he wakes up this is still the composition of the group. So wrong.

Yoko alert: The episode tracks the band's rise to fame, falling out and return for a reunion show, with the middle section driven by Zack blowing off the band when their publicist Mindy (Stacie Foster, who apparently was in two episodes of "Saved by the Bell: The New Class" as a different character) says he doesn't need them. Her agenda for Zack to go solo emerges so quickly it is a bit curious why ultra-enthusiastic record producer Brian Fate (Nick Brooks) doesn't get to intervene at all.

Zack's lies: None!

Possibly the most surreal moment: Zack Attack wins a prestigious award (assumedly a Grammy, though the show probably couldn't say that), and it's presented to them by Michael Jackson and Madonna (not being played by the real people). Then Zack has a faux pas of thanking people for listening to "my music" rather than "our music" (he quickly corrects himself), Slater thanks his dad for his first drum set, Lisa thanks her hairstylist and manicurist and Screech thanks his dad for giving him electric trains when he was 3.

Deja vu: Following "No Hope with Dope," "Rockumentary" represents the second consecutive episode featuring the guys at a happenin' Hollywood bash and marveling at all the hot babes there. Sorry, "babe heaven." Perhaps a bit much to do this twice in a row.

Inappropriate history: Zack claims that he used to sneak into Paula Abdul's dressing room twice a week. This seems improbable and very difficult to execute (did she have a residency in L.A.?), though it doesn't really seem like he's lying so we'll just chalk it up to him not respecting other people's boundaries as usual.

After the breakup: With each band member going their separate ways, Screech searches for the meaning of life by seeking the wisdom of "The High Geek," who says the secret of happiness is to "Marry a cheerleader and live at the beach." He also gives Screech a retainer for good luck and performs a painfully awkward handshake. Better is Kelly becoming an actress, Lisa becoming a gladiator (Lethal Lisa) and Slater performing stunts that send him to the hospital, bringing them all back together and Zack away from Mindy. I admit that during this sequence I was thinking about something similar (the going of separate ways, that is) happening in "The Muppets Take Manhattan."

Taking it literally: Screech has an issue with a song called "Friends Forever" because "We haven't known each other forever. If we sing that, we'll be living a lie."

Armchair analyst: This is a fascinating dissection of Zack's subconscious in that when he dreams he is still susceptible to betrayal and female influence but is less deceitful (hence the zero lies) and able to reconcile with forgiving friends. Once more for those in the back, though: Why isn't he dreaming about Jessie too?

Hyperbole alert: Casey Kasem (making his return to the show) says, "Not since the Beatles and the Rolling Stones so captured the hearts and minds of young America ..." In other words, Zack Attack is even bigger than MC Hammer!

*****Interview with Derek Berry, co-founder of the Saved by the Max pop-up restaurant in Chicago and L.A.:** "I've always loved the Zack Attack episode. I just love how it was shot. I always watched those 'Behind the Music' growing up, and it was just funny to see something shot a little bit differently than a normal 'Saved by the Bell' episode but to have them involved in it. It was just memorable. The songs to this day, those are bangers. Everyone knows them. And it was on one episode. People just remember those; it's crazy. They play in the restaurant, and everyone knows every single word." *["Like 100 people singing to 'Did We Ever Have a Chance?' in unison?"]* "Yeah. Like six days a week, every three or four hours. It's crazy. That and 'Friends Forever.' I had one of my friends cut a bunch of stuff, like the 'Snow White and the Seven Dorks" rap that Jessie did. [Editor's note: See page 159.] When that comes on in the restaurant, people know it. I'm like, 'How do you know that? That's insane.' It just shows that people continue to this day to either quote it or rewatch it. And it stays relevant because of that." *(Read more from Berry on page 332.)*

Episode 23: "Cut Day"

Aired December 7, 1991

Plot: The titular event means everyone gets to hang out at the Max and go to the movies and the beach. Well, except Zack, who will be suspended if he gets his tenth unexcused absence. So it's a perfect time to bet Slater $100 that he can ditch each class and meet up every place they go!

Useful tension: This episode effectively creates new pairings that question levels of commitment and connection in relationships. Slater and Kelly have a blast hanging out all day (multiple comments are made about how much more fun she is than Jessie) while Jessie hits it off with Graham (David Kriegel of "Speed"), who is just as passionate as she is about ending the school's use of plastic foam cups. Ultimately Slater and Jessie handle this with shocking maturity, recognizing that they both enjoyed spending time with other people and should take that as an opportunity to spend some time apart. This then leads to a several-episode arc in which both new couples explore the highs and lows of new relationships. (Nope, nothing happens between Slater and Kelly, and Graham is never seen again.)

Plus: "Cut Day" is also fun because of the battle between Zack and Slater, which escalates when Slater tries to outmaneuver Zack by sending away sight-impaired Ms. Culpepper (Maris Clement, which is the name of the student who bids on Herbert in the date auction episode!) so Belding will watch over the class. What Slater doesn't expect is that Zack will feed Belding Screech's chocolate-covered grasshoppers and get sick. Come on, Slater, anyone could have predicted *that.*

Zack's lies (6):

- Telling Franklin he'll support his "Mr. Ed resolution" if Franklin lies and says Zack has to go pay late fees at the library (2)
- Painting the curb red so Belding's car gets towed for parking in a red zone
- Telling Belding he's in the hallway to exercise his right to protest
- Pretending to be the custodian while the custodian poses as him to take his French test (2)

Status alert: For some reason Zack is in the student council meeting and introduces a petition by saying it was signed by "Four nerds, two dorks and a dweeb." He is not nice.

Also very bad: When Jessie says she and Graham were just discussing the benefits of a long-overdue U.S. female president, Zack's response is, "Just like a woman. Always late."

Recall the episode in which Zack ran against Jessie for president, and commence screaming now.

Trivia: Jessie's suggested protest sign: "Plastic Foam: The Choice of Idiots."

Episode 24: "Home for Christmas (Part 1)"

Aired December 7, 1991

Plot: Winter break means working at the mall, where Slater does a lousy job of wrapping presents; Jessie takes pictures of kids with Santa; Zack helps his mom put on "The Christmas Carol"; and Kelly works at a men's clothing store with Laura (Jennifer McComb, who apparently played "Mugatu Model" in "Zoolander"), who is both the inevitable object of Zack's affection and, as it turns out, homeless.

Brief good judgment: Laura calls off her planned lunch with Zack after he says he hopes the homeless man he gave money spends it on food, since "When you give a guy a handout you can't be sure if he's really hungry or a wino or worse." Seeing as that guy is Frank (Stephen Mendel of "Mad Men"), Laura's dad, you wouldn't think she'd later shake off Zack's comment and be interested again but (shrug emoji).

Plus: Zack's statement pretty much undoes the nice scene in which he recognizes that Frank, who is shaving in the mall bathroom, is homeless, helps Screech not be awkward about it and then leaves cash in the pay phone change slot so as not to make Frank feel uneasy about accepting the money. Why couldn't that just be a good gesture and that's it, Zack?

Zack's lies: None!

Of course: Baking with his mom, Zack makes "gingerbread women," prompting Slater to say "gingerbread chicks" so Jessie can say "For you, they should have made gingerbread pigs." Just a bit of deja vu here.

Truth in humor? Once again, the show winks at Zack's aggression toward women: Vouching for him, Kelly tells Laura, "He's safe. If you eat near a security guard." She's joking, of course, but keep in mind that Laura's known Kelly about four minutes and Zack roughly 40 seconds so not sure how she's supposed to take that?

Aggression toward Jessie: Was it really necessary for her to deal with a bratty kid who not only steps on her foot but returns to apologize by saying, "I'm sorry, you ugly old bag"?

Continuity! At the hospital where Lisa volunteers and Frank goes after passing out, Monique (previously seen giving Zack a massage when he went in for surgery) is still working as a nurse! This callback is nothing less than shocking.

Because now we have to mention it: Another MC Hammer reference! This comes when Slater says he got a job doing gift wrap, with Screech wondering if "Gift Wrap" is an MC Hammer Christmas song. Or would it be "Gift Rap"? Regardless, we can all agree this would just sound like Vanilla Ice's "Ninja Rap" from "Teenage Mutant Ninja Turtles II: The Secret of the Ooze."

*****Interview with Rogers on the dynamic between Zack and his mom:** "As characters and as actors, we had a really good relationship. I was not the strict, overbearing mom, as you know; you saw that. I was going to make sure that bad things weren't going on, but I was trying to be a friend too. I think we had a really great mother-son relationship. If I had a son, I would like to have that kind of a relationship. I didn't fool around, but my son knew what was right and what was wrong, at least in my eyes. And when I saw him, like with the nightclub, I would get him. But there was always a sense of, I would say, friendship too. I sort of based this a little bit on my relationship with my mother. I wasn't a boy, but she was a fantastic mom, but she didn't let me get away with anything. We always had a great relationship." *(Read more from Rogers on page 303.)*

Episode 25: "Home for Christmas (Part 2)"

Aired December 14, 1991

Plot: The gang learns more about Frank and Laura while grumpy clothing store manager Mr. Moody (Lew Horn) refuses to give Laura time off to be in the Christmas play with everyone and accuses her of stealing a sport coat that Kelly set aside to buy for her.

Some good, some bad: While the episode overdoes it a bit on the warm-and-fuzzy holiday cheer and makes Frank seem rather saintlike, credit the show for showcasing Frank and Laura as people who are homeless, not homeless people. Frank's description of how they wound up in that situation is heartbreakingly simple (his plant closed, he couldn't find another job, couldn't pay the rent and no employer will hire someone without a permanent address), and Laura also notes how friends shied away from her after that happened. "It's almost like they think it's contagious." She also misses simple things that many take for granted, like listening to music in her room and talking to friends on the phone. For a sitcom that often struggles to make its points effectively, this counts as daring and impactful.

Zack's lies (1):

- Telling Laura he likes to get up early after just telling his mom that he doesn't

Funny way to turn a lie into a truth: It seems disingenuous when Zack tells Mr. Moody that allowing Laura into "A Christmas Carol" will double his business, but the play's constant reference to characters wanting to become more stylish by shopping at Moody's store (with sizes ranging from Tiny Tim to Gigantic George!) provides welcome lightness amid the expected holiday hokiness.

More messaging: It's nice that when Kelly starts to blame herself for telling Moody that Laura was homeless Zack corrects her and says, no, only Moody is responsible for unfairly believing Laura is a thief just because she is homeless. A good reminder about character and culpability (followed by the inevitable redemption of Moody as he apologizes and gives Laura and Frank the sport coat as a gift).

Worth noting, though: Interesting that, compared to some other brief relationships, Zack's flirtation with Laura remains pretty chaste, never going beyond a kiss on the cheek. Certainly Laura has bigger concerns at the moment than her relationship with Zack, but she's obviously interested in him, and the episode not letting them exist as a couple in the same way Zack and (insert any girl) do in most episodes seems to set aside Laura as a partner because of her circumstances.

Trivia: The episode closes with the entire cast singing the aforementioned MC Hammer song "Gift Wrap." (No, it's "Silent Night," and not MC Hammer's version.)

*****Interview with Mendel, who said he wore his "oldest, rattiest pants and a cardigan sweater and a plaid shirt that I buttoned up to the top button" to the audition, on capturing the difficult circumstances and emotions of Frank's character:** "For me as a human being, to connect with a person who's been down on their luck is not a big stretch. Because unless you've been extraordinarily fortunate as an actor, sometimes there's long periods of time where you don't know if you're going to work again. So to be able to find in my own emotional history times when I felt, 'Jesus, oh my god, what am I going to do? When am I going to work again? What the hell do I have to do? I know I'm good at this, why can't I [catch a break]?' So finding the places of truth and reality in that situation for 99% of the actors in the world who are worth their stuff … that was not a difficult place for me to go to and to find reality, find truth within myself, find a way to connect that story to some real places of emotional truth within me, within my own personal history. Have I ever been homeless? No. Have I ever not had enough money for food? No. But I've been hungry. So I explore that, and I take that further." *(Read more from Mendel on page 308.)*

Episode 26: "Mystery Weekend"

Aired December 21, 1991

Plot: When a radio contest awards Lisa a weekend at a murder mystery mansion with a +5 that no other guests seemed to have received, the gang attempts to identify who killed the piano player with a very "The Game"-esque question of what is and isn't part of the fun. Featuring a classy and, well, mysterious turn from Larry Cedar ("Deadwood") as mansion host Steven Jameson.

On that note: It's amusing to wonder what's really involved in the weekend's entertainment, but the show doesn't quite know what to do with, you know, the gang even briefly considering that Zack is a murderer. Seeing as this is the season finale, imagine if the episode ended with everyone wondering if they've learned something shocking about their friend! Obviously "Saved by the Bell" would never do that and shouldn't, but it's an opportunity for a cliffhanger is all I'm saying.

Nevertheless: This has always been one of my favorite episodes because of the pep and playfulness that isn't always written into the episodes. Normally each storyline is pretty predictable and safe, but here viewers actually have incentive to pay attention to the personalities and how they interact. It's mostly about the fun of solving a mystery (and one-liners like "Care to take another stab at it?" after someone suspected of the crime falls to the ground with a knife in his back), but it also includes an irritable maid (whose pillow-fluffing technique is pretty porny), off-putting butler and Screech doing his best Sherlock Holmes impression, claiming that he knows who the murderer is: the stableboy! "There is no stable, you dork," says Slater. "Ah," deduces Sherlock Screech. "Then the dog lied." Classic.

More where that came from: Screech has a lot of good lines here, including determining that a man who grabbed his throat before dying strangled himself to death. He also thinks, after the inspector is killed right before he can identify the murderer and only able to say "Argh!," that they know the killer's identity now, just not whose real name is "Argh!" Clearly spin-off shows don't work and no one's trying to give Dustin Diamond more opportunities, but if there had been a four-episode series in which Screech attempts to solve crimes, I would have watched that.

Zack's lies: None!

And yet: Quite the fitting sequence when Zack is being questioned for being a jewel-thieving killer (the theft of the diamond necklace is reminiscent of "The Great Muppet Caper," the second Muppet reminder in the last few episodes) and his friends attempt to defend his character, only to make statements about his penchant for selling fake IDs, stealing the principal's car and Valley's mascot, and tying Screech to railroad tracks. What a guy.

Either lack of continuity or just not learning: Lisa says her dad bought her a new watch, but "He won't find out until he gets his Visa bill." What happened to the important lesson from "The Lisa Card"?

Back to the presentation of old people: I'll just leave this exchange here:

Older guy, speaking with very trembly, over-the-top old guy voice: "Enough funeral music, play something we can dance to!"
Piano player: "I'll play what I want, Pops!"
Older guy: "Careful who you call Pops, Sonny!"

Once again: The tone of that eighth-grade science video was not my fault.

*****Interview with "Zack Morris is Trash" creator Dashiell Driscoll:** "The first season of 'Zack Morris is Trash,' I was hoping the murder mystery weekend could be the Halloween episode. Because that's the one I really remember as a kid. For some reason, the ones that stood out episode-wise were that one and the Malibu Sands Beach Club episodes. Maybe because they were different literally, so it was easier for them to stand out. But when I went back and watched the murder mystery one – and I've done it a few times, and maybe it will be in a "Zack Morris is Trash" episode, I don't know; not all of them quite fit the formula – he didn't seem to be that bad. You're right; his friends do suspect he could be a murderer, but the way he handles an actual murder happening seems to be, 'Let's pack the bags and get out of here.' I was actually surprised, especially when I was that deep in the research the first season of saying, 'How far does this all go?' that amidst a murder he actually buttons up and drops it a little bit." *(Read more from Driscoll on page 339.)*

*****Interview with Cedar**: "A lot of our most famous characters in art and movies, film, TV, theater, in general, are bad. We tune in to watch people behave badly. The appeal of it is that it's easier to deal with in TV than it is to deal with in life, and we can watch it unfold. Clearly there was enough good in him or fascinating enough in him or appealing enough in him that people weren't turned off by his behavior. If anything, they wanted to see more of it. They were fascinated by it. I don't know that the show ever claimed to be a moral standard for kids. 'Tune in to watch 'Saved by the Bell' to learn how to be a good person in life.' I don't think it ever claimed to be that. It claimed to be an entertaining show that you would always find interesting. And apparently people did. So they succeeded in that. I guess it's up to parents and individuals to say, 'Well, that may be a hit, that may be a success, but to me that's teaching a bad lesson.' That's up to the individual. I don't remember how much my kids watched it or didn't watch it. I don't remember them thinking about it particularly about Zack, if he was a good person or a bad person. We never said, 'You shouldn't watch that show; Zack lies all the time." I don't remember thinking that. If I recall anything, it's, 'That show's funny.' We just watched to be entertained. It's a gray area." *(Read more from Cedar on page 295.)*

Stats/Looking Back on the Third High School Season

Wow. In this 26-episode season, eight of the episodes feature zero lies. That's 31 percent! Here were the percentages of zero-lie episodes in the previous three seasons: 38 percent, 19 percent, 17 percent.

In other words, after two consecutive high school seasons of being a pretty rampant liar, Zack demonstrates growth that brings him closer to his behavior in junior high. That certainly isn't to say that lying nearly 70 percent of the time is good, but it represents improvement. Plus, while overall this season's 72 lies marks a new high of 2.8 per episode, those numbers are significantly skewed by the two 11-lie episodes, as this is the only season so far containing two episodes with double-digit lies. Remove those two and the average dips to an even 2 lies per episode, which is a new low.

Point being: Zack is generally a more honest person this season, especially when it comes to the six Malibu Sands Beach Club episodes, which feature four zero-lie episodes and only six lies total, resulting in an average of just one lie per episode. That's an enormous improvement, suggesting (maybe) that responsibility and work in a non-school environment lead to growth for Zack, along with dating someone (Stacey) who challenges him and provides balance to his personality in ways that other girlfriends mostly haven't.

Meanwhile, only 23 percent of the episodes feature Zack being bad to women, a huge decrease from previous seasons (62 percent; 56 percent; 56 percent). By now it's not terribly surprising to see this operate in tandem; while Zack certainly doesn't only lie to and about women, that is a major factor, so treating women better does seem to result in fewer lies.

However, 50 percent of the episodes still feature aggression toward Jessie, a big jump from 28 percent in the previous season. It seems as the characters get older and sometimes take on more adult opinions and situations (again, sometimes), the show does more to undermine its loudest feminist voice. Other than Screech (who rarely makes strong points of his own), no one else is cut down to size like Jessie is, with many of the indictments against the others (mostly Zack) disintegrating so we can still think he's a good guy.

Otherwise, this might be the best season so far, with a lot of diversions from the usual school-based episodes and some different, worthwhile challenges presented to the characters, including Kelly's feelings for Jeff, Kristy wrestling with the boys, Jessie and Slater preferring to spend time apart and the fun of imagining rock stardom and solving a murder mystery. Maybe "Saved by the Bell" is kind of good after all!

High School Season 4 (1992-1993)

The final high school season is another big batch of 26 episodes, more focused on shenanigans inside the school and only occasionally grappling with the impending end of a major part of a young person's life. And, duh, Tori arrives for a little while in place of Jessie and Kelly, then vanishes when they return, and everything goes on as if nothing ever happened. Because, as this show has often argued, it's just easier not to talk about it.

Episode 1: "The Fight"

Aired September 12, 1992

Plot: A season that actually starts at the beginning of the school year, not just with some arbitrary dance! Anyway, they're seniors now, which enhances not just feelings of status vs. underclassmen but competition between each other as Zack and Slater battle for the affections of Joanna (Shana Furlow), who just moved from Idaho and assumedly soon moves back there based on how things go for her at Bayside.

Wait, speaking of dances: Yes, there is one (without chaperones, hubba hubba), and Lisa's excited to go with Darren (Jon Clair) until she realizes he's a freshman. Of course she eventually learns she shouldn't care about that, although it's notable how different her relationship is played after she recognizes she's being rude than Zack's was in "Date Auction" when he finally felt comfortable with Wendy. Shame on the show for minimizing the romance there because of her size, which was supposed to be the thing we're saying doesn't matter.

Zack's lies (9), his worst season-opening tally since junior high:

- Telling a freshman he has to go home to use the bathroom
- Adding that he can't go to the roof without a pass
- And that he also needs a stairway pass and hallway pass (2)
- Identifying himself to Joanna as part of the senior welcoming committee
- Telling Joanna that Slater is clumsy after Zack kicks Slater's chair out from under him
- Saying it's a proven study technique to literally touch your heads together
- Paying a woman to pretend to be Slater's mom
- Tasking Screech with maintaining the ruse about Slater's mom

Armchair analyst: Zack's behavior is really extreme in this episode, suggesting not just that he's again forgotten his junior-high lesson about not letting a girl get in between he and Mikey but that he's lost sight of his improvements from the previous season. It's discouraging to see him open a year that might result in a sense of maturity with only fear and cruelty, seeing Joanna merely as an acquisition and his close friend Slater (who actually makes conversation with Joanna, rather than just telling her she's beautiful) as an enemy to be vanquished. This includes sabotaging dates and throwing punches, though the dudes of course shake off their battle very quickly and fortunately Joanna wants nothing to do with either of them. So in the end everything's back to normal and maybe the guys learned something about friendship and how they treat women, though they seem pretty distracted by laughing at Belding's terrible wig falling off so who knows.

Trivia: While Slater tells Zack that the girl he met has a smile out of a Tic-Tac commercial, Zack's description is somewhat more of the moment: "She makes Madonna look like Bart Simpson."

Episode 2: "Student Teacher Week"

Aired September 12, 1992

Plot: It's right there in the title as Kelly becomes a history teacher, Screech and Lisa teach gym and Zack takes over as principal, a perfect chance to exploit his position of power as if he's never learned a lesson about it before. In this case, it's trying to get Slater (who notes, "It's good to know low people in high places") and the rest of the football team out of a test Kelly's giving so that they can focus on beating – you guessed it – Valley.

Zack's lies (2):

- Telling Kelly he wants his students to enjoy learning and not worry about grades
- Affirming her belief that he's taking his job seriously

Reminder and resonance: This episode has echoes of "Clubs and Cliques" when Bliss and Belding switched places, with this time the students meant to learn about how hard the jobs of principal and teacher are. And it works: Kelly, still the most inspiring and appealing character on the show, really connects with her role as educator and forces Zack to examine his priorities more seriously than usual. His speech to the students at the Max when he tells them the players are suspended (and later when he reminds Slater he wouldn't have ditched the test if Mr. McGee were giving it, identifying that Slater was taking advantage of Kelly) showcases strength we don't often see from him.

More on Kelly: There are several nice, nuanced moments in this episode, including when Slater questions how Kelly could be cheering for the team at the Max while still asserting the importance of the test. "I want the team to win too, Slater," she says. "Just not your way." She also stands up to Zack and questions if he deserves how much she has invested in him over the years. Thiessen is great here, and the conflict and lessons between friends with different perspectives works well.

Here we go again: When Slater invites cute blonds to take over for the football team's broken tackling dummy and Jessie says that's sexist, Zack jumps in to note, "She's right; all brunettes and redheads are welcome too." This obviously prompts laughs on the laugh track, undermining Jessie and encouraging the guys. Groan.

Even worse: Zack's first agenda is "enlarging the peepholes in the girls' locker room." Enlarging?

Continuity: Another mention of Muffin Sangria, though she's only included because termites ate her ventriloquist dummy, postponing the talent show. Thinking of you in this difficult time, Muffin!

Trivia: This is Troy Fromin's first appearance as intelligence-limited Ox ("If we take that test, we'll flink!"), even though he already played Scud in "No Hope with Dope." What were we saying about continuity again?

*****Interview with Fromin, explaining the above**: "I went and auditioned and got the part, and I did my Scud thing. And a day or two later my manager called and said, 'They want you back on the show. They love you, but they don't want the character Scud any longer. They want to try you as this football player named Ox. They want you to come in and read a couple lines in front of producers and everybody real quick.' So I did that and they said, 'You're Ox.' They just wanted to make sure I could deliver the lines the way they expected … I didn't think about it [being confusing to viewers]. Not many people put it together earlier, but later on they did. All I thought was, 'Great, another acting job.' I never expected it to be as big as it is, and I'm thankful that it is." *(Read more from Fromin on page 241.)*

Episode 3: "Screech's Spaghetti Sauce"

Aired September 19, 1992

Plot: In a storyline entirely copied by Phoebe's grandma's Nestle Toll House chocolate chip cookies on "Friends," Screech becomes the talk of the school (much like in "Beauty and the Screech") when he markets his own sauce on the students' cable access show, only to get in legal hot water when the "Betsy Crocker" cookbook threatens to sue for copying its recipe. Meanwhile, there's yet another new girl in school: Beverly Hills-native Robin (Soleil Moon Frye of "Punky Brewster"), a shameless gold digger who aims to manipulate Screech for whatever he'll buy her before he wises up.

Zack's lies (1):

- Introducing himself as Screech's business manager

Hard-hitting expose: It's a pretty funny scene when Jessie prefaces her interview with Belding with a bunch of softballs about his favorite songs, but as soon as the conversation actually starts she presses him about a $500 petty cash discrepancy discovered by the school board. Belding's response: "I thought we were going to talk about Pokey, my pet turtle?"

A+ exploitation: Robin really goes for it, asking for a watch and then immediately wanting the matching necklace, getting a silver necklace and wanting the gold one too. She even orders lobster thermidor at the Max, prompting Screech to also put in his order for "lobster thermometer." The gang's team effort to trick Robin into buying the company and paying off their debt to the school is fun, and we'll excuse Zack's deception (pretending to be Wolfgang Von Schmidt, who's interested in buying Screech's sauce) because, well, Robin deserves it.

What to even say about this: The commercial for Screech's sauce is a festival of over-the-top Italian stereotypes, complete with Jessie's "Wassamattayou" and Screech's slogan "The sauce you can have, but the secret she's-a-mine!" Fortunately it does not appear there are any Italian students to complain, so bravo!

More "Arrested Development": Screech's sad walk after he overhears Robin bashing him is not far from George Michael Bluth's (Michael Cera) classic mopey stroll.

Trivia: Lisa's new perfume is Eiffel Power.

Episode 4: "The New Girl"

Aired September 19, 1992

Plot: Here we go: Kelly and Jessie are gone and not acknowledged at all while Bayside's never-ending roster of new girls in school continues with Tori (Leanna Creel), who quickly becomes part of the gang and shockingly appears in 10 of the season's 26 episodes. She wears a leather jacket and isn't impressed by Zack (at first), so you know she means business! Oh, and of course there's a dance coming up, the fall ball, which Tori brilliantly suggests should have a theme of … fall.

Whiny preppie: We don't often see Zack throwing a temper tantrum, but his performance in Belding's office after Tori takes his parking space goes way beyond immature. Not only does he complain that everyone knows this is his spot she can't have it why oh why life isn't fair, but he scours the student handbook in search of loopholes. A good reminder that, deep down, Zack's attempts to be a swaggering stud mask a lot of fear, insecurity and need for control.

Future famous co-star: Bridgette Wilson-Sampras ("Billy Madison") plays less-than-brilliant Ginger, whose core concern is if she has lipstick on her teeth.

Growth from Screech: Refusing to pair up with Zack for a class assignment, Screech aligns himself with Slater (who also wants to exploit his academically inclined friend) instead. "You may be a dumb jock, but at least you'll appreciate me." Obviously Zack has to partner with Tori, who isn't thrilled either, until like five minutes later when she develops a crush on him.

On femininity: As it did previously with Kristy, the show again grapples with how it believes a woman should behave to attract a man. "You've gotta turn on the femininity," Lisa tells Tori. "I'm not asking you to be a bimbo; just soften your image." This leads to Tori wearing heels and a dress and flirting with Zack through lines like, "How's the punch? I'm really thirsty." While it's good to see her recognize that she should be herself (ending the episode with her leather jacket over the dress), it's disconcerting that her edge is mostly set aside in favor of a more benign, conventionally feminine personality. Her best moment in the episode (not including her initial good judgment not to be swayed by Zack's arrogance) might be telling Lisa she won't help her plan the dance unless Lisa (who just alienated her team and is all alone) changes how she treats people.

Zack's lies (2):

- Claiming he wrote "Pretty Woman" after using the lyrics to hit on Ginger

- Saying that Tori's absence from class is intentional as part of their presentation (when in fact Tori overslept after helping Lisa until 4 a.m.)

Status check: When Pete suggests making math the theme of the dance (everyone dresses as their favorite number!), Lisa snaps, "Who asked you to speak, geek?" Cue laugh track and another instance of the show looking down its nose at anyone outside the core group.

Trivia: After arguing with Zack at the Max, Tori storms into the locker room and attempts to come up with a nasty nickname for Zack. She dubs him Zack "The Jerk" Morris. Uh, zing?

Episode 5: "The Bayside Triangle"

Aired September 26, 1992

Plot: And now back to a world with Kelly and Jessie but no Tori, as Screech's determination to finally win over Lisa hits a big, blond wall when suddenly Zack and Lisa, collaborating on her showcase for a recruiter from the Fashion Institute, experience a spark that after more than a decade of friendship finally grows into a very small, lightly kissed flame.

The aggression is back too: This is a brutal episode for Jessie. After she tells Screech it's never going to happen for him and Lisa, he responds, "Did you know your Adam's apple shakes when you're judgmental?" That is a pretty terrible thing to say to a friend (I recognize Screech doesn't want to hear he has no chance with Lisa, but still). Later Jessie is shown to be terrible at sewing, with no one really caring when she SEWS HER THUMB TO A ZIPPER.

Plus: Jessie flips out when Slater actually uses the word "women," which really is an accomplishment for him. She's thrilled and should be! But the rest of the gang just stares at her and does not care, which is disappointing though not surprising.

"Friends" forever: Just like when Slater and Lisa hit it off in a new way during the Malibu Sands episodes, the Zack/Lisa pairing has the feel of Joey and Rachel, where a previously unexplored chemistry emerges that has promise … but the show refuses to take it seriously and then just sets it aside. Zack and Lisa legitimately have a different rapport in this episode, a testament to Gosselaar and Voorhies embracing a narrative that might have seemed like a stretch on the page, and their moments are sweet.

Even better: "The Bayside Triangle" hinges on a relatable adolescent experience and offers good lessons, recognizing that Zack should have talked to Screech about his feelings for Lisa before acting on them and Lisa also letting Screech know that she is not his and he cannot dictate her life for her. Situations like these involve a lot of confusion, possessiveness and heightened emotions, and the way it resolves (Zack and Lisa giving it a go, Screech feeling like he's over her at last) is rewarding. Needless to say, the plotline ends as soon as the episode does.

Zack's lies: None!

Notable: Kelly isn't jealous or upset at all when Lisa talks about her kiss with Zack, which we'll chalk up to Kelly being a remarkably levelheaded and emotionally generous person and not the show punting the complex awkwardness that might have ensued between these friends and their overlapping romantic experience within their small group.

Creepy: Screech claims to have 16 of Lisa's broken nails at home, a tribute to her beautiful hands. Anyone who was rooting for her to give him a chance, this was your moment to let that go.

Funny: After Screech's narration of Lisa's fashion show involves lines like "Lisa has created a rugged yet scholastic look; I hate it!" Belding takes over, and his ineptitude is hilarious: "Zack Morris is modeling ... a very nice pair of pants. Loooong pants. And they are lovely. Handsome. And tan? Tan! And a very manly tan they are too, Zack."

Episode 6: "Teen Line"

Aired September 26, 1992

Plot: Not only is Tori back but again the episode hinges on an idea she presents in Belding's office, this time a teen line that apparently no one remembers already doing in "1-900-Crushed." It leads to Zack connecting with Melissa (Jennifer Blanc-Biehn of "Party of Five"), who uses a wheelchair and is reminded of that seemingly every 30 seconds by Zack, who says ignorant things like, "Even though she's handicapped, she gave Cathy perfect advice."

Value: It may not be subtle, but this episode does a good job identifying that Melissa wants to be seen as a person and not defined by her disability. "Most people get so freaked out about it they never stop thinking about the chair," she tells Zack when he asks why she didn't tell him over the phone. "I wanted you to meet me first." Eventually he recognizes that he feels far more uneasy than she does, and she says that she has lived with it her entire life and is not only used to it but can do the majority of what anyone else can do. Teen sitcoms like this can and should be used to help young viewers understand other people's experiences and why it is important to be tolerant and understanding. For a change, "Teen Line" finds "Saved by the Bell" doing this well.

That said: Once again, just as with Wendy (who was heavier than the girls he normally dates) and Laura (who was homeless), when Zack goes out with someone outside his comfort zone the show really dials back the romance. By the end of the episode he has learned not to be a jerk and the girls forgive him, but everyone's interest in taking things further has subsided. Just once it would have been nice to not only accept these girls as they are but be interested in them as a partner too.

Also terrible: Lisa advises a caller who's feeling overweight to never wear white because "You'll look like Shamu at a wedding." Just because she provides the number for Overeaters Anonymous doesn't mean her joke is OK.

Zack's lies (2):

- Telling Melissa to set her clocks back two hours before she goes out so her parents won't know when she gets home late
- Adding that if her dad (who wound up being late for work as a result of the adjusted clocks) asks to just claim the power went out

Good advice: Melissa tells Cathy (who feels uncomfortable about her height, just like Jessie), "Stop looking at being tall as a problem; think of tall as beautiful, and the rest will fall into place." The moment when this washes over Cathy, who happily and gratefully hugs Melissa, is really nice, and same for when Tori tells Zack, "Maybe she'd rather be your friend than your cause," reiterated when Melissa insists, "Don't treat me like I'm broken." For a show that often does not find the right words, it's worth celebrating when it does.

Continuity: In the junior high episode "The Showdown" Zack refers to Screech's brother, yet here Screech (dealing with a 10-year-old nuisance named Tommy) says he's an only child. WHAT DID KEVIN DO TO YOUR BROTHER, SCREECH, AND WHY ARE YOU COVERING UP BOTH OF THEIR DISAPPEARANCES?

*****Interview with Blanc-Biehn, when I note that Zack didn't kiss the girls he dated who made him uncomfortable and ask if anything more romantic was ever shot or discussed:** "I think that's a really, really great [point] – you're obviously a good reporter. [Laughs] I didn't ever really think about it. I don't remember that being in the script, so that was probably more of a network choice, which is my guess. It's a total guess because you're bringing it up. That's interesting. That anything that was normal and streamlined for him was OK to be romantic, but the others were not. No, we didn't shoot anything like that, and I never thought of that or knew that. There was a part of me that thought maybe once he realized Melissa was in a wheelchair it was going to be too hard for somebody like Zack to really be in a relationship even though he was trying to date her, but that was just specific to that episode for me. But, no, I never knew that, and I never thought about it. The romantic part never came up on our episode. It was all seemingly like he was into it, then he met her and was happy for a second, and then when he realized she was in a wheelchair it all spiraled into more of a cause for him than a real relationship." *(Read more from Blanc-Biehn on page 265.)*

Episode 7: "Masquerade Ball"

Aired October 3, 1992

Plot: With the students about to don masks for yet another dance, Zack and Slater bet $50 on who can kiss Tori first, though Zack soon grows uneasy because he actually likes her and doesn't want his kiss to be motivated by the wager. Such a complicated life this guy leads.

Surprisingly: This episode actually has the goofy, freewheeling tone of a farce, with misunderstandings piling up and inevitable confusion once the masks go on and no one can be sure who's who (with Tori also trying to set up Zack and Screech to accidentally kiss while in their costumes). Add in Screech, in disguise, doing a Groucho Marx impression ("Maybe I'll join a club and hit myself over the head with it") and "Masquerade Ball" achieves old-fashioned silliness that's a good fit for the material.

Although: There's definitely a hint of the junior-high episode "Love Letters" here, as Lisa searches for the identity of her secret admirer (she should have learned by now that it's Screech, and her thinking it's Zack is weird after what happened between them a few episodes ago, which of course is not acknowledged) and Belding mistakenly thinks Ms. Culpepper has feelings for him. So far this season is not delivering an abundance of new ideas.

Notable: Tori is perfectly likable and still maintains a point of view ("Why don't you little boys try growing up?" she asks Zack and Slater), but the way in which she becomes much more restrained and conventional on her date with Zack is a bit of a cop out for a character who seemed to be different. Instead, she winds up being a mash-up of Jessie and Kelly in an effort to take the place of both simultaneously, which is a ridiculous thing for the show to have attempted.

Zack's lies (1):

- Just the bet and the deceit involved

Trivia: Slater's pathetic effort to win the bet involves getting Tori to pose for a sculpture he claims is called "Young Girl on the Verge of Kiss." Also: When Tori tells Screech Lisa's secret admirer, who Tori thinks is Zack, is a hypocrite (for going out with Tori too), Screech, who is actually Lisa's secret admirer, quips, "No, he's not; he's a Methodist!"

Episode 8: "Day of Detention"

Aired October 3, 1992

Plot: Once again Zack's desperate to win a free trip somewhere, this time to Hawaii if he can be the 10th caller for a radio contest hosted by Rappin' Ken Kelly (Jeremiah Birkett, who had small parts in "Seinfeld" and "L.A. Confidential") and being held, yep, at the Max. Needless to say, Zack rigs the contest, gets detention for using his giant cell phone in school and then comes up with elaborate schemes to get out of detention and win the grand prize, though he underestimates how much attention to pay to Belding's bonsai tree.

Zack's lies (8):

- Pretending to be from the phone company to rig the contest and have Screech intercept other calls so Zack can be the 10th caller (2)
- Getting Slater to fake an injury to distract Belding and get Zack out of detention
- Having Lisa say Zack's mom needs him home right away
- Having Tori pretend to be his mom to say Zack needs to go home
- Getting Screech to don a wig and pretend to be him to fill in at the Max for an interview with Ken (just like when he was in line for U2 tickets, Screech runs away when asked a question he doesn't know how Zack would answer)
- Leaving a skeleton in his place in detention
- Claiming everything he did was a setup so Belding could win the trip to Hawaii

Continuity: Even though they kissed at the end of the last episode, now it doesn't seem like there's anything between Zack and Tori. Sure, fine.

More repetition: Zack gets rid of Belding by discussing cow brains and frog intestines, just like he did with the principal getting nauseous eating chocolate-covered grasshoppers during "Cut Day." Stick with what works, preppie.

Low-key psychological insight? When Zack finally arrives at the Max, Ken is expecting to see the Screech version of Zack, telling the real Zack, "Nice try, kid, but Zack Morris is a skinny little nerd!" Maybe this is the perception Zack most fears? Or not, but at this point throwaway episodes like this demand a degree of analytical stretching.

Episode 9: "Wrestling with the Future"

Aired October 10, 1992

Plot: Recalling the pre-college anxiety of the SAT episode, Slater struggles to tell his father that he wants to go to the University of Iowa, not into the army. Meanwhile the gang receives college acceptances and rejections, which mostly is an opportunity to stress out Jessie.

Zack's lies (3):

- Impersonating Slater to do his West Point interview for him
- Saying he calls his dad Major Dad when he doesn't know who "Martin" is
- Telling the government dudes "I didn't do anything" when they arrest him

Wow: The interview sequence is really something, with Zack (as Slater, curly wig and all) turning over a chair and using it as a machine gun, describing an attack on Canada and raving, "I hear those commie chicks are red hot." Really.

Continuity: Jessie says no one offers college acceptances in person even though that's what happened to Lisa with the Fashion Institute, after which the Iowa wrestling coach approaches Slater's table at the Max, offers a full scholarship and leaves. Totally normal!

Perspective: With Jessie fearing she won't get into the Ivy league, Kelly attempts to help her be thankful she can even afford those places, since Kelly will be going to community college and getting a job (obviously no one told her about "The College Years" yet, which also applies to Zack, who says he's going to Yale as if only SATs and not grades or character or anything matter). As Jessie stress eats, Lisa advises, "Pigging out like that is only going to get you a curly tail and a snout," which is a really awesome way to describe someone who likes to eat!

Message: As usual, Zack suffers no real consequences for his lies and everything turns out just fine. Thankfully, Slater's dad respects his son's wishes, although it's not like the episode would end with them having a falling out or something.

Reminder: When Slater tells his dad "They're not our plans, they're your plans," it's hard not to think of James Van Der Beek barking "I don't want your life" in "Varsity Blues."

Trivia: The schools Screech applies to include Emerson, Princeton, Duke, Cal Tech, the Barbizon School of Modeling and Fisher College for Women.

Episode 10: "Drinking and Driving"

Aired October 10, 1992

Plot: One of the series' most memorable episodes/lessons as the gang has a couple beers, Zack thinks he's OK to drive and lies pile up while they try to secretly fix Lisa's mother's car before she comes back into town.

Zack's lies (13, a new record for an individual episode):

- Telling his dad a dog ran in front of the car and Lisa swerved to miss it (2)
- Claiming they can't get the car into Lisa's garage because of boxes of tools for homeless people (2)
- Having Lisa call his dad, pretending to be her mom
- Pretending to be a ringing bell so Lisa can get off the phone with her mom
- Getting Screech to sneak into the auto shop to steal the water pump (this kind of deception counts as a lie)
- Telling Belding Slater hurt his shoulder in practice because he was so intent on winning Saturday's game that he threw too hard (we'll call that 2)
- Saying the wax clogged the fuel injection and the extent of the clog will impact how long it takes to fix (2)
- Trying to get his dad to go inside by saying a guy called wanting to buy 100 computers (this may have been true but probably not)
- Desperately claiming the accident his dad's referring to is the accident of getting wax in the car

The message: Obviously this is more after-school special material, but I'm sure I wasn't the only one who saw this as an elementary school kid and absorbed the blunt statements about responsibility and the dangers of drinking without any questions. Sure, the episode suggests that drinking at all will make you feel horrible the next day, which of course is a stretch even for high school kids having a couple light beers. But the degree to which Zack thinks nothing bad can happen to him feels accurate, and the flailing attempt to cover up what happened plays as desperately as it should. Lying to skirt accountability is nothing new for Zack, but the fear it sparks in his father, unsettled by how irresponsible his son has shown himself to be, achieves an impact that a lot of the late-episode lessons don't. ("You risked throwing away the rest of your life for a couple of beers, then you lied to me about it! … You need to think about this one, son. I love you. I don't want anything bad to happen to you.") The same goes for Lisa's punishment from her mother, who had been so supportive about Lisa winning homecoming queen but is now understandably furious and forbids her from going to homecoming at all. It may be heavy-handed, but it lands.

Also: Tori, now occupying the voice of the audience, sets Zack straight quickly and accurately when he laments "What did I do to get into this mess?" and she snaps, "Drove drunk and drove into a telephone pole, remember?" Noteworthy that the show allows her to be the voice of reason without undermining her the way it does Jessie.

Slightly less convincing: The song that Zack, Slater, Screech and Lisa sing in the car as Zack stops paying attention to the road is "Wild Thing"? What, were the rights to "U Can't Touch This" too expensive?

Also not great: Once again the plot involves raising money to fix a car (though it is clever that Zack sells ad space for love notes on Slater's jersey, which backfires when Slater's too injured to play). Exactly how often does the average teenager deal with this?

Worth noting: This is yet another episode in which Tori's ideas instantly catch on with others. In this case it's making the party (at Ox's house) a toga party, which may or may not have been a low-key troll job when suggested to the football team.

Speaking of which: Credit Troy Fromin for making Ox (who now reminds me of Billy Bob, in case anyone needed one more "Varsity Blues" reference) a funny doofus during exchanges like:

Ox: "Let's trash this place!"
Slater: "Ox, this is your house."
Ox: "Bad idea!"

*****Interview with Fromin**: "I myself had a DUI many years ago. It's a bitch, and it's expensive. I wouldn't want to have to go through that again. Maybe it happened four or five years after the episode. Maybe later on I pondered [the overlap with the episode], but not at the time. I was drunk off my ass. My wife and I, we were drinking and partying. We were young, and we got in a fight, and I got in the car and drove off, and that's when I got my DUI. I was stupid." *(Read more from Fromin on page 241.)*

Episode 11: "Love Machine"

Aired October 17, 1992

Plot: Sheesh, yet another episode that aired out of order, which means that there's no Tori, Slater and Jessie are still dating, and everyone looks younger. As if that weren't enough of a continuity whiplash, we're also supposed to buy that Bayside has ANOTHER new girl in school, and of all people she happens to be Jennifer (Stephanie Furst, who was a mermaid in "Hook" and a former girlfriend in "Jerry Maguire"), Slater's longtime girlfriend in Germany.

Major breaking news: The A.C. in A.C. Slater stands for Albert Clifford! This doesn't really get the onscreen emphasis it deserves.

Science: Returning to the sort of love triangle that drove apart Zack and Kelly, the show again does a nice job exploring compatibility and change. Slater and Jennifer still blow up the love machine that Screech and Kelly design for their science project (Zack and Jessie's micro-listening device of course catches Slater asking for Jennifer's number), but after a less-than-explosive date they realize that Albert and Jennifer were good together, but A.C. and Jen (who no longer agree regarding Mel Gibson vs. Kevin Costner!) are now better off as friends.

Zack's lies (1):

- Pretending to be an old lady to go with Jessie (an old man) to the movies to spy on Slater and Jennifer

Awkward: When Zack takes out Jennifer to try to diminish the heat on Slater (and also because Zack wants to date Jennifer), he arrives with her at the Max and says to his friends at their usual table, "You all know Jennifer." Why does he do this? It's an odd moment that suggests someone needs to be re-introduced to people they already know before they can speak?

Once again: Kelly is clearly the best person here, doing a great job of being supportive to Jessie during a difficult time and helping her realize holding too tightly to Slater won't be the way to keep him around. "I don't want to lose Slater," Jessie says, crying. "I love him." It's a moving, vulnerable moment between friends.

Aggression against Jessie: Fearing retribution, Slater observes, "Jessie's going to rip my eyes out, punch my face in, then break up with me. It's her usual pattern." Why is Jessie always the butt of the joke even when she's the victim?

Foolproof line: At the Max, Zack orders for himself and Jennifer by requesting "How about one burger and we'll meet at the pickle?" Sounds romantic until you actually do it, dude. So I've heard.

Episode 12: "Class Rings"

Aired October 17, 1992

Plot: Belding makes the brilliant decision to put Zack in charge of acquiring the senior class rings, leading to Zack's equally wise move to negotiate with a blatantly bottom-feeding dirtbag named Gem Diamond (the late Gary Beach, who apparently reprised the role on an episode of "California Dreams"?!). When the rings prove to be fake gold, the other students (and their green-stained fingers) demand Zack fix things or be melted into a ring himself. (Well, no, but they are pretty mad.)

Again with the phony business genius swagger: Zack claims "Deal is my middle name" even though he has done little if anything to earn that. This guy is the king of doth protesting too much.

More effective plotting: Tori may have rough edges but she's kind and clear-headed, so it makes sense that she would ask why Lisa treats Screech like dirt and then bet that if Tori can make it through a date with him, Lisa has to be nice to him for the rest of the year. Though it just causes the show to play up Screech's oddities/bug fixation as if he can't ever suppress them, and it's a bit unsettling that Lisa is so horrified by the idea of not being mean for a while. But as an engine for the story and continued evidence that Screech is quite lonely, it works.

However, that continuity thing: It's rather insulting to have Lisa tell Tori she'd want to kill Screech before they bought tickets if the two ever went to a movie together considering the one time Lisa and Screech caught a movie it was Screech who grew frustrated with Lisa, not the other way around. It's … odd that the characters don't remember their own lives.

Zack's lies (2):

- Telling Belding she and Tori were in the library studying (wherever they were, they were not studying)
- Pretending to be sad about losing Tori to Screech
- (Giving Zack a pass for lying to Gem, who is very sleazy and deserves it)

More fun with Ox: Who would have guessed that this guy (a reminder that Troy Fromin originally played a different character named Scud) would become a recurring character? Obviously the show only wants him around to insult his intelligence, but the comic timing is there. "It actually makes sense," Zack exclaims after Ox shares a good idea about what style to use on the class rings. "Did you have brain surgery over the weekend?" Replies Ox: "I don't think so?"

Trivia: One of the details on Gem Diamond's business card is GGTK, which stands for Good Guy to Know and is not an acronym used by anyone, particularly a good guy to know.

Episode 13: "Isn't it Romantic?"

Aired October 24, 1992

Plot: We made it so far without a clip show of repeated segments from past episodes, but here we are with a Valentine's Day-related montage that aired in late October. Sure.

Zack's lies: Nothing new that comes up during the short connecting bits that are just meant to be introductions to the clips.

Continuity: Now Zack and Kelly are dating again? Who can follow this?

Aggression against Jessie: When Slater mentions that he also pursued Kelly a while back, he adds, "Until Jessie threatened to beat me up if I didn't go out with her." Yes, he's kidding, but it's another shot at Jessie that undermines her and Slater's feelings for her. Stop it.

Weird comment: "It was fun chasing Kelly," Zack says, "But nothing could top the feeling of catching her." This notion of acquisition fits in with Zack's constant demonstration that he just likes Kelly because she's pretty.

Incident we sadly never got to see on screen: Apparently Screech once shaved "I love you" into his head and stood under Lisa's bedroom window. It would have been so easy to include a clip of this here!

Episode 14: "The Will"

Aired October 24, 1992

Plot: Because it's been about 10 minutes since the episode about Bayside striking oil, now a wealthy alum (he invented waist bands for underwear) has left the students $10,000. With rampant sexism clearly an ongoing problem here along with a lack of firm leadership, it makes sense that the money will be given exclusively to boys or girls (stemming from a dispute about guys vs. girls sports). Cut to a "Battle of the Sexes" competition involving gender-normative activities such as baking (in which the guys of course cheat; see below) and putting together a carburetor (which Tori nails), plus a more neutral scavenger hunt.

Zack's lies (1):

- Secretly replacing the girls' oven knob so their cake will burn (everyone seems to have forgotten Slater was once a top-notch baker)

The central debate: It's good that the show gives women a voice against the guys' sexist perspective on sports (even if there's no denying where the most revenue comes from). Perhaps even better is that the episode ends with a tie-breaking event (limbo!) to determine the actual winner rather than just giving it to the girls because of the cheating, which would have been justified but not allowed them a real victory. Overall, not bad.

Unexpected inspiration: After the girls discover what happened in the bake-off (thanks to Screech casually tossing the oven knob in their presence), they refuse to date the dudes until they confess, which is like a PG-13 version of "Lysistrata."

Never-ending fountain of kindness: Slater explains that the football team is feeling the school's budget crunch by stating, "We're starting to use fat nerds as tackling dummies." If there's going to be a laugh track, there should also be a boo track.

Bad sign: When the money is announced, Zack blurts out that they should rent out the Forum and have a private party with the Laker girls. When Tori, his girlfriend, reminds him that she's sitting right next to him, Zack explains that it was simply a reflex action. Oh, in that case no problem.

Trivia: Attempting to decipher visual clues to win the scavenger hunt competition, Screech guesses that the statement (which is actually "Honor thy principal") is "Honor thy neighbor's bucket of chicken!" Also wise words to live by.

Episode 15: "The Teacher's Strike"

Aired October 31, 1992

Plot: Once again Zack wants to go skiing, which apparently has to mean scheming his way out of school by fostering conflict between Belding and the teachers. This does not sit well with Jessie, Lisa and Screech, who have been prepping hard for the Academic Bowl, one of many things that will be canceled if the teachers are picketing.

Zack's lies (3):

- Telling Belding it's customary to interview him to pump up the team
- Using Belding's answers in a new, false context to manipulate Tuttle and drive a strike
- Claiming Belding came up with his own proposal for changes he'll make to meet the teachers' demands

For a change, undermining Jessie! Kelly is "away" so Jessie occupies her job at the Max, explaining, "I hate wearing this demeaning sexist uniform, but the tips are great." Once again, the person with the message is painted as a hypocrite. (It's also not awesome that Lisa describes Jessie with "Smart chick, lousy attitude" and Tuttle tells Jessie and Lisa, "The hard work you put in will be the winning complement to Screech's brainy energy," suggesting that only through effort, not intelligence, can the girls succeed.) Whyyyyyyyyyyyyyy.

Status check: To the surprise of no one, the Valley competitors are a bunch of stereotypical nerds that have nasally voices and awful fashion sense. Wouldn't it be more engaging if the opponents were both smart and well put-together like the Bayside team? (This obviously excludes Screech, who gets very sick while carrying Zack and Slater's luggage on the ski trip and is even more of a mess than usual during final battle prep.) Also, Zack comments, "Sometimes the biggest dorks have the best ideas" in reference to Screech, a super-nice thing to say about your best friend.

Reminder: This episode now brings to mind the Mathletes competition on "Freaks and Geeks," which was juuuust a bit more sympathetic to the outsiders of the high school community.

The message: There's so much manipulation in this one, and Zack taking Screech's place on the team and helping them win feels unearned to say the least.

Trivia: Led to believe they should study football but then tested on basketball, the Valley team's guesses about the names of basketball legends include Kareem-Abdul Montana and Air McMahon. They also guess that O.J. Simpson invented basketball, and let's just move on.

Episode 16: "Slater's Sister"

Aired October 31, 1992

Plot: As it's been 30 seconds since a new girl has shown up in school, here's another one! Somehow J.B. (Rana Haugen) has a long-established relationship with the rest of the gang (not including Tori) even though she's never been seen before, and of course Zack's now interested in her. Which Slater justifiably doesn't love.

Zack's lies: None!

Emotional healing: Belding takes a male sensitivity seminar at his wife's request, leading to the male students sitting in a circle around a fake fire and expressing their feelings as long as they're holding the talking stick. This allows Slater to come clean that he doesn't want Zack dating J.B., during which Zack is remarkably clueless about who Slater's discussing. Unlike their recent war over Joanna, however, Slater ultimately gives Zack his blessing, leading to Zack and J.B. dating for the rest of the series. (Nope, never seen again.)

Continuity: So I guess Zack and Tori aren't dating anymore, and it's not weird for them at all when Slater forces a double date with him and Tori and Zack and J.B.? Makes sense.

Tori as fill-in for Jessie: Recalling that J.B. used to be a real tomboy, Screech says, "Hey, just like you, Tori, not feminine at all!" Tori asks someone to hit him hard, but clearly the joke is at Tori's expense, not Screech's, and later he tells J.B. "You're a girl now!" and notes to Tori, "Hey, there's still hope for you!" Blech.

More sudden musical achievement: Out of nowhere the gang comprises a barbershop quintet called The Five Aces, with plans to perform at a '50s-inspired sock hop. And the best part is the cast isn't lip-synching! (Yes, yes, they are.)

Feel! Feel! Brought together during the male bonding session, Screech laments feeling burdened by his intelligence while Ox wishes people didn't think he was just a dumb jock. It's a nice moment, and come on, Ox knows the capitals of all 48 states!

Episode 17: "The Senior Prom"

Aired November 7, 1992

Plot: As they say, dance #5,967 is the most special, as the gang figures out who they'll go with to a square dance-themed prom (necessitated by decorations for "Oklahoma!" that can't be taken down). Of course Zack waits too long to ask Kelly, requiring him to sleazily get rid of the dude that does, a seemingly nice guy named Matt Wilson (Andrew Bowen of "MADtv").

Zack's lies (9):

- Claiming he doesn't ask Jamie to the prom because "I never noticed it before, but she's left-handed; I don't want to deal with that"
- Saying he didn't ask Cathy because he just remembered she used to wear braces in junior high
- Telling Matt that Kelly's dad used to interrogate prisoners of war and sometimes gets carried away, plus her older brothers will break his hand if he tries to touch her (and Zack's thumb is messed up as a result) and maybe Kelly's curfew will be extended to 9:30 p.m. for prom before her brothers hunt him down (calling this 6)
- Deflecting Matt's reference to Kelly's family as Matt just being a weird guy

Again with the appearance: When Kelly notes that no one has asked her to the prom yet, Zack responds, "Kelly, you're one of the hottest girls in school, a lot of guys are going to ask you." A reminder that they've been close friends for years and dated for a long time and he has nothing to say about her except for "You're hot."

Also uncomfortable: After Matt dumps Kelly based on the misinformation he received and Zack swoops in, Kelly says gratefully, "You're always there when something bad happens." Once again, this really recalls the line "If you're seeing me, you're having the worst day of your life" in "Nightcrawler," and that Zack could be compared to Jake Gyllenhaal's unforgettably creepy character in that movie says something.

Continuity: Zack claims that Kelly is "the only girl I've ever cared about." She's certainly been the biggest presence in his life, but there's no way he shrugs off his time with Stacey as easily as the writers do.

Much sweeter: Obviously Lisa has countless prom options she'd rather go with than Screech, but after seeing many girls be mean to him, she snaps back at Cathy (insulting both her character and fashion sense) and has a really nice moment with Screech at the Max. Screech promised he wouldn't ask Lisa so she asks him, and his joy (and her sincere happiness, rather than pity) make this a surprisingly rewarding culmination of years of his inappropriate pursuit. (It would have been better to give Lisa a true romantic partner and not just use her to make Screech feel better, but if not that then this is OK, especially with how Voorhies delivers the line, "I couldn't pick between all of the favorites, so I went with the underdog.")

Typical sitcom business: Slater and Jessie are both going with other people (who we never see) but get locked in the boiler room, causing them to miss most of the dance as well as rekindle their spark. On the list of "mandatory incidents to include in a sitcom," accidentally locked in a room has to be Top 20.

Because of course: The episode finds a way to squeeze in a dig at Jessie, making her look dumb when she says the heat in the boiler room is "like a furnace," to which Slater responds, "It is a furnace."

Memorable: Let's set aside how Zack has no consequences for his lies (he explains that he did it because he just had to go with Kelly, and she thinks it's sweet) and recall Screech's great hoedown lines, including "Promenade home and don't look back, Kelly go out and talk with Zack!" and asking Belding, "Want me to call the Arkansas hog with the chicken in the skillet?" Who could say no to that?

Episode 18: "The Video Yearbook"

Aired November 7, 1992

Plot: Yet another episode that would make more sense if it ran in the earlier season it was meant for, considering now suddenly Zack is 16 again and back to not having a car. He's also still sleazy and selfish, secretly converting the video yearbook he and Screech are filming into a video dating tape of Bayside's best-looking female students to be sold to every lonely guy in the area.

Instant aggression: After Slater recalls buying a yearbook when he arrived at Bayside to "check out the babes," Jessie calls him shallow, noting that you can't judge a person by a picture of their face. "You're right," Slater says, "I couldn't even see their legs." Eye roll, laugh track, completely botched message, etc.

Bleccccccccchhh: After the tapes sell like crazy and the women of Bayside receive tons of dates, Screech says what they're doing feels slimebally. "Yeah, isn't it great?" Zack says, assumedly also thinking about when he made a calendar of his female friends in their bathing suits without their permission. What a guy.

Impressive continuity: Slater completely freezes up on camera, which fits with how terrible he was on the radio. "I bet it feels good to be the captain of the football team?" Zack asks. Slater: "Oh. I bet it does." Then his message to the graduating class is just "Goodbye." Hilariously awkward.

Not-as-worthwhile continuity: After the gang figures out what Zack has done, Kelly insists they teach him a lesson he never forgets, herself apparently forgetting that there has never been a lesson that Zack has remembered.

On that note: When Zack tells Screech he's the dumbest person on earth for including Kelly, Jessie and Lisa in the video, Screech shoots back, "You hired me; what does that make you?" Well said.

Zack's lies (1):

- Just the video

Oops: With Slater pretending to beat up everyone who's interested in Jessie, Zack calls a timeout to acknowledge how desperately he needs to resolve the chaos he caused. The timeout also leads to Slater accidentally punching Belding in the face, which reminds us that perhaps society is simply not ready for timeout technology.

Episode 19: "Screech's Birthday"

Aired November 14, 1992

Plot: After they forget you know what, the gang schemes to throw an epic, belated bash in Belding's office, which requires replacing evil hall monitor Neil (Jesse Wilson) and giving the job to Screech.

OH MY GOD: This episode was supposed to be part of the first high school season but didn't air for another three years, which must have been so weird when viewers suddenly saw the cast look so, so much younger.

Zack's lies (2):

- Recording Neil and playing the tape to get him in trouble with Mr. Dewey
- Making an announcement claiming to be Belding's new secretary Miss Johnson

There is truth in all humor: When Zack asks Kevin (still around because this episode is old) if Screech is in the bathroom shaving his cat, Kevin says, "No, he only shaves his cat on Halloween." Yeah haha *that's so creepy.*

Acting opportunities: Because Kelly, Lisa and Jessie are all auditioning for a drama festival, they're working on accents that they get to utilize as part of their deception toward Belding. Lisa's a Southern belle, Kelly's Eliza Doolittle from "My Fair Lady" and Jessie's Joan of Arc. Slater is glad because Joan of Arc dies, yet another example of the show's aggression toward Jessie.

Speaking of which: When Jessie says the plan to take over Belding's office makes her nervous, Slater exclaims, "Will someone shoot her with a tranquilizer dart?"

Manipulation: When Zack requires a secret password to enter Belding's office, he forces Kelly to say, "Zack Morris is the most awesome guy in the world. He's so hot I just want to be with him forever." ("You missed stud muffin," Zack notes.) Beyond groanworthy.

Surprising influence: The super-fast party that winds up taking place is reminiscent of the super-fast date that Ted executes for Stella on "How I Met Your Mother."

Episode 20: "Snow White and the Seven Dorks"

Aired November 14, 1992

Plot: Whaddayaknow, another leftover episode from a previous season that now feels really out of place. When the drama class decides to put on a rap version of "Snow White," unexpected sparks fly between longtime platonic best friends Zack and Jessie, who have to kiss in the play and wonder if a particularly heated rehearsal means more.

Important to note: Zack has now officially had single-episode flirtations with both of the non-Kelly female leads, and both times the relationship is given a chance (he and Jessie eventually realize they're just friends while he and Lisa want to give it a shot, which of course we don't get to see). By comparison, Slater also had episodes in which he seemed to be getting closer to Kelly and Lisa, yet the show never really indulged those possibilities. (Screech had moments with all of them too but never anything romantic that went both ways.) Too bad.

Zack's lies: None!

New levels: It's fun to see Kelly initially give a too-sweet audition as the Wicked Queen but turn darker after Mr. Bainbridge (Henry Polic II) asks how she'd feel if Snow White were picked as head cheerleader and won a recount for homecoming queen. Kelly's also not upset when Jessie gets the lead role and is gracious in appreciating Jessie's gesture about being cast instead. Worth repeating: Thiessen is an underrated asset of this show, and Kelly is the gang's best person.

Good platform for Jessie: It's actually really good how she rewrites her lyrics to give Snow White more agency, such as telling the seven dorks, "You sexist pigs and that's no lie, treat me like this I'll stay at the Y." For a change, the episode gives her room to be herself and doesn't judge her for it.

Plus: There's a lot of solid stuff in this episode, between addressing the challenging emotions for actors performing a love story, the flicker that may appear between longtime friends at potentially inconvenient times and the clever way Zack and Jessie adjust the lyrics to reassert their loyalty to Kelly and Slater after Zack and Jessie determine that they don't feel anything more for each other. All that plus rap lines like "To make her pulse accelerate, she needs a kiss from dork number 8"? Bring it on.

Double entendre? Anyone could have predicted that Zack would suggest making the dwarves "tall blond chicks and put 'em in bikinis," but the way Slater says "I'm down for that, hi ho hi ho!" may or may not suggest his "hi ho" has more to it than song lyrics.

Episode 21: "Earthquake!"

Aired November 21, 1992

Plot: Congratulations to Mr. Richard and Mrs. Becky Belding (the late Louan Gideon), expecting their first child in their early 40s. Would you believe that she goes into labor during an earthquake and Zack and Tori have to help with the delivery while trapped in an elevator?

Zack's lies (2):

- Manipulating his way out of the physics midterm by claiming the gang had a baby shower planned for Mrs. B
- Defending his possession of a key to the faculty elevator as a safety precaution in case all teachers are rendered helpless

Typical Zack: He runs a pool predicting the birth date of Baby Belding but takes the due date and several dates around it for himself. "Still ripping off the nerds?" Tori asks. "I prefer calling it overcharging the less cool," Zack says. Clearly acceptable then.

Quick question: How does Mrs. B have a relationship with all of the students? We've never seen her before, which is actually surprising considering how often Belding has mentioned her over the years. Good to finally put a face to the name.

Worth mentioning: No one is saying the scene should have been graphic, but the elevator birth has to be the cleanest delivery of all time (not to mention being pretty fast and shockingly low on pain). Why write an episode like this if it's going to have such a warped sense of reality? There's merit in showing how to stay calm in stressful situations, but perhaps that could have been done without DELIVERING A BABY AT THE SAME TIME.

Proof that people absorb what they see on TV: Trapped in Belding's office after he pulls the knob off the door, Screech asks the principal to hand him the baby key ring and soap on a rope that Screech gave Mrs. B at the shower. The reason: He saw it done on "MacGyver."

Episode 22: "The Best Summer of My Life"

Aired November 21, 1992

Plot: Another clip show! New ideas really are not in abundance here. Especially because the timing of this is absurd as Zack stays home the first week of school and reflects on the Malibu Sands episodes and the two-part excursion for Jessie's dad's wedding, both of which by now happened more than a season ago and don't need to be recapped no matter how long it's been.

Zack's lies: Nothing new added in the short bits that lead to the clips.

Shady: As soon as Slater mentions how much he made in tips at the beach club, Zack asks, "Did I ever tell you about the Zack Morris Investment Program?" This proposed to a close friend from a guy who has proven to be irresponsible with money and indifferent to losing other people's funds. Sigh.

Better: As a way of introducing clips of the female characters, the show at least recognizes that the girls had just as much fun as the guys. It doesn't mean they drove the plot as much, but considering how often it seems like the guys get to have the most fun on the show, even a little balance is better than none.

Devastating: Screech bursts into tears as he reflects, "I've never had so much fun in my entire life … and I bet I never will again." There's a surprising amount of fear and paranoia lurking under the surface of this show, and anything that counts as an added psychological layer is progress!

Episode 23: "Slater's Friend"

Aired November 28, 1992

Plot: Another instance of babysitting/surrogate parenting as the gang must watch Slater's best friend, a chameleon named Artie who movingly has been the only consistent friend he's had while traveling all over the world. Artie's inevitable death leads to even more inevitable deception, followed by redemption and a funeral in which everyone sings about bugs to the tune of "Oh, Danny Boy." ("Oh, Artie boy, the bugs the bugs are buzzing!")

YOU MUST BE KIDDING: This was yet another holdover from the beginning of high school. Really wonder if there's anyone out there who noticed this at the time and was baffled at the emergence of these lost, old episodes appearing from the past to interrupt the series' progress.

Just shut up, dude: When Zack tells Slater that, unlike Slater's fondness for Artie, Zack prefers to hold something "cute and female," Kelly quips, "Oh, buy a poodle, OK?" By now in the series we're a long way from when she saw through Zack's garbage.

As if that weren't enough: After telling Kelly he'd be happy to help her with her speech for class because he's "a generous, caring individual," he turns to the camera and adds, "And she's gorgeous!"

Oh yeah, and and and: Now Zack has a life-size cutout of Kelly in her volleyball uniform, which is in addition to the poster he has of her that descends from his ceiling. Zack. Is. A. Psycho.

Zack's lies (4):

- Claiming that Artie's at Zack's house, asleep
- Buying a new chameleon and pretending he's Artie
- Saying the chameleon the girls bring in is only called Artie because it's short for Artesia, Artie's date for a slumber party
- Claiming the volleyball cutout came with his wallet

Wow: During a vision in which the gang is part of a police lineup with Belding as the cop and Slater playing Artie in a full-body chameleon costume, Slater as Artie tells Kelly she was always "a hot little number." It's always uncomfortable to see the show objectifying Kelly, but it's especially weird when a chameleon does it. (Also, Brooklyn stereotype Coach Rizzo, played by Frankie Como, calls her "Miss Dollface Kapowski.")

Funny yet undermining: Jessie and her mom try to picket an oil company but never make it to the protest when they run out of gas and refuse to fill up on principle.

Credit where credit's due: When Slater starts disrupting class because he's sad about Artie and goes to Belding's office, they share a nice moment and a hug. Lopez also proves capable of capturing emotion, something, for example, Matthew Perry couldn't do on "Friends."

*****Interview with Como:** "The comedy is in a speech teacher with a thick Brooklyn accent. It doesn't matter to me if they are laughing with him or at him; it was a kids' show, and I was hired to make kids laugh. My ego was not involved. If people were laughing, I did my job. Caricature or stereotype, it doesn't really matter to me, and frankly I am delighted that there is any discussion at all about a character I played over 30 years ago. I did indeed grow up in Brooklyn and knew many 'Coach Rizzo' types, so I knew going into the audition that a thick Brooklyn accent would be funnier for a speech teacher. So I purposely thickened my accent to match many of the characters I grew up with when I read for the part. Years later they needed a Brooklyn type to play Big Al Gambino on 'Saved by the Bell: The New Class,' and I got a call and was on the set the next morning without auditioning at all … In this day and age, I think it would be inappropriate to call Kelly 'Dollface.'" *(Read more from Como on page 318.)*

Episode 24: "School Song"

Aired November 28, 1992

Plot: Zack's perspective is so warped that he thinks winning a rigged contest will still endear him to future students forever. So with the senior class deciding its gift to the school will be a new official song, he does anything necessary (translation: screwing over his friends) to ensure his track, the toe-tapping, guitar-driven "Cool School," can defeat Screech's underdog candidate, set to the tune of "Home on the Range."

Zack's lies (2):

- Starting a fight between Slater, Lisa, Screech and Tori, misrepresenting everyone to drive them apart (let's call this one)
- Messing up the piano for Slater and Tori's audition

This guy: Obviously Zack's idea for the class gift is every girl getting a kiss from him. The bravado is exhausting and in a very small way kind of sad.

Logic: Everyone agrees that Zack is the school's biggest goof-off, yet he's participated on several sports teams and many clubs? Makes total sense.

For what it's worth: The psychology here holds up as Zack struggles to accept how his bad behavior has established his identity as a deceitful person, and it's no surprise his first instinct ("I love contests; they're so easy to fix") about how to solve that is driven by something desperate and selfish. That he gets what he deserves (after his friends spike a drink with lemon extract and ruin his performance in the finals of the contest) and doesn't make any progress in his legacy is justice – even if it comes with yet another instance of forgiveness from friends who by now are probably a bit tired of a guy who's eager to throw them under the bus whenever possible. His ridiculous performance after ingesting the tainted drink is pretty hilarious as the glee club sings along with botched lines like "Ah bippy boo."

More status stuff: This episode hinges on wanting to "sway the dork vote," with Zack romancing Louise (with whom he shares an awful kiss) because of her influence over dudes like Pete and Sylvester. Certainly high schools have cliques and perceived social tiers, but "Saved by the Bell" really worked overtime to emphasize people's behavioral differences rather than recognizing what they have in common.

Fun with words: Even though he ties Zack in the initial vote (prompting the live final showdown), Lisa, Slater and Tori rewrite the entire song (and, to be fair, make it much,

much better), and Screech doesn't care because, as Slater says, they keep words like "the," "and," "it" and "Bayside." Good point!

Episode 25: "The Time Capsule"

Aired December 5, 1992

Plot: Yet another clip show? That's the third one of the season, which clearly is limping to its conclusion. Here members of the class of 2003 join Belding in his office to watch a video from his favorites from the class of '93, who reflect on memories that apparently were being filmed "The Office"-style all along, albeit without on-camera interviews.

Zack's lies: No new ones, thankfully.

Aggression against Jessie: Did she really have to comment on her life with, "Even when I did something stupid, I could always count on Zack"?

Creepy: Screech tells any high school girls watching that he's still single. No no no no no no no no.

The new class: The characters watching the video include an arrogant blond dude named Josh who calls Belding "Mr. Building," an intellectual girl named Robin who calls sexist guys "pig" and a much-insulted guy called Duddy who admires Screech. Can you believe we never saw these people again?

Episode 26: "Graduation"

Aired May 22, 1993 (on a Saturday night, six months after the previous episode)

Plot: High school's about to end for everyone but Zack, who finds out that he's one credit short because of a class he dropped sophomore year and because obviously Bayside's terrible at record-keeping or they would have known this a long time ago. So Zack attempts to get his last credit by joining the ballet class' performance of "Swan Pond" while Screech declines the honor of being valedictorian because he knows how much it means to Jessie, whose GPA is .1 lower.

Zack's lies (2):

- Getting Pete to claim he's injured and needs to be replaced in the show
- Claiming he's been taking dance lessons for 10 years

Clever: Attempting to deflect Belding, Screech insists that he can't be valedictorian because he got the answers in biology from a frog he hid up his sleeve, "Ratatouille"-style. (Which would be worth celebrating, not punishing, if that were true.) When he eventually gets serious and storms off it's good to see Screech being strong about something he believes in, although then he explains Jessie would be better to speak at graduation because "I'm just a geek with a squeaky voice." Not great that he still sees himself that way despite his accomplishments.

On that note, status check: Couldn't Pete have gone along with the scam without Slater patting him on the head and saying, "Good nerd"? Rude. Though it is good that when Jessie refers to Screech as a dorky guy, Lisa defends him (leading to her spilling that Jessie is only valedictorian because of Screech's character, dorky or not).

Logic: This episode doesn't really make sense in that after the supporting cast of "nerds" gets the flu Belding says the ballet is being canceled, prompting Zack to recruit the rest of the gang to help out. It seems likely that is not what would really happen, or at least there first would be an effort made to save the show rather than just shrugging and saying it's off despite the work of all the others involved. Oh well.

Choice of words: It's pretty moving to see Belding address each character as they receive their diploma, but I'm sorry to say his message to Zack just sounds weird. He tells him that he has something very special inside of him, and "I hope I'm around to see it when you let it all out." I can't be the only person who hears that and now remembers multiple characters saying something similar about something very different to Eddie Adams/Dirk Diggler (Mark Wahlberg) in "Boogie Nights."

Foreshadowing: Zack's speech at graduation (prompted by Jessie bringing up Screech, who just hands off to his best pal) is far from great (he claims to have had 86 girlfriends, which is not even close to true though we're not counting it as a lie because we'll accept we don't see his entire life on screen). But he does mention "I may even let Screech do my homework in college," which isn't a terrible tip-off to the idea that Zack isn't actually going to Yale (duh) and will wind up at Cal with Screech. And it's nice to see him feel the sense of loss that Kelly thought he didn't have as their time in high school closes out. This is not a fantastic episode, but good luck not feeling touched by having to say goodbye to these characters as they say goodbye to each other. Just kidding, they don't really say goodbye and to varying degrees they all come back!

Stats/Looking Back on the Fourth High School Season

The season total of 70 lies (2.7/episode) comes in just below the previous season's tally of 72 (2.8/episode), though this data is skewed by the presence of three clip-show episodes in which Zack has zero lies added. Remove those and you get 3.0 lies per episode over the remaining 23, which again reflects increased dishonesty from the blond truth twister.

Throughout this final high school season Zack shows a surprising amount of desperation, risking his friendship with Slater over a girl he barely knows, his closeness with Kelly over very temporary priorities, his bond with Screech over a sudden escalation with Lisa and the wellbeing of himself and his friends because he thinks he's capable of driving after drinking. Throughout the series Zack is an incredibly selfish person, and as a senior he more often leans into his narcissism than shows substantial progress thanks to having created these situations for himself over and over again. "School Song" shows how even toward the end of the year he is still flailing, and the sentiment of "Graduation," which has to make any fan of the show get at least a little choked up, is a bit undercut by Zack only getting into the ballet by conniving his way on stage because Pete pretends to be hurt. What progress it would have been if Zack just accepted his fate, went to summer school and grew as a person, though of course then there's no show.

Unfortunately there's more bad news: Setting aside the clip shows, in this season Zack is bad to women in 39 percent of the episodes, a significant increase from 23 percent the previous year. Part of that is from his continued treatment of women as acquisitions, but it is also in offhand comments and a continued emphasis on his own needs without any consideration for what a woman (or anyone) wants. Looking back now, it's sort of stunning that the last episode didn't end with more about Zack and Kelly's relationship, especially considering how they come back together (justly or not) at the end of the senior prom episode.

Meanwhile, for the episodes that include Jessie (which is only 62 percent of the season), a whopping 69 percent of them contained aggression toward her, even higher than the 50 percent of the previous year. As the series goes on the presentation of this character becomes more and more as a way of criticizing her, and the instances in which she's able to speak out about important issues without being undermined are few and far between.

It's hard not to see this last high school season as a disappointment compared to the strengths of the year before it. Senior year contains not just three clip shows but five that were meant to air in previous seasons as well as 10 episodes featuring Tori, who became part of the group while Kelly and Jessie were mysteriously absent and then disappeared as quickly as she arrived without any incident or discussion. It doesn't speak to anything other than a show without a ton of good/even moderately sensible ideas left, although that's not to say this season doesn't have its highlights, from the affecting messages of "Drinking and Driving" to the fun of "Snow White and the Seven Dorks."

Yet a more emotionally curious show would have better dialed into its characters' individual and group experiences as this period of their lives wound down, rather than using a few moments at a dance or in the hallway to achieve a sense of reflection and weight. Of course, sometimes "Saved by the Bell" was the most fun when it allowed everyone to exist on the same playing field, so the gang banding together for a ballet (of all things) makes for a reasonably rewarding memory for them and experience for us as viewers who were a part of their lives. Now whatever happened to that never-seen deleted episode about the insane graduation party where they trashed the school and shut down nine miles of Los Angeles highway?

"Saved by the Bell: Hawaiian Style"

Aired November 27, 1992

Note: On Hulu this is presented as four distinct episodes, but it originally ran as a full-length movie (without a laugh track!) so that's how it should be assessed. It aired before "Slater's Friend," "School Song," "The Time Capsule" and "Graduation" but is included here afterwards to keep the previous season intact. If that isn't confusing enough, the movie is set during the summer before senior year, meaning it should have aired before the start of the previous season, not after 22 episodes already ran.

Plot: Two weeks at the Hawaiian Hideaway, which is owned by Kelly's grandpa Harry Bannister (Dean Jones of "The Love Bug" and "Beethoven"), turns into a collision of romantic possibility, real estate sleaziness and ancient prophecy. In other words, Zack starts dating unavailable single mother Andrea (Rena Sofer of "General Hospital" and "Melrose Place"); Kelly gets close to Harry's lawyer Brian (Dan Gauthier, who played Chip Matthews on "Friends"), who claims to be an ally in Harry's fight against the Royal Pacific Hotel's attempt to put Harry out of business; Slater and Jessie try to win a bet with Lisa that they won't fight for the whole trip; and the local Pupuku tribe believes Screech descended from a powerful chief and his foretold return will save their sacred land from being taken over by the Royal Pacific as well. Also, Belding's leading a tour group of principals and at first wants nothing to do with the kids' trip (even though normally he always wants to hang out with them) but winds up a major part of keeping the Hideaway alive.

It should go without saying, but: Every scheme here involves absurd disguises, ridiculous voices or secret recordings (and possibly all of the above), particularly once it's identified that Brian is actually a double-crossing pawn of the evil Royal Pacific Hotel, whose second-in-command Derek Worthington (Blake Boyd) is of course Andrea's dopey boyfriend. The quality of these deceptions is … mixed, but they're entirely justified by Belding's wildly over-the-top accent while impersonating a professor. When he doubts it will work, Zack offers a foolproof, stunningly direct defense: "Why not? We've done stuff like this a million times in your office."

Zack's lies (4):

- Pretending to be a fumigator at the Royal Pacific as he and Screech do their best Wayne and Garth impressions, complete with wigs and lines like, "Party on, dude, blast away!"

- Telling Belding he's only at the Royal Pacific because he had to try the buffet when he's really there to motivate the group of principals to leave
- Participating in fake banter with Slater to get Belding interested in staying at the Hideaway
- Getting Belding to do the professor act to fool Brian

Real quick about age: Uh, Kelly just finished her junior year of high school, and Brian must be at least 25 if not closer to 30, what with being a practicing lawyer and all. So that's not great. And Zack, perpetually a lothario who is also looking for love (almost like he's first-season Ted Mosby with Barney Stinson swagger), may be incredibly sincere/naive in his pursuit of Andrea and kindness toward her 4-year-old daughter Jennifer, but this often seems like a pretty different, unselfish version of Zack. If anything holds up, it's that he has always fallen fast (for seemingly any girl that crosses his path), and that being away from Bayside (like in the Malibu Sands episodes) can be good for his personality and his interactions with women. For him, only four lies across the length of four episodes is quite good, especially since zero of them are directed toward Andrea.

Speaking of credibility: Andrea has lived in Hawaii her whole life yet isn't particularly tan and has no accent and really doesn't have any characteristics of a native Hawaiian? More concerningly, the Pupuku stuff is rather embarrassing, with characters like Keanu (Donald Li) and Pono (Glen Chin) used as exaggerated comic relief for the inane Screech-as-savior subplot. Considering the show's penchant for minimizing anyone identified as an other, this isn't especially shocking. For what it's worth, though, their chant ("Manaleo manaleo manaleo, Pupuku manaleo Screech") is really catchy.

More status stuff: When the Pupuku first assert their beliefs to Screech, Lisa attempts to say they have the wrong person simply with, "This guy is a dork." At no point in the movie does she praise Screech for coming to the Pupuku's rescue (and he really doesn't do that much, actually), but the good guys win and Screech gets to have fun, so Lisa actually winds up losing out by being relegated to an also-ran in other characters' storylines. Karma for not being that nice sometimes?

Poor Jessie: As usual the goal is to make her look annoying and stupid as she overcooks a ham, starts fights with Slater and directs him to a shortcut that only leads to disaster. Nice that the couple winds up celebrating their connection anyway, but it's a reminder of just how frequently she's presented in a negative light. Sheesh, after Lisa brings TV dinners for the principals (who move from the Royal Pacific to the Hideaway after the gang impersonates horrible Royal Pacific staff members) and says, "You didn't expect me to stay inside on a day like this?" Slater responds, "Lisa, you're just as bad as Jessie." Cold!

Is this charming? Andrea swoons, but it may be debatable if Zack should be so proud that his mom says he hit on the first nurse who gave him a bath, and his dad says Zack ran a football pool in the nursery. Class act.

More mature: Slater has some wise words for Zack, who claims to love Andrea (who eventually refuses to let Zack make the same mistake she did and grow up too fast) even more than he loved Kelly and wants to figure out how to stay in Hawaii permanently. Slater gently but firmly reminds Zack that he just met her and speaks for himself in that he knows he's not ready to be a father. It's a necessary conversation to have for the storyline, and kudos to the movie for including it.

Must be said: The likewise Hawaiian-set "The Descendants" (for which Shailene Woodley should not only have been nominated for an Oscar but should have won!) clearly stole its property-related subplot from (the admittedly not original at all) "Hawaiian Style," right?

Line to use in casual conversation: "Frosted flakes are sweet," says Lisa, raving about Brian being "a 10 going on 11." "This man is the whole enchilada."

*****Interview with Boyd:** "At LAX, the scene at the international terminal, that's real traffic and that's real people. There were extras walking around there, but that's outside the Bradley international terminal. It was underneath – I think we were shooting downstairs where the arrivals are. Or maybe the arrivals are upstairs, I can't remember which. But we would get into the limousine, when I'm picking [Andrea] up from the airport and she's with Zack and I take her luggage and I try to tip him and I realize he's not a bellman and I snatch the bill back away. And I get in the car, and we had to make the entire loop of the airport. We couldn't just stop and back up and do it again; we had to continue around the whole loop because that was real traffic. They can't stop traffic at LAX. Even though we quote-unquote owned the location, we didn't own the traffic. So Rena and I driving in the limo together had on body mics, and we would look at each other, and we'd start talking because actors tend to talk when you're not working, you chit-chat. And Rena looked at me and put her finger up to her mouth and was like, 'Be careful what you say.' I would never disparage another actor or director or whatever, but we were reminding each other, 'Don't talk because we're mic'd, and they can hear us.' [Laughs] I don't know if she was having any difficulty or not on the show, I don't think so. I remember sitting around and talking about Biblical history with Peter Engel, the producer of the show. He's a Biblical scholar. A friend of mine joined us one day; he was also very, very well-versed on Biblical references and scripture, and that was pretty interesting to talk to a Hollywood producer about the Bible … I will tell you I think I was smoking then. And I would have a cigarette, and Victor Brandt, he played my father, he was talking about he had quit smoking, and Mark-Paul Gosselaar said, 'Yeah, I used to smoke, but I quit because I wanted to be big, and I felt like cigarettes were suppressing my appetite. And I wasn't able to be big, so I quit smoking.' He was at that age when teenage boys say, 'We want to get big.' I don't know if you did or not, but I know I wanted to be big, be muscular … He was really, really into lifting weights. He was really, really into fitness at the time, and he wanted to be as big as he could. That was his goal." *(Read more from Boyd on page 310.)*

"Saved by the Bell: The College Years" (1993-1994)

So I guess Zack isn't going to Yale after all. No, he, Slater and Screech all wind up at CalU, which I remembered as being the actual University of California-Berkeley. But it's not; the CalU mascot is the Falcons (rather than the Bears) and, well, their wrestling gym looks an awful lot like Bayside's did.

More importantly, going to college would seem to be an opportunity for the series to grow up, what with moving into primetime (!) and no longer having to lie to anyone's mom about where they're going and when. Plus, the guys live in a suite in which a shared living room connects their bedroom to a room with three girls: Leslie Burke (Anne Tremko), Alex Tabor (Kiersten Warren of "Desperate Housewives") and Danielle Marks (Essence Atkins of "Marlon"), to whom, well, you shouldn't grow too attached.

Because clearly these kids need another mentor who focuses an unexpectedly high percentage of his attention on them, there's also Mike Rogers (Bob Golic, who played for the Cleveland Browns and Oakland Raiders), an ex-NFL star who isn't here to take any crap from Zack. So surely this is the time preppie will finally turn into the stand-up guy we always wanted him to be, right? Right?

(Crickets.)

Episode 1: "Pilot"

Aired May 22, 1993

Plot: Welcome to an extremely tame, network sitcom-appropriate version of college! As expected, Zack relentlessly hits on Leslie while Slater struggles to adjust to a higher level of wrestling competition and Screech is the only one who seems to care about communicating with his family. Mike also asserts that he will not tolerate loud parties during the week or any alcohol on premises, which you'd think would be addressed during a building-wide meeting or via flyer rather than a personal announcement to every dorm room but alas.

Zack's lies (5):

- Telling the girls, "Believe me, I am not the kind of guy to break the rules"
- Running a fake contest to collect surveys even though there won't actually be a Hawaii trip given out
- Secretly paying a girl $20 to boost Slater's ego
- Claiming that he has a date to save face with Leslie
- Saying this is the first time he didn't get the girl

Memory is selective: Unable to process how many girls are around him in college, Zack is very quick to note, "If I would have known college was this good, I would have skipped high school," as if he didn't spend his entire high school career skipping class and for a while doing everything possible to hang out with a college girl. This clearly isn't a lack of continuity but merely a young person struggling to handle his emotions. Or both.

Remind me why we're supposed to like this guy: Identifying that his major is investment banking, Zack adds that "all my heroes are in jail." In another version of "Saved by the Bell," Zack would be the nemesis, not the lead. Surely it's not too late to make that.

The best of the newbies: Tremko makes the strongest impression of the girls (possibly because Leslie is a decent character while Alex is just an overly dramatic caricature and Danielle is forgettably snooty and, again, will be gone soon), particularly when Zack throws her an unsanctioned 18th birthday party and Leslie says, "You're immature and selfish; you didn't throw that party to make me happy, you did it to impress me and make yourself look good. I guess it doesn't matter if somebody else has to pay the price." If she only knew.

Worthwhile adversity: Even though this episode is less than stellar, it's useful to see Zack's swagger challenged a bit and Slater have to recognize that he will need to deal with tougher competition if he wants to continue wrestling and maintain his scholarship. Both consider quitting and leaving, and it's a decent lesson to young viewers that adaptation isn't always easy, but it's necessary to grow and get what you want.

College being a place to start over: Kinda nice to see Screech seeming to have a little more of a carefree attitude as well as impressing a girl at the party. She's also interested in cybernetics but is even more interested in "having a slow dance with you." Hubba hubba.

Because Rhode Island isn't big enough: The first time he sees Mike, Screech observes, "It's Ohio, and it talks!"

*****Interview with Tremko on what her role was initially supposed to be**: "My agent had put me up for the part of Alex, and when I got there the casting director was like, 'You know, you look more like a Leslie; why don't you read these Leslie sides?' Then I had a callback, and then I had a callback with the producers, and then I went to the test. And then I found out I got the role … When I originally auditioned for the show, my character was supposed to be the love interest, and that was because they couldn't negotiate Tiffani's contract. And then at some point in that summer between when we shot the pilot and when the series started they were able to negotiate a contract with her, so they had to fire one of us, and I had no idea any of that was going on. In fact, when I found out the show got picked up, I called Essence [Atkins, who played Danielle], and her boyfriend answered and I was like, 'Hey, the show got picked up. She can come out and stay with me if she wants to look for a place,' and he was like, 'Well, she didn't get picked up with the show.' And then they had to somehow explain why they kept me, and I became kind of the voice of reason, and then they wanted me to take on a little bit more comedy. So my character kind of changed a little bit where I got to be sillier, but I couldn't be the love interest anymore. So I think they just didn't know what to do with me." *(Read more from Tremko on page 236.)*

Episode 2: "Guess Who's Coming to College?"

Aired September 14, 1993

Plot: Just when you wanted to learn more about Danielle (nope) we find out that she transferred and, whoa, Kelly's back! Which creates just a few complications when she takes Danielle's spot in the room and is inches away from where Zack's using all his moves (e.g. lying, being an idiot) on Leslie.

Zack's lies (7):

- Telling Leslie that he wasn't crying during "Free Willy," he just had a Good & Plenty in his eye
- Claiming he's afraid to get too close to a woman again because Kelly drowned after falling off a sailboat (3)
- Saying it's a miracle Kelly is alive
- Identifying his story about Kelly's death as "a little fib"
- Snooping on Leslie's class schedule to get closer to her

Screech's powers: Not only did he pull strings to get himself into the room with Zack and Slater, he also apparently wields enough clout to get Kelly into Leslie and Alex's room as well. Needless to say, this is not addressed further but raises several intriguing questions. (He also rents his bike to a revolving door of attractive girls, continuing the narrative that in college Screech's stock has elevated considerably.)

On Kelly: Despite being her usual, bubbly self, Kelly's also lonely, wanting stuffed animals to feel better about being away from home and fearing having to eat alone/in her room because of not knowing anyone at the student union. When she reminisces with Zack and says she wants to start things up again between them, it's not hard to see the psychology of clinging to something safe out of uncertainty rather than genuine feeling.

Of course: When Zack can't decide who he likes between Kelly and Leslie (and therefore who to take to the REM concert), he has nothing positive to say about Kelly except for that she's beautiful. Just awful every time. Fortunately, his waffling blows up in his face and Kelly and Leslie, both commanding instead of mad, declare that neither one will date him and they're going to the concert together.

Is that right? When I was in college we registered for classes online over the summer (at least as far as I can remember). At CalU everyone participates in a mad rush to line up and get what they want in person at various booths, causing Alex to fret over missing out on crucial acting classes and Slater to rejoice at his blow-off schedule for athletes. That is, until Mike sets him straight about the minimal job opportunities out there for people who excel in "Physics of Frisbee."

Justified embarrassment: Leslie does an excellent job showing Zack that she won't be manipulated, causing him to duplicate a fake schedule and accidentally sign up for Advanced Mandarin Chinese 503, in which no English is spoken. It really pays off by the end of the season when Zack becomes fluent! (No.)

Timely reference: After attempting to romance Leslie by giving her Pop Tarts on a tray, Zack turns to the camera and says, "Rumor has it that's how Lyle Lovett snagged Julia Roberts." Note the very deliberate use of "snagged."

Harsh: After celebrating that a kid in drama class got mono and thus opened up a spot for her, Alex adds, "If Jodie Foster gets hit by a bus, I am on my way." Considering she's rooting for this despite the "Somersby" poster on her wall shows how ruthless Alex is. In other words, she's got what it takes in an "All About Eve"/"Showgirls" kind of way.

Good policy: When Screech asks if a package he received smells like mothballs and Polident (meaning it's from Grandma Powers), Mike replies, "I'll do a lot of things for you, kid, but I won't smell your mail."

*****Interview with Tremko, when I note Zack's remarkable dishonesty**: "I mean, I guess that was just his character: 'Watch Zack try to manipulate and watch him try to do all these stupid things.' And most of the time he got caught, I think. Maybe he didn't. You probably know better than me. I don't remember him getting away with a whole bunch of things. In fact, [Editor's note: spoiler alert if somehow you didn't know this] Kelly was the one having two relationships, with a teacher [Professor Lasky]. That's kind of a big, bold thing to do, have a young, college girl having a relationship with a professor. That's a fireable offense. It was just supposed to be like a caper. Like a corny caper. If you compare it to college, a lot worse goes on in college than making up ridiculous stories like your girlfriend is dead, and then she walks in the door. It's a little innocuous." *(Read more from Tremko on page 236.)*

Episode 3: "Zack, Lies and Videotape"

Aired September 14, 1993

Plot: Besides for making all the girls in class swoon, anthropology professor Jeremiah Lasky (Patrick Fabian of "Better Call Saul") also tells Zack he can sleep in all semester (thus missing class) if he can complete a field study of what women want in the next few days. Seeing as Zack only cares what women want if A. they're cute and B. what they want is him, he's either the best or worst possible person to execute this project.

Zack's lies (2):

- Trying to buy a copy of the midterm for $20, not knowing that the guy selling him the test is the teacher
- Secretly recording his female suitemates while lying behind the couch

A revolving door of sleaziness: Man, this episode. Recalling the shadiness of turning the video yearbook into dating ads in high school, Zack utilizes his interviewing efforts to get girls' phone numbers and claims "Hitting on girls is like breathing to me." Fortunately, Lasky calls him out after Zack says he's been "scoping chicks" since the third grade and Kelly (who you'd think would have had this conversation with Zack sooner, or maybe it's believable that it took until college) tells Zack that girls won't open up to someone who's aggressively trying to pick them up. It really shows how little the two ever actually had between them, though any opportunity for the guy to learn something as basic as "women want different things" and "stop hitting on every single girl you see and listen for a change, you dope" counts as a small win. Until he tries to negotiate his B into an A by offering Lasky footage of the girls' swim team (something else he pulled in high school, hello repetition and unlearned lessons) and we're back to the same old perv.

A little more on that: This is an interesting episode as far as men and women go, what with Mike being afraid to be mocked for not having a date until he was 20 and his mom still calling herself "Mikey's mommy," plus Slater needing to gain weight for wrestling and then lose it to the satisfaction of Alex, who normally has to watch it both because she's a woman and she's an actress. Meanwhile, Zack's documentary footage finds women searching for connections that aren't based on physical desire, male emotions not driven by football and a mix of intelligence, sincerity, kindness and a guy who hasn't done time. All good things.

Such a good friend: After Screech (who identifies himself as Samuel Powers) gives a good answer in class and says that he read Lasky's book, Zack blurts out that Lasky shouldn't be excited because Screech also read "Garfield Goes to the White House." Clearly Zack wants to make sure Garfield isn't forgotten and isn't just a selfish jerk who can't stand anyone else, even a supposed close friend, being the center of attention.

Lack of continuity or inside joke? Alex notes that she has to lose two pounds due to "That Tori Spelling look that's in right now." Major missed opportunity for a Violet Bickerstaff reference here.

Definite lack of continuity: Mike said he played for the 49ers, yet in praising his own giant hands he says, "They were great for crushing Joe Montana." I guess that could be in practice, but could the writers not think of a quarterback on a different team?

And even within the same episode! Zack's mission is to be more understanding toward women, yet Mike, who agrees to help Screech bulk up if Screech helps Mike write his book "The Other Side of the Jock," describes Screech's hands with, "Those are the fingers of a sickly young girl." Here's to airtight messaging, the cornerstone of "Saved by the Bell."

#goals: That said, Screech's reason for wanting to work out is something we can all aspire to: "I'd just like to be able to lift the toilet seat without getting a hernia."

Episode 4: "Rush Week"

Aired September 21, 1993

Plot: Extremely reminiscent of the Rigmas episode from junior high (while of course not addressing that ever), "Rush Week" finds Zack and Slater desperately trying to join (Mike's fraternity) Sigma Alpha, whose members aren't as impressed by Screech's fondness for balloon animals. On the sorority side, Leslie considers whether to take her legacy spot in Kappa Theta, while Kelly and Alex hope someone, anyone, will want them.

Zack's lies (7):

- Telling Sigma Alpha leader Rick (Matt Letscher of "Scandal") that he's a jock and plays hockey (2)
- Asking Slater to tell Rick that he's loyal, honest and Cindy Crawford's new cohost on "House of Style" (3)
- Changing Screech into a guy named Brad who loves sports (2)

Deja vu: Being embarrassed by Screech has been a running theme for Zack, so it's a bit less than uplifting to see him learn once again that a good friend doesn't sell out someone else to benefit himself. Leslie is justifiably appalled that Zack and Slater are so eager to turn their backs, and somewhere underneath this episode is a more intriguing examination of how people can take different paths in college and when loyalty can also result in holding yourself back. That Zack and Slater ultimately bow out of the house only for Screech to be welcomed in is satisfying from a friendship standpoint but oversimplified in terms of what everyone actually wants. The girls' plotline works better, with Leslie backing away from the competitive spirit of rushing as Kelly and Alex embrace the camaraderie.

Funny: Screech, who's so excited to be in a house with his friends that he tells his dad it's the greatest thing that's ever happened to him (something, to be fair, Screech has said multiple times throughout the series), wonders why his underwear says Screech if his name is now Brad. To avoid any confusion, he greets the Sigma Alpha guys with, "Hi, guys, I'm Brad, but you can't see my underwear." Always good to get out ahead of a problem.

So close: Just when you thought there could be an episode without Zack being lousy to women, he wants to swap Screech for a Pakistani exchange student simply because "If she loses her mustache, she's a babe."

Timeless references: Bickering over their rushability, Alex suggests Kelly dresses like Margaret Thatcher, and Kelly says Alex looks like one of the B-52s. Surely there's a sorority out there with a tin roof?

Episode 5: "Slater's War"

Aired September 28, 1993

Plot: Zack thinks he's finally onto something with Leslie when she agrees to go skiing with him … as long as someone else comes along. That proves surprisingly difficult when Slater decides his Chicano heritage (and Theresa, played by Ara Celi of "All My Children") are more important to him than the getaway and Zack's crush.

Zack's lies (2):

- Assuring Leslie, "I'm not going to try anything, you can trust me"
- Telling Alex that he didn't mean to read her diary

Canyon-sized continuity issues: Not only do Zack and Slater never refer to the time Zack learned about his own heritage (which, oddly enough, was the episode "Running Zack" and not "Zack's War") but Zack suggests Slater's type is girls with blond hair and blue eyes. Slater has to assert that he's gone out with girls who have dark hair and dark eyes AS IF JESSIE NEVER EXISTED!!! They don't mention her name, and Zack doesn't seem to be facetious when he makes the initial comment. Just astonishing.

More unacknowledged repetition: Mike takes sensitivity training (just like Belding did) and looks after a mouse for a research project, recalling Slater's chameleon Artie as well as the animals from the pond that the class cared for before they died in an oil spill. Fortunately, Mike's mouse X97, or "Exey" for short, enjoys a happier outcome, though it's a shame Kelly, who feared something bad happening, doesn't reference the oil episode because why would she it's only her own life she's remembering arrrrrrggggghhhhhhh.

Troubling relevance: Theresa and Slater's class engages in a good conversation about hidden bias in the media, and the episode hinges on how difficult it can be for minorities to even get a chance to be heard, much less actually get to exist on the same playing field. Reminder that this aired in 1993, and about the intolerance a certain president has supported for his entire life.

That said: Like "Running Zack," "Slater's War" has a few deeply painful lines, such as "You can tell Pancho Villa I'll never forgive him for ruining my big chance with Leslie," "Why did you have to pick this weekend to be a Chicano?" and "I'm not a busboy, I'm an oppressed minority." (Alex saying "Word up, my brothers" as a force of habit because of a protest the previous week isn't great either.) Fortunately, when Zack tries to be a white savior during the sit-in that Theresa and Slater lead, his efforts are sincere but pointless, as the chancellor agrees to meet with the group before Zack's speech. It really would not have been a good look to let Zack be the reason that Theresa and Slater's efforts were recognized.

Speaking of recognized: For a minute I wondered if this is a different version of Kelly that we're seeing, as she fights to defend X97 here and begs for sorority acceptance in the previous episode. In fact, it's just that we haven't gotten to see her featured prominently very often before, and it's nice to see the character have more opportunity to carry a storyline that doesn't involve Zack.

Trivia: The show never did an episode called "Screech's War."

Episode 6: "The Homecoming"

Aired October 5, 1993

Plot: Very much recalling what Zack learned about Rod Belding, this time around he invests infinite trust and admiration in football legend Johnny Walters (Charles Grant), insisting that Mike (Johnny's former teammate at CalU and on the 49ers) is just being jealous when he says the star quarterback only cares about himself. Meanwhile, things heat up between Slater and Alex because why would these people ever try to date outside their own suite.

Zack's lies (1):

- Telling Mike he came to his room to talk about his term paper (when that is just a ruse to come talk to Johnny)

Armchair analyst: Zack begins the episode extremely dismissive of Johnny, suggesting the guy's merely "another jock" who thinks he's special just because he's rich and successful. The envy and self-consciousness practically drips off of Zack, and it definitely fits with how desperate he is to be the center of attention and only care about those who can do something for him. (He only wants to get on Johnny's good side after finding out he's on the board of three major corporations.) For what it's worth, this counts as consistency of character, even if it's a lousy person who rarely learns or grows.

Of all the questions: One of the first things Zack asks Johnny is if girls in car commercials are really as beautiful as they look on TV. 1. Are you 14 years old? And 2. What does it say about you that you're doubting them?

Much better: No matter how self-serving and awful Zack is throughout the episode, he somewhat surprisingly believes Kelly right away when she tells him how sleazy Johnny behaved with her in the limo. (He kicks her out after she turns him down.) Zack definitely doesn't deserve points for this, as believing women should be the rule, not the exception. Still, happy to see him effortlessly discard his own agenda and stand up for his friend once he finds out what happened to her and the true nature of the guy he's been idolizing.

Law of attraction: Setting aside the show's insistence on pairing up the main characters (not uncommon in sitcoms, obviously), it doesn't quite land when Slater, trying to be nice to Alex after telling her that she looks "like a nut" practicing to audition to be school mascot Freddy Falcon, claims that her pecking is kinda cute. I can't be the only one who will watch this and think of George Michael praising the cuteness of Ann's "mayonegg" on "Arrested Development."

More status stuff: Wanting to upset her snooty parents, Leslie brings Screech as her date to the homecoming banquet, where he accidentally pulls everything off the table and tells her dad (Edward Winter of "Herman's Head") he plans to take over the family business. It's kind of funny, but by now this concept is more than sad. Especially when Screech accepts the invitation and says, "I'm great at scaring parents; I scare my own all the time."

Challenging line to use out of context (delivered by Slater to Alex in a bird costume): "Will my lips fit inside your beak?"

*****Interview with Tremko on Screech:** "He was one of the most bizarre characters outside of [Kramer] on 'Seinfeld.' Screech was, like, talk about an odd person. [Laughs] I mean, he was not functioning, not interacting with reality a lot of the time. He was off in his own world and not really understanding how the world operated. He was definitely an outsider." *(Read more from Tremko on page 236.)*

Episode 7: "The Poker Game"

Aired October 12, 1993

Plot: Probably because Maxwell Nerdstrom does not attend CalU, the guys are back at the poker table, now competing against a dude named Tony (David DeLuise of "Wizards of Waverly Place") who agrees that girls should not be invited to their game. When not appropriately angry with Zack, Slater and Screech for being sexist morons, Kelly, Leslie and Alex participate in a karate class, mostly because they have a crush on the teacher (Danny Lee Clark), marking the second consecutive episode to feature a guy named Johnny.

And because Mike always needs a subplot too: He's so bad at flirting that he nearly blows it with Judith (Nancy Stafford of "Matlock" and "Scandal"), a literature professor he likes, and won't stop inserting himself into his favorite male students' plans and forcing them to play board games. Are there not RA rules about this?

Zack's lies (1):

- Telling Mike that Leslie heard Judith say he was cute to try to give him confidence/get rid of him

To the surprise of no one: One of the women suggested to Mike is Sally (Heather Elizabeth Parkhurst of "Bikini Summer III: South Beach Heat"), a very porny vending machine operator who would love to see Mike's room. Since the show can't handle characters like that for more than a few seconds because then they'd actually have to be treated like people, Mike does not show her his room.

Great response: When Screech foolishly says poker is "real men sitting around scratching and burping" and Leslie suggests the girls go off and do something only women can do, Alex declares, "Yeah, we'll go … give birth."

Then back to undermining women: After Slater claims women can't play poker because they're too emotional, Alex shouts that she's not emotional and hits him in the face with a pillow. When they finally do play the game, Alex braids Leslie's hair and they talk about how many kids they want to have, and at karate the desire to defend themselves fades away once they swoon over Johnny. Enlightened this is not.

The best message: In the midst of a lot of redundant garbage is the mildly sweet interaction between Mike and Judith, the former thinking he needs to talk endlessly about Emily Dickinson and the latter intimidated to be dating "her first hunk." Though him insulting aerobics instructors seems odd considering Jessie's stepmom Leslie, it's a nice lesson about varying perceptions as a relationship kicks off and the communication necessary to get everyone on the same page. That they ignore the fire alarm and a room full of smoke to continue hooking up perhaps sets less of an example.

Episode 8: "Professor Zack"

Aired October 19, 1993

Plot: Zack pretends to be Professor Lasky to impress Lasky fangirl Jennifer (Brittney Powell of "General Hospital" and "Friends"), really showing he's put his immature high school deceptions behind him. Alex and Kelly also attempt to make a calendar of hunky dudes to help pay for a big-screen TV in the dorm rec room, which raises several questions that go unanswered.

Zack's lies (11):

- Telling Lasky he's taking notes and then reading Alex's notes out loud in class
- Posing as Lasky to impress Jennifer
- Insisting he doesn't usually date girls Jennifer's age because they're so immature
- Claiming that Screech is one of his students and he spent a year living among the Zulus (2)
- Saying he's just about to start class and no one is allowed to audit them (2)
- Referring to the real Lasky as an older student who is so eager to learn
- Having to look in the mirror every morning and tell himself "You've done the right thing, Professor Lasky"
- Getting both Alex and Kelly to pose as his significant other to drive Jennifer away (2)

Zack is just the worst: He repeatedly tries to justify his scheme by explaining "The girl is gorgeous," and his solution after finding out that Jennifer is the chancellor's daughter is initially just to avoid her and hope she gets the hint. The only upside is Lasky recognizing how Jennifer's appearance doesn't justify anything and ultimately Jennifer, drooling over the real Lasky, showing Zack that she didn't actually want him, just her perception of who she thought he was. Which Zack then really takes to heart and uses as a motivator to change his behavior. (No.)

Good line: Lasky tells Zack they aren't friends, Zack is his student, and "This is college, not high school. No one's going to make you learn." It's an important statement … until Lasky shields Zack from serious punishment and for no legitimate reason decides it's OK for them to be friends.

Where have we seen this before? For the second time in three episodes, Screech is called on to be awkward and annoying, this time while messing up Zack and Jennifer's date.

He also claims he could only be in a calendar if someone invented the month of "Geekuary," leading to his head being pasted on Slater's body for the final image, with coloring inconsistency surely only 99.9% of people would notice.

Calling Jessie: Leslie finds the idea of a pin-up calendar offensive and continually goes to shooting locations to protest, only to crumble at the sight of the models. "This is demeaning; I'm leaving," she declares. Then Slater takes his shirt off. "In an hour," she adds, really suggesting she's committed to her principles. Somewhere Ms. Spano is nodding emphatically.

Really need to hear this: At the beginning of the episode Zack has headphones on in Lasky's class, cramming for an English test by listening to "War and Peace" *as read by Joey Lawrence.* As they say, war and peace may be heavy concepts, but ain't nothing his love can't fix.

Episode 9: "Screech Love"

Aired October 26, 1993

Plot: Nearly duplicating the episode where Screech tutored Kelly for a science test and the spark that resulted, now Screech shares astronomical facts and swoony eyes with Zack's tennis-star girlfriend Linda (Hillary Danner), who just wants a normal collegiate education like her pop star best friend Stevie. (Not true, but that would have been great.)

Big, important thing: It is not new for Zack to undermine Screech or think of him as less than a person, telling him, "If this was someone other than you, I would get the feeling you're trying to horn in on my girlfriend." Zack always uses Screech and assumes his so-called best friend is a non-sexual non-threat who is just there to help Zack. Yet the show finally creates a situation in which Screech and the relevant female character have something legitimate together (beyond the series' diagnosed geek love between Screech and Violet). It's great to see Screech refuse to take Zack's crap ("You have so little respect for me that you can't even picture one girl liking me more than you. I'm not going to live with anyone who thinks I'm beneath him") and Linda tells Zack she already chose Screech before Zack tries to step aside. Congrats to Screech and Linda, and have a great time on your honeymoon! (In other words, after this episode, yep, she's never seen again.)

Zack's lies (3):

- Typically, as referenced by Slater, using "Excuse me, I seem to have lost the keys to my Ferrari" as a pickup line
- Telling Linda "I've got a tennis court reserved and my partner just canceled" (2)

Sleaziest of the sleazy: The first time Zack sees Linda he blurts out, "Whoa! Check her out. What line do you think I should use?" He also notes "Linda is beautiful, rich and famous; I usually settle for one out of three" and cuts off Linda as she tries to tell him she's a good tennis player. Even if this is just meant to set up him literally getting served and identify what a shady dope he is, uh, I think we know that already and are ready to see him not be.

What year is this? Kelly exclaims multiple times about hearing that Screech and Linda were at places unofficially known as "Makeout Point," "Liplock Lane" and "The Old Necking Tree." This can mean only one thing: Kelly needs to find someone. (Can it not be Zack, please?)

On that note: A subplot in this episode involves Kelly and Leslie hosting a party to try to meet more sophisticated guys, which mostly involves Leslie offering everyone pate and the guys eventually being distracted when Linda arrives. This seems like juuuuust a bit of a stretch.

Before they were famous: Eddie Cibrian ("The Young and the Restless," "Third Watch") plays a hunky janitor at the party.

Meanwhile: Slater and Alex agree to support each other at wrestling and plays, respectively, with Alex's disinterest in "barbaric" wrestling turning into her fighting Slater's opponent's girlfriend during the match – from which Slater is disqualified for breaking up the girls' fight. So clearly the message is (trails off, shrugs and backs away slowly).

Really funny personal detail: Screech doesn't follow sports but delights in cheering for the refs during football games. Believe it or not Mike does not like this, even though Screech points out that refs never lose and, come on, "Did you ever see a guy throw a flag like that?"

Very, very obscure trivia: The name of the official that Screech cheers for is Bill Plankman.

*****Interview with Danner on what was her first big guest-starring role: "**I never had a very big ego, and I think part of my personal nervousness in that role was I didn't have an ego and personally, not as Linda but as Hillary, would never have thought that I would have the Zack. Which is maybe why this worked on screen – if it worked, if you're saying it worked. In terms of doing the show and at the time, it seemed to me that this was just normal behavior. Being in Hollywood, you deal with those people all the time, so it didn't seem that strange to me. It seemed like it sucked, and I personally would not want to be friends with that person anyway. I wonder – if you think there was a chemistry there – if you would have a different reaction if there was an actress who maybe had more self-confidence at the time. It maybe wouldn't have worked or been believable. I don't know. I remember feeling very comfortable in the scenes with Screech and less comfortable with Zack … If I had to go do the [episode] over again, what I think would happen is I would be much stronger in my scenes with Zack and internally taken him to task a little bit more. I could see myself at least internally feeling less – I don't think I was googly-eyed. I don't think the character was into him really? I don't remember her being torn between the two of them. I think she was probably already questioning – I think she was more worldly and more attracted to a genuine person. Because she was an outsider; why the heck was she even at this school? [Laughs] This famous tennis player running around, what the heck was I doing there? My sense was she was popping in and wasn't going to fall for him anyway. That's what I remember. And that when the character meets Screech, I think she immediately recognized the character as someone she'd want to hang out with." *(Read more from Danner on page 313.)*

Episode 10: "Dr. Kelly"

Aired November 2, 1993

Plot: With all college students needing money and apparently all college guys needing a place to grunt in women's direction, Kelly and Alex take waitressing jobs at Skeeter's, a sports bar known for skimpy outfits and bros responding to "Would you like an appetizer to nibble on?" with "No, you'll do just fine."

Credit where credit's due: Like the early "Friends" episode in which the gang's varying salaries impacted what they all felt comfortable doing for fun, "Dr. Kelly" addresses difficult financial decisions (and corresponding social implications) for young people still figuring out their path. Kelly enjoys working at the health center but it doesn't pay nearly as much as Skeeter's, and Zack's absolutely horrendous input into her dilemma ("No offense, but you don't exactly seem like the doctor type," continuing his pattern of undermining women) makes her feel lousy about having any prospects beyond flirting for tips. Meanwhile, even if there's obviously more to unpack about sexism, it's useful for Slater's endorsement of the bar to be challenged by his girlfriend working there and forcing him to recognize that guys are ogling her just like he's ogling the other waitresses. With Screech also having to discover that Debi (Donna Barnes) is calling other diners "Sugar Britches" as well and he shouldn't take her kindness as romantic interest, there are actually a few decent lessons here.

The inevitable "that being said": It wouldn't be "Saved by the Bell" if the message weren't suppressed, with Leslie commenting on Skeeter's with "Is this what our mothers burned their bras for in the '60s?" and Kelly replying, "My mother once burned her bra. She fell asleep, and the Virginia Slim fell out of her mouth." In other words, the mission was pointless and women are reckless, got it!

Age ain't nothing but a number: Even though Mike is in his mid-30s, he gets a tryout to return to the 49ers, resulting in him recruiting Zack, Slater and Screech to help him train. That Mike makes the team but decides he's more interested in working on his thesis is a nice point about changing priorities that at least somewhat helps us forget lines like "It's always fun to crack a few heads."

Breaking news: Zack is bad: After getting hurt in a very sensitive area on the football field he claims, "I think I've now experienced what childbirth feels like," and he hits on Kelly at Skeeter's (not realizing it's her) by declaring, "Pardon me, but a body like yours is a felony in most states, but if you turn around I'll let you off on good behavior!" That this episode labors to rekindle feelings between them is less than desirable or necessary.

Zack's lies (1):

- Taking money from Screech by selling him shares of Zack Industries

Comic timing: One more tip of the hat to Thiessen, whose energy continues to brighten the mood and elevate the material. Highlight: Alex saying she's helping humanity as a waitress and Kelly noting, "I hear that's how Mother Teresa started: serving brewskis at T.G.I. Fridays."

Episode 11: "A Thanksgiving Story"

Aired November 23, 1993

Plot: Even if you haven't seen this special holiday episode, you can probably guess what's in store: The gang struggles to get home for Thanksgiving and winds up helping out/goofing up Mike's "Feed the Kids" program, which of course is featured live during Marv Albert's halftime show.

Zack's lies (5):

- Telling Mike he wants Raiders tickets for his brother Teddy, who's in the Peace Corps and just got back from building schools in Guatemala (3)
- Claiming he knows exactly where they are when the car breaks down
- Pretending to be a doctor so the airline will help him out with a ticket

More breaking news: Zack is bad: Sometimes he's so exhausting. After lying about his nonexistent brother Zack admits he just wants to sell the tickets for profit; later in the episode he sits in a chair Kelly pulls out and only tries to get himself on standby despite Kelly being desperate to fly home; after shopping at 7-Eleven he unloads an extremely stereotypical Indian accent not once but twice, saying "Just be glad I did not buy a turkey slurpee!"; and he really does not deserve Kelly's affection just for eventually getting her a ticket because "Making you happy is even more important to me than money." Kelly, your bar for Zack to impress you is way, way, way too low.

More questionable taste, to put it mildly: It's great that Mike hosts an event for 20 underprivileged kids. Not as great is the show perpetuating awful myths about the children, like saying that the kids are considering stripping the dean's car and Slater worrying that they will mug someone. Although Mike's line early in the episode ("These are tough street kids, not the Olsen twins!") probably should have been a clue what type of less-than-sympathetic presentation we were in for.

So much positivity for this one: This episode is just awful toward women, and it's way beyond Zack's treatment of Kelly. It's getting lost in the woods and Zack snarling, "Even in the woods they have to go in pairs" when Kelly asks Alex to join her when she goes to the bathroom. It's Leslie being a horrible cook who doesn't even know what "tsp" stands for. And it's Alex trying to connect with the kids only for them to dislike her and Slater to tell them to go play video games. Bad bad bad.

Different kind of question: Clearly sitcoms subscribe to their own logic and that's fine, but in what world is anyone believing Mike (who inevitably throws out his back) asking Screech of all people to help him lift a pool table?

On a happier note, guest stars! Folks wandering into the Thanksgiving dinner include Mr. Belding (pff), Jenna Von Oy of "Blossom" (Belding asks her to sign his mashed potatoes), the late Jonathan Brandis (who Kelly identifies as "of seaQuest" for maximum NBC promotion), Marsha Warfield ("Night Court") and Brian Austin Green ("Beverly Hills, 90210"). Unfortunately we don't get to hear what conversation transpires between these people.

Plus: That's Marty York (Yeah-Yeah in "The Sandlot") as one of the underprivileged kids. Really nothing else to say about that other than that "The Sandlot" is extraordinary and legends never die.

Episode 12: "Teacher's Pet"

Aired December 7, 1993

Plot: Because this primetime show is still sort of trying to be safe for kids, Zack gets up the courage to ask Kelly (his long-term, on-and-off girlfriend) to, oh boy oh boy, go steady! As has happened several times before, however, she's not in the same emotional place and prefers to babysit for Lasky's daughter and get closer to the professor.

On Kelly, Lasky and Abby: This is very reminiscent of Zack's relationship with Andrea and Jennifer in "Hawaiian Style," with the added tension of Lasky trying to resist getting closer to a student but finding a lot to like in Kelly. In his words: "Any man on this campus would kill for a woman like you. You're beautiful, you're smart, you're great with kids. Abby adores you; it's hard not to. You're very loving and sensitive. Everything a man could want in a woman." Still, he holds strong and walks away. (Nope, they kiss.)

Zack's lies (1):

- Telling Lasky he caught Kelly in front of the mirror wearing a veil and throwing rice at herself (based on Kelly's behavior this may have happened, but safer to assume it's just Zack saying absolutely anything if it helps his cause)

Bad detective: Zack's first reaction to hearing that Kelly is seeing another guy is "Who on this campus is cooler than I am?" because he is just a super-quality guy. He eventually proceeds to smell every dude he sees in hopes of figuring out who's wearing the Yacht Club cologne that Kelly bought her mystery guy. Shockingly, Zack does not get punched.

Worth noting again: Even when Zack is supposedly sure that "the search has ended," as if he's really been rotating among all these women (BTW: Zack is delusional about his romantic abilities), he still has nothing to compliment about Kelly besides her appearance. Their connection continues to be completely superficial and forced, and the show has a welcome lightness when she's free to feel something for/with someone else.

Also annoying: We just saw an episode in which Zack learned not to underestimate Screech. Yet once again, when Zack is wondering who the other guy could be, he briefly considers Screech only to turn to the camera and say "Nahhhhh!" He. Never. Learns.

Something to discuss: When Slater comes into the room and Zack says he thought Slater was Kelly, Slater notes, "If I were Kelly, I'd wear something skimpy and stare at myself in the mirror." Replies Zack: "That's what you do now." If nothing else, these guys know each other well.

How have we made it this many episodes without: A monkey! Screech babysits Lucy, the chimpanzee from Lasky's class, hoping to show the university that she can communicate and should not be sent to the zoo. "Screech and Lucy and Ross and Marcel" coming to theaters soon, we can only hope.

Episode 13: "Kelly and the Professor"

Aired December 14, 1993

Plot: Can Kelly and Lasky comfortably exist in public? Should Mike's compatibility quiz lead Slater and Leslie to get together, and the same for Screech and Alex? Most questionably, will Zack behave like someone older than 10?

Zack's lies (4):

- Telling Kelly he'll keep her relationship with Lasky quiet and then announcing it in front of the class
- Sending Screech under the pool table to eavesdrop on Kelly and Lasky's conversation
- Asking the person at the costume shop what Lasky is wearing to the sorority masquerade ball so Zack can also dress as Zorro and even kiss Kelly, knowing she thinks he is Lasky (2)

Ugh: We're in just a dreadful period of Zack behavior, which is saying something. He's possessive and jealous and immature and inappropriate (especially in his aggression toward Lasky) in so many ways. Yes, he's hurt that Kelly is more interested in Lasky, and hurt people hurt people, as they say. But still: He's remarkably awful throughout this episode, with the aforementioned kiss 100% qualifying as sexual harassment. Perhaps the only thing worse is that after Lasky decides he can't handle being with Kelly, Kelly winds up apologizing for being insensitive to Zack. (Thankfully she resists his advances but is not sufficiently angry for the garbage he pulls, and she still wants to be good friends.) This show is not teaching us lessons about conduct if Zack always winds up getting what he wants no matter what he does.

A lot of back and forth: This episode has a lot of potential yet mostly wastes it. The Slater/Leslie/Screech/Alex storyline recalls previous episodes exploring unexpected chemistry, but as usual the show punts complexity and returns to the status quo. Meanwhile, the Kelly/Lasky narrative would be compelling to see Kelly deal with the realities of being with an older man who is also a father, and Lasky also align his perception of Kelly with the reality of dating a student. Instead they succumb to the easy dismissal of Lasky's theoretical discomfort and the suggestion that Kelly was just being naive to think this was someone she could spend the rest of her life with. Imagine if the show was willing to let her pursue something meaningful with someone like Lasky and Zack kept in touch with Andrea and anyone discussed anything that previously happened to them.

But wait: A shocking example of continuity does occur as Slater references the other time they went to a masquerade ball and he and Screech accidentally danced together. Kudos to the writers for occasionally remembering there were other episodes before.

That being said: Zack refers to his feelings for Kelly "since she walked back into his life." How did they leave it after high school? Did they agree not to talk for a while or something, in which case her showing up at CalU would have been a major, confusing violation? Leaving out the details in ongoing relationships like this is such a missed opportunity.

Memorable line: After Slater asks to switch costumes (Tarzan and Peter Pan) with Screech, Screech observes, "Wow, this is a big loincloth. Can I borrow one of your loins?" Sometimes this show actually is kinda funny.

Timeless reference: Briefly keeping Kelly's secret, Zack claims Kelly's guy is Joey Buttafuoco. No, I'm not going to detail who that is, and I am not proud that I remembered how to spell that.

Billion-dollar box-office smash: Screech says a past compatibility quiz told him his perfect match was Whoopi Goldberg. Come on, Hollywood, this is still the romantic comedy everyone wants to see! (For the love of God, no.)

Episode 14: "A Question of Ethics"

Aired December 21, 1993

Plot: In one of the series' most straightforward narratives, hard-edged new ethics professor Dr. Hemmings (Robert Guillaume of "Benson" and "Sports Night") "accidentally" leaves behind a copy of the midterm, and the gang all considers whether or not to cheat. That's it. (OK, Screech also covers for Slater clearing tables at the student union, but best to ignore that as much as possible.)

This is what the series should be! Sure, on some level "A Question of Ethics" just achieves what "Boy Meets World" would go on to do better and more consistently (at least, in high school; those college episodes weren't good either). Yet it's still worth praising how this one presents a chance for the characters to challenge how their beliefs and behavior match up in a way that feels appropriately suited to their lives as college freshmen. (Hemmings' tactic of having the students grade themselves based on their own conduct is clever as well.) Plus, Zack experiences a rare moment of conscience as he and his friends are searching in a dumpster for scraps of the test that Leslie threw away and he realizes how low they're stooping. Even if it's out of character, it suggests his ability to develop, and any shred of evidence that he is a human being who can learn and feel is progress!

That said: His first reaction after finding the test is turning to the camera and asking if he should give the test to his friends or sell it to them. As may have been mentioned before, this is not a good person, and it's weird and bad that he's the hero.

Zack's lies: None!

Rules to live by: Hemmings insists students never speak unless he recognizes that he is ready for them to speak, and "If you do speak, say something interesting." A bit harsh, but maybe worth trying?

Real quick about the Screech subplot: Passing along a plain chicken sandwich order to lunch lady Clara (Mindy Sterling), Screech calls out, "I need a naked chick with hot buns!" Mike assures Clara, "Screech couldn't sexually harass himself," and somehow the rest of the episode isn't a social/moral/ethical/legal dissection of this.

Almost makes you miss MC Hammer: Since apparently people didn't care about "U Can't Touch This" by this point, pop culture references now hinge on stuff like Zack describing Hemmings with "They call him Hannibal Lecturer." And "The Silence of the Lambs" came out nearly three years before this episode aired, so it's super timely!

Memorable line (from Alex): "I'm an actress, so ethics will never apply to me."

Episode 15: "The Rave"

Aired January 4, 1994

Plot: Needing to raise thousands to fund a Mexico trip for himself, Kelly, Slater and Alex, Zack decides the best route is hosting an "illegal rave" (as opposed to a legal one) while Mike is out of town and Dean McMann (Holland Taylor of "The Practice" and "Two and a Half Men") immediately diagnoses him as trouble. Possible expulsion takes a backseat to the thought of Kelly in a bikini, which is a questionable perspective for many reasons, not least of which is that Zack and Kelly have dated extensively before and he shouldn't still see her as such a one-dimensional fantasy.

Speaking of which: When Kelly says she doesn't exist anymore after finding out that Lasky transferred her out of his class, Zack notes, "For a girl that doesn't exist, still turns me on." Aren't we supposed to think that Zack is a good friend of hers, not just some perv waiting for a chance to go after her?

Both confusing and revealing: Clearly Kelly's hurt and misguided in thinking the lesson to take away from her relationship with Lasky is "Men are filth," as Lasky may have ultimately led her on and crushed her but was neither filthy nor exploitative in his treatment of her. Yet it's really something to observe the degree to which she only goes to Zack because of her own vulnerability and lack of other options. It's why she wants to go to Mexico and why she enjoys a night to take her mind off Lasky, while Lasky's highly contrived act of saving Zack's hide just because he loves driving the dean crazy causes Kelly to remark, "Isn't Jeremiah wonderful? He's so brave and selfless, I could fall in love with him all over again." Zack should see that Kelly doesn't have real feelings for him, but it's not as if he has real, non-physical feelings for her either. So maybe this match makes more sense than it seems, and than it should.

Armchair analyst, continued: This is a standout episode for Screech, as Slater gives him a really hard time and then, when Screech asks what's up, explains it's because Screech is a screw-up and needs to grow up now that they're in college. It revives the narrative of the fraternity episode, validly calling into question how certain friendships maintain or fade over time. The issue is mostly suppressed by the time Slater apologizes and helps Screech out of a jam (providing a tank of nitrous oxide, which turns out to be helium, to a jerky dude from class), but it creates the right frame of mind for Screech to be taken advantage of while feeling lonely and dismissed by his friend. Not bad.

Zack's lies (3):

- Telling Dean McMann "Let me get Zack for you"

- Adding that there's no furniture in Mike's room because they wanted to surprise him by painting
- Claiming that the rave is a class project

Early-'90s trivia: The dean says Zack has been added to her list, which also contains her ex-husband and legendary Dallas Cowboys fumbler Leon Lett, who cost her hundreds in a bet. Ouch!

More startling honesty: After Leslie talks about Donna Karan dropping off an outfit at her house, McMann says, "You are rich. I like that in a person."

More obscure trivia: Alex's rap name is Snoop Ali Dogg.

The kind of line you couldn't get on Saturday morning (from Screech, to Mike): "I know your body better than I know my own, and, trust me, I've explored mine extensively!" Apologies for the mental picture.

Episode 16: "Bedside Manner"

Aired January 11, 1994

Plot: Zack's desperation to reconnect with "his" Kelly drives him to work alongside her at the hospital, where Zack just winds up having to look after the dean while trying to prevent Kelly from giving Lasky (suffering an ulcer due to post-Kelly stress) any sponge baths.

Zack's lies (6):

- Telling Kelly he took the job because he's devoted to the sick and injured
- Assuring the dean he cares deeply about patients
- Claiming his Uncle Harry died from pneumonia when he is actually alive and in jail in Texas
- Saying he is suffering from headaches, fainting and loss of memory (3)

The ongoing saga of Zack and Kelly: Zack's attempt to use skywriting to steer Kelly back in his direction is typical, grand romantic gesture stuff, and that she finds the idea adorable if it came from Lasky but ridiculous from Zack should speak volumes about her emotional position. Yet Zack keeps at it, ignoring hospital patients and injuring Dean McMann (he lets her roll away in a wheelchair, which just happened to Mike a couple episodes ago) so he can lurk near Kelly and interrupt any possible sparks between her and the professor. That this ultimately leads her to feel touched about how much Zack will go through to be with her and angry with Lasky that he won't do anything for her just represents the show contorting itself to bring its central couple together, even though Kelly still says "Maybe" to Zack asking if there's a chance for them. It is worth repeating how much they seem to be relying on past chemistry and superficial feelings to get them through an uncertain time, further complicated by the show reinforcing the '80s/'90s pop culture trope that the way to get a girl to like you is to persist and persist and persist until she gives in. Can't Kelly just be single for a while?

Casual creeping: Kelly barely bats an eye when telling Zack that Pops the security guard always has his binoculars fixed on her window. Shiver.

In subplot news: Screech solicits Leslie's help to draw a fake Sigma Alpha tattoo when he doesn't want to go along with the other pledges getting real ones, leading to standard peer pressure/mocking of Screech and a worthwhile lesson that what seems cool at one time may not 10 years down the line. For example, Mike's butt tattoo of Tweety Bird, which Screech insists is now Big Bird. For family-appropriate tattoo humor, that's not the worst.

More tattoo action: Alex laments that Slater won't get a tattoo of her name, of course leading him to do it and her to bail on getting her own of Slater. What's weirder is that she makes it up to him by agreeing to attend a film festival of every movie Sylvester Stallone ever made, with Alex particularly unhappy about seeing all the "Rocky" movies. Seems like she'd be much more upset during the "Rambo" franchise, but maybe I just don't know Alex that well.

Unexpected contemporary relevance: When Leslie wants to come to Lasky's office to discuss a paper, he says that after what happened with Kelly he no longer allows female students in his office. More than two decades later this is still happening, with women suffering the consequences of men in power who can't control themselves and therefore keep women out of leadership positions, conference rooms or otherwise as if that's the right and fair solution. It's not as if "Bedside Manner" was going to advance the dialogue on this issue in 1994, but it didn't help either.

Episode 17: "Love and Death"

Aired January 22, 1994

Plot: While baffled about where he stands with Kelly (a product of her not actually liking him!), Zack experiences a quarter-life crisis after the sudden death of Professor Rich (Victor Raider-Wexler of "The King of Queens"), a popular history teacher despite his casual quoting of Mussolini for inspiration. Cue motorcycles, rappelling down university buildings and skydiving.

Zack and Kelly update: As usual, Zack is a possessive, insecure bozo, telling Kelly she can't go out on Saturday night because they've been dating for weeks and Saturday is date night. He continues to be petty and awful throughout the episode, insisting on knowing if she loves him or not (she doesn't!) right before the funeral and snapping "It's not like you're my girlfriend" after wondering why she cares if he jumps out of a plane. This is not the development of a beautiful relationship, it is a weak dude prodding a young woman into guilt and pity that mixes with her own fears into a couple that doesn't recognize how little they actually have together and how much they don't work. Despite that lesson being learned like 500 times!

Philosophy class: Rich tells Zack that he's been a fraud for a long time, actually going to his sister's in Fresno when he tells students he's taking big international trips. This time, though, he really did plan to go to Egypt, so dying on the main characters' couch was particularly ill-timed for him. Zack's behavior certainly represents a person experiencing something major, even interrupting the dean's eulogy to say that the professor wouldn't have wanted them to waste a nice day inside. If only the episode could have been a legitimate exploration of how best to use the time we have, not just manipulation to make Kelly confuse not wanting Zack to die with being in love with him.

Zack's lies: None!

Masculinity: Slater, who doesn't want to go skydiving and believes the professor's death means you need to be careful, is mocked for his decreased bravado, with Screech saying he used to motivate himself by pretending to be Slater but "If I acted the way you do now, I'd be a real girly-man." This is not useful, though all three guys ultimately determining they don't want to jump (but fall out of the plane by accident) perhaps indicates the truth behind the posturing.

Screech Powers, standup comic: Explaining that he's not kidding when he says he doesn't want to go skydiving anymore, Screech says a joke would be, "Waiter, what's this fly doing in my soup? The backstroke!" About as modern as the previous paragraph, but better.

Karma chameleon: A sad lack of continuity as Slater wonders what you're supposed to do at a funeral, as if the service for Artie never happened. We will now all sing "Oh, Artie boy, the bugs the bugs are buzzing!" in unison.

Episode 18: "Marry Me"

Aired February 8, 1994

Plot: Blech. Blech blech blech. Will explain why, but right now just need to say blech.

The Zack and Kelly saga: I thought we already identified how wrong it is to try to inhibit someone's big-time opportunity for purely selfish reasons? Wasn't that what Zack learned when he attempted to prevent Kelly from modeling in Paris but eventually saw that he should think of her needs first? Well, apparently not, because in "Marry Me" he cares less that she has a chance to spend a semester at sea and visit places like the Parthenon and Colosseum and more that she won't be with him. He tries to tell the dean he speaks for Kelly (thankfully, Kelly shuts that down very quickly) and then tries conniving his way onto the ship himself, complaining that it's not fair that the dean cares about the fact that Zack has no character. His way of dealing with anxiety over Kelly getting closer to a guy on the trip is to wake up from a bad dream, go into Kelly's room and wake her up to propose marriage. That is not a good reason to tie the knot, and Kelly's right to be hesitant. Zack can only address her concerns about education and finances with "I do know we can make this work if we love each other," which is very generic and goes along with his inability to process Kelly or his relationship with her on any level whatsoever. That she accepts his proposal after he comes to the ship to apologize and say goodbye, only for them to BOTH RUN OFF THE SHIP, is so wrong I really cannot imagine any fans of the show being happy about it. No. Way.

And if you were? Then maybe remember that Zack shrugs off the awfulness of backstabbing Screech and trying to take his oldest friend's place on the trip just because it means getting to see Kelly in a string bikini. Argggggggggh. (And not in the sea-relevant pirate sense.)

Zack's lies (7):

- Telling Lasky how much he enjoyed the lecture this morning even though he slept through it
- Claiming he wasn't sleeping, just closing his eyes in intense concentration
- Adding that he wasn't drooling, just salivating over Lasky's intense insights
- Paying a stoner named Stingray (Jake Beecham) to try to scare Screech away from the semester at sea and take his spot
- Pretending to be on Screech's side in that conversation
- Suggesting that someone who died at sea was playing with his Mr. Potato Head collection, which would be of particular relevance to Screech

- Putting new slides (like a ship on fire and a shark attack) into the dean's presentation to freak out Screech

More on masculinity: After Mike cries watching "Love Story," Screech assures him there's no shame in a man showing his feminine side. "I don't have a feminine side," Mike says. "Even if I did, it would be really macho." This actually works much better because it has a sense of humor about Mike's attempt to perpetuate a stereotype while showing his true self. There's obviously a lot more to say about the culture that encourages the bluster, but still. Small victories.

That said: It's weird how the show continually tries to turn Slater into such a meathead, lifting weights during "Love Story" and preferring to see a Steven Seagal movie. He's also mad Alex won't go to a car show with him and gets into a tough situation when Christy (Ami Dolenz of the short-lived "Ferris Bueller" TV series) shares that interest with him, as well as a kiss that Leslie accidentally witnesses. Fortunately the show demonstrates another one of its rare moments of sound relationship analysis when Slater tells Alex, "It's not Christy. It could have been anybody. It's our relationship; it's just not working out." Of course, because the show writes itself into a corner with people dating their roommates/best friends/whatever, Slater and Alex manage to part on very good terms and it's not a huge deal. It's all very reminiscent of Slater and Jessie, except much less emotionally involving.

Continuity issues, er, continued: In the Palm Springs Weekend episode, Screech reads a book called "Everything You Need to Know About Girls." In "Marry Me," Zack gives Screech the book "100 Ways to Pick Up Girls," whose cover looks a lot like the other book. Guess it's OK 'cause he still has a lot to learn? (No.)

Episode 19: "Wedding Plans"

Aired February 8, 1994

Plot: Zack and Kelly are getting married and they want to do it ASAP, which really makes you feel great about Kelly's state of mind regarding this decision. Unfortunately the giddiness fades as their parents say they're making a huge mistake, Slater doesn't support it either and their off-campus apartment (which they can only rent because the dean wants to get rid of Zack, even if it means Kelly ruining her life) is a total pit.

Zack's lies: None!

One more thing about continuity: It seems odd that the main things we knew about Kelly's family is that they were loving but didn't have much money, yet Kelly's parents' disapproval of the wedding is communicated through refusing to give even a penny for it. Was Kelly expecting them to pay for it in the first place?

Plus: Lisa Turtle returns! Which means Kelly claiming that Lisa is her lifelong friend despite not meeting until like four years earlier, and Lisa fighting with Leslie and Alex over who gets to be the maid of honor. As with many of the college episodes, it provides Kelly a chance to get frustrated with the idiocy of people around her and really stand up for herself, which is in stark contrast to how much the show forces her to give up everything else she seems to want and feel to be with an awful guy who doesn't actually know or appreciate her. But I think we may have addressed that.

Just one more thing about continuity: Zack wanting to buy rings from an extremely sleazy dude who's trying to get change from the pinball machine really suggests Zack learned nothing from his experience with Gem Diamond, who searched for quarters in pay phones! Shady jewelry sales people weirdly have a lot in common.

As you'd expect: Zack and Kelly's attempt to make a good impression with a reverend goes horribly wrong when he comes over at the exact time their friends throw them surprise bachelor and bachelorette parties, leading Alex to think the reverend is a stripper and tell him to take it off. Says Screech (more in reference to the female stripper who handcuffs herself to Zack), "I knew we should've gone with Barney."

New glimpse into Screech: Wanting to throw the bouquet and wear the garter, he laments that the bride gets to do all the fun stuff. "What are you trying to say, you want to be a bride?" Zack asks. "No, of course not," says Screech. "But it would be nice to be asked." Perhaps if this weren't the last episode Screech could have further explored these ideas about himself. (Actually, he appeared in a lot of "The New Class" episodes, which I only watched sparingly but am pretty sure didn't deal with this part of Screech's identity at all.)

Call the police: The dean pulls strings to get Zack and Kelly (who ultimately decide to get married in Vegas) into the university chapel, bumping the funeral of the unknown Professor Fink. That makes two dead professors in the last three episodes. What is going on at CalU?

Stats/Looking Back on the Only College Years Season

I remember liking this season when it originally aired. Now it's appalling, featuring many episodes that feel like watered-down versions of storylines we've already seen and behavior from Zack that he should have moved past a long, long time ago. In fact, college finds him at his worst rate of lying, with a total of 66 lies in 19 episodes. That (3.5 lies/episode) is by far his highest for a season, considering the previous year was 3.0 after removing the zero-lie clip shows. In college, Zack is a somewhat steadier liar, with one episode of double-digit lies (11), two with seven each and otherwise a lot with three to five lies. However, Zack has three zero-lie episodes in the last six, really showcasing how the series changes as it tries to move toward getting Zack what he wants or just wind down the season with less despicable conduct.

Along with that, in two of those three zero-lie episodes Zack is not bad toward women, something you can only say for three of the 19 episodes of the season. That means that he is bad toward women in a massive 84 percent of the episodes, which is by far the highest instance of this. (The previous high was 62 percent in junior high.) In college Zack is totally flailing, desperate to reclaim the status and attention he so craves and failing time and time again to establish the honesty and empathy that would demonstrate real growth. Meanwhile, his refusal (and the show's) to maintain the lessons he supposedly learns puts him in the same situation over and over, to the point where we keep waiting for scenes in which people get really upset with him for a long period of time, but it never comes. (Why does Slater insist Screech needs to get his act together but doesn't demand this of Zack, who is also embarrassing and infuriating?)

Instead, we get a Kelly/Lasky storyline that mostly exists in a vacuum and to drive her back to Zack, episodes about identity and love that are often corny at best and, occasionally, some moments of meaning or perceptiveness, like when Screech connects with tennis star Linda and Zack instantly supports Kelly when she's treated terribly by football star Johnny Walters. (Both popular athletes. Hmm.) Leslie, Alex and Mike all have some standout scenes and work as part of the ensemble, but the series mostly defines these characters as narrowly as the others and shrugs in their direction while focusing on the central couple.

Even as a Saturday-morning sitcom, and in college as a primetime comedy with a few dramatic elements, "Saved by the Bell" had an opportunity to really help teenage viewers explore ideas about personal development, friendship and how to treat others in a relationship. More often than not, it dismissed these chances and just gave the main character, the least likable, least deserving person on the show, a free pass.

In other words, there are plenty of moments to like across the series, but "The College Years" really leaves a bad taste. Now, uh, on to the wedding!

"Saved by the Bell: Wedding in Las Vegas"

Aired October 7, 1994

Note: On Hulu this is presented as four distinct episodes, but it originally ran as a full-length movie (without a laugh track!) so that's how it should be assessed.

Plot: With the recent release of "Speed" seemingly leading Zack and Kelly to believe that if they slow down they will explode, the engaged couple, Slater, Screech and Lisa head to America's capital of urgent, family-unapproved weddings. After a police mix-up means Zack has to bribe a small-town sheriff (Pat Corley of "Murphy Brown") to get the guys out of jail, Zack and Screech take some short-notice jobs (caddying, male escorts!) to make back the funds. Because Zack has learned nothing, particularly about what kind of person his fiancé is, he labors to hide this from Kelly, preferring to behave suspiciously rather than be honest and direct and show that the marriage will start off on the right foot.

Zack's lies (7):

- Getting Slater and Screech to help prevent Kelly from knowing their $1,200 wedding budget is gone because Zack says she'll kill him
- Telling the golfers that they've caddied the course many times before
- Secretly taking a job as an escort to make his money back
- Saying he's been running all over town looking for the right tuxedo when Kelly wonders why Zack is late and he was actually training with Bert Banner (Gilbert Gottfried!)
- Assuring Kelly he's not hiding anything when obviously he is
- Claiming he's going to the restroom at the restaurant when he's really going to meet the woman who hired him as an escort
- Explaining he was gone a long time from dinner because of long lines in the bathroom

On the subject of lies: For Zack, lying seven times over the length of four episodes is not a lot. However, it should be noted that he only lied four times in "Hawaiian Style," and none of those involved Andrea. In "Wedding in Las Vegas," all but one of his lies pertain to deceiving Kelly, who of course gets to the point where yet again she feels she can't trust Zack (even calling him "scum"). However, Zack again puts himself in a needlessly dangerous situation (nearly falling to his death while climbing from his hotel balcony to

Kelly's when she won't talk to him, which was a common practice in the pre-cell phone era) that causes Kelly to forget everything that happened and how she felt about it just because she doesn't want Zack to die in a terrible accident. At no point do they have a serious conversation about their present or their future or how badly he treats her or how little they ever talk about or do to show they can successfully navigate their lives together. But otherwise how beautiful that these two are finally tying the knot!

More plot: Much like in the episodes surrounding Jessie's father's wedding, Slater hits it off with someone, only this time Carla (Liz Vassey of "CSI") is connected to jealous mob dude Freddie Silver (Mark De Carlo), whose goons chase the gang all over the place and create the necessary chaos to push this otherwise very slow-paced endeavor closer to its anticlimactic finale. A great film this is not.

Many random issues with all this:

- At the beginning of the movie Zack, Slater and Screech visit Bayside but only look at it from the outside, which we've never really seen before and thus feel none of their nostalgia. Couldn't an old favorite teacher have been there too for a dose of something more specific?
- It's weird that Zack's dad is so broadly against the wedding despite Zack and Kelly's long-standing relationship. Certainly his concerns about them being too young are fair, but they never discuss in detail why they have to get married now or anything in depth that would actually be worth addressing. Plus, Zack's mom says she's on his side but that she can't go against his father. More to unravel there.
- Kelly tells Lisa that Zack is "a whole new person" since they fell in love and that he's now mature and responsible. 1. Weren't they in love before? 2. What kind of person did she fall in love with? 3. How many pieces of evidence does she have for this claim?
- Kelly had previously noted her parents' disapproval and that it meant they wouldn't give any money for the wedding, which was odd considering seasoned viewers wouldn't expect them to have much to give in the first place. Now her parents are on board emotionally but not financially, meaning that when they didn't want to they wouldn't and when they wanted to they couldn't. So why approach this matter this way in the first place?
- The show really can't decide when things took place. Lisa asks Kelly if she remembers when they dressed up as brides in seventh grade, even though we saw that they didn't go to junior high together. Zack also says he's been in love with Kelly since grammar school even though they met as high school freshmen. It's sort of fascinating that only Belding has the accurate version, noting that Zack and Kelly met in his school, which technically could have been any time considering Belding has been the principal in every school these people have attended but you get the idea.

- Failed shortcuts are such a lame plot device. That already happened in "Hawaiian Style" and it does again in "Wedding in Las Vegas" as Zack attempts a shortcut because "No girl's going to beat me to Vegas." What a guy.
- There is so much saxophone used as transitional music here. That's not a complaint, just an observation.
- The restaurant scene in which Zack darts back and forth between Kelly and his other date is so bad, and not just because the first time he sees Katrina (Marina Maximova) he says, "Oh, boy, she would have to be gorgeous," as if that should matter. When Kelly looks at the menu and says "The Russian dish looks really good" just so Zack can say "No, she doesn't," it should only make us wonder, "What Russian dish is on the menu?!" And it's odd that Carla asks if Slater had girls in every country he's lived in and Slater responds, "No one special," which is not true (Jen! Jessie! Um, Alex?) and suggests overcompensating to impress someone he just met. Carla sees through him and storms off! (No, she likes it.)

As a finale: I remembered enjoying "Wedding in Las Vegas" when it originally aired, a little bit before I turned 12. Now it makes for an upsetting end to the series proper, suggesting that the whole thing was a beautiful will-they-won't-they story of Ross-and-Rachel proportions, even though Zack and Kelly had maybe two episodes featuring sweet moments. He was constantly awful to her, and putting so little focus on surrounding characters only further reminds us of how little was done to establish the pair as a strong couple. Even on a high-school-set, Saturday-morning sitcom, that sends a lousy message, and the pair not sharing vows that would have provided Zack in particular an opportunity to go in depth about Kelly as an individual and his partner prevents any sense of adult closeness and growth.

Jessie returns: We shouldn't be surprised that she's not part of the movie's plot but arrives late to the wedding, dropping her shoes to ensure that the show is still making her look bad/sloppy/etc. whenever possible. She apparently left her finals to attend the wedding and is fine going to summer school as a result, showing that she has changed her priorities since high school, which really wasn't long ago and it's weird how the characters act like years have passed. Also, Jessie tells Zack, "You take care of her or you will hear from me" and Zack quips, "Anything but that!" Which I guess is a lighthearted demonstration of rapport but also just a reminder that the writers don't like Jessie.

Not a huge deal but: The characters should have at least mentioned Leslie's absence, seeing as Belding, Alex and Mike all attend the wedding but Leslie isn't there and no one comments on that at all. Maybe she's hanging out with Tori?

For what it's worth: After the wedding Zack does share a nice moment with his dad, who calls him Zachary for the first time since he was a kid. Maybe this is just because of the emotions that come from weddings, family bonds and the end of an era, but it feels good, and same with Zack and Kelly leaning into the married-couple vibe of "I'm sure the little lady will let me out once in a while"/"If you're good." Maybe they'll show that a flawed couple can improve things by getting married! (Hahahahahaha.)

Easily forgotten but kind of good: Curt Martin (Spencer Rochfort), who fixes Lisa's car and hitches a ride to the Stardust, where he works in a number of jobs because his dad owns the place, actually makes a nice addition to the crew. He's laid-back and challenges Lisa on her material priorities, eventually leading them to travel to an Indian reservation together. Where's our spinoff movie about that?

Shocking continuity! At this point anything done to show a consistent world within the "Saved by the Bell" universe counts for something, so the fact that Zack and Kelly's parents are still played by the same actors as they were previously is worth celebrating. Yes, sometimes you have to look to little things for elements to praise.

Look who it is! Richard Schiff ("The West Wing") appears for a split second as a cop named Dano just so Corley's character can say, "Book 'em, Dano." Because clearly all "Saved by the Bell" fans love "Hawaii Five-O."

Another moment out of "Arrested Development": When Thorpe (Corley) suggests the guys could buy their way out of jail and tells Screech the $1,200 they have is exactly what it costs, this is the identical exchange that happens between Tobias and Carl Weathers when they meet in the airport shuttle. Funny.

And more "Muppets"!: I know this is not the only story of a jewel heist, but Freddie scheming to steal the $4 million Considine diamond just reminds me of "The Great Muppet Caper," a much, much, much more fun movie than this one.

One more unexpected reminder: As an escort Screech goes dancing with his date and they do the tango, which also featured prominently in "True Lies," which came out in July of 1994. This is more than enough to label 1994 as the year tango peaked.

Accurate Screechism: Discussing guy stuff like swimsuit models and burly actors on the drive to Vegas, Zack and Slater consider if Seagal or Van Damme is tougher. Offers Screech: "You know who's tougher than he looks? Martin Short!" Please make another "Expendables" movie, Sly, just so we can see this showdown.

*****Interview with Rogers:** "I think oftentimes parents are not in agreement with what their children are going to do. I don't have children, but I've certainly been around enough with my friends with kids. I think that a woman does usually – this was a while back, this was 30 years ago – try to go along with her husband, and I think that if Melanie really thought that this was a horrible thing to do, she would have somehow not let it happen. I do remember that I adored him, I loved him, I wanted the best for him, but I was always going to try and make sure that he stayed on the straight and narrow, even though he would deviate from it. Like most mothers of young boys, I think. But I just was never aware of all this [lying]." *(Read more from Rogers on page 303.)*

So What Have We Learned?

Let's start with all the stats in one place:

Eighth grade:

28 lies in 13 episodes = 2.2 per episode
Zero-lie episodes: 5 of 13 = 38 percent
Bad to women: 8 out of 13 episodes = 62 percent

High school season 1:

35 lies in 16 episodes = 2.2 per episode
Zero-lie episodes: 3 of 16 = 19 percent
Bad to women: 9 out of 16 episodes = 56 percent
Aggressive toward Jessie: 3 out of 16 episodes = 19 percent

High school season 2:

47 lies in 18 episodes = 2.6 per episode
Zero-lie episodes: 3 of 18 = 17 percent
Bad to women: 10 of 18 episodes = 56 percent
Aggressive toward Jessie: 5 of 18 episodes = 28 percent

High school season 3:

72 lies in 26 episodes = 2.8 per episode; removing two 11-lie episodes brings average down to 2.0
Zero-lie episodes: 8 out of 26 = 31 percent
Bad to women: 6 of 26 episodes = 23 percent
Aggressive toward Jessie: 13 of 26 episodes = 50 percent

High school season 4:

70 lies in 26 episodes = 2.7 per episode; removing three zero-lie clip-show episodes elevates average to 3.0
Zero-lie episodes: 3 out of 23 = 13 percent
Bad to women: 9 out of 23 non-clip-show episodes = 39 percent
Aggressive toward Jessie: 11 out of 16 episodes she appeared in = 69 percent

"Hawaiian Style":

4 lies across the length of 4 episodes
Not bad to women!

College:

66 lies in 19 episodes = 3.5 lies per episode despite zero lies in three of the final six episodes
Zero-lie episodes: 3 out of 19 = 16 percent
Bad to women: 16 of 19 episodes = 84 percent

"Wedding in Las Vegas":

7 lies across the length of 4 episodes
Very bad to women (well, just Kelly)

Series overall:

329 lies in 123 episodes (removing clip shows) = 2.7 lies per episode
Bad to women: 62 out of 123 episodes = 50 percent
Aggressive toward Jessie: 32 out of 76 episodes = 42 percent

Episodes with the most lies:

13: "Drinking and Driving," high school season 4
12: "Aloha Slater," high school season 1
11: "Fake IDs," high school season 3
11: "The Wicked Stepbrother (Part 1)," high school season 3
11: "Professor Zack," college

Character ranking:

1. Kelly (very kind and deceptively mature; doesn't deserve the narrative forced on her)
2. Jessie (strong voice for important issues but also a hypocrite who can be very judgmental)
3. Screech (somewhat funny, usually well-intentioned but frequently the henchman for Zack's evil schemes)
4. Slater (some sincere moments, many boorish ones)
5. Lisa (very self-centered and shallow, rarely given opportunity for more)
6. Zack (duh)

Positive conclusions:

- Zack's best behavior took place in the third season of high school, in which he was "only" bad to women in 23 percent of the episodes, his lowest amount by far. If you remove the two 11-lie episodes that represented outliers in the season, it lowers his per-episode average to 2.0, which is also his lowest of the series, albeit with the asterisk of removing those two exceptions. In that season the show was all over the place, departing from Bayside for the Malibu Sands episodes, the two-part "Palm Springs Weekend" and "Home for Christmas" episodes, the "Rockumentary" and the "Mystery Weekend," plus the two-part "Wicked Stepbrother" saga that changed the usual dynamic of the group. More often than not, those storylines served him well. Yet what I'm still thinking about is how much better he seemed over the summer while he was dating Stacey. He connected with her in ways he never really did with Kelly, and it made the end of their relationship feel legitimately sad instead of justified. Young people absolutely absorb messages about relationships from pop culture, and it's really something to wonder to what degree the featured pair of "Saved by the Bell" was mismatched and forced together in direct contrast with the way they actually operated as a couple.
- Similarly, Zack's rhythm was different with Andrea during "Hawaiian Style." There's an ease about him that leads to sincerity and curiosity instead of insecurity and lust confused as love. If we take "Saved by the Bell" as an extended examination of its main character's conduct, and that conduct as a direct result of how he treated women (which usually stemmed from whether or not he was interested in them), it would have been fascinating if "Hawaiian Style" had been the controversial but surprisingly rewarding finale to the series, in which Zack makes a big decision to stay with Andrea and Jennifer and we're left to wonder if he did the right thing and how his life will turn out. By continuing on to "The College Years" and "Wedding in Las Vegas," the series fell into an obligatory arc that certainly wraps up the central relationship in the expected way but, on further review, the wrong one.
- Despite "The College Years" being mostly terrible, at various points the show found its characters growing into themselves in new ways. Slater challenges his work ethic, connects with his heritage and questions Zack's choices in difficult moments. Screech stands up for himself with Zack and projects more confidence and stability (at least, as far as the show will let him), which leads to his first love interest since Violet (who the show labeled a geek and was therefore undeserving of attention from any non-geek). And Kelly comes into focus as more than a sweet person who is constantly disappointed in Zack, making us feel like we've never actually seen her before. Even if the series' trajectory ultimately suffered for its continuation (especially in what it brought out of Zack), at least these dimensions defend it a little.
- It wasn't often, and there was almost never any follow-through, but on rare occasion "Saved by the Bell" managed to identify some trenchant points for

young viewers. The importance of taking accountability, as seen in "Drinking and Driving"; the value of vulnerability and shared humanity in "Cream for a Day"; the benefit of standing by your principles, which usually earned Jessie judgment but landed in "Pipe Dreams." That's just a sampling, as many other themes were explored to varying levels of success. But even bad attempts can create a discussion, and there are more than enough examples of that throughout the series. Speaking of which:

Not-so-positive conclusions:

- 329 lies. That's so many. Maybe not in the modern era (insert rant), but for the so-called hero of a so-called innocent teen sitcom, that's startling. Perhaps even more troubling is that his ratio got worse almost every season, starting at 2.2 lies per episode in junior high and rising to 3.5 in college. Before beginning this exercise, I thought maybe we'd see fluctuations in Zack's behavior as he figured himself out and saw consequences for his behavior, growing and relapsing, growing and relapsing. But outside of the third season of high school (which, again, is greatly skewed by the two 11-lie episodes), much of the series finds a wall-to-wall liar scheming and deceiving, sometimes failing to acquire what he wants but never facing sobering results that make him question what he does moving forward.
- That is only reinforced when looking at Zack's treatment of women, who he treats poorly in an astonishing 50 percent of the episodes. It should be noted that the percentage often fell throughout the series, beginning at 62 percent, dipping to 23 percent in the third high school season and leaping to 84 percent in college. While those percentages don't evaluate the extent of the behavior, only the binary assessment of good and bad, it remains very disturbing that Zack treats women badly so frequently (obviously treating anyone badly with any frequency is not good) and that he was the worst at the point that he might have been the most enlightened. Clearly what we now see as toxic masculinity wasn't defined that way at the time, but that doesn't make it OK or any less predatory. Are there any other series about how a show's main character was trash? Nope.
- I hadn't planned to chronicle the show's treatment of Jessie. But it stuck out in three episodes in the second half of the first season in high school and then it was impossible to miss. Throughout high school, the percentage of episodes featuring aggressive behavior toward Jessie rose from 19 to 28 to 50 to 69 percent, leaving the series total at 42 percent overall, or 32 of the 76 episodes in which she was featured (I didn't count the ultra-brief appearance in "Wedding in Las Vegas," FWIW). As previously mentioned, Jessie was the character with by far the strongest opinions, and often the moral compass of the show. So for there to be so much negativity toward what she believed and how she spoke her mind reflects a really unpleasant bias beneath the surface.

- And that's not the only example: Throughout this book I make mention of how obsessed "Saved by the Bell" was with status, segmenting its characters in a way that perpetuated stereotypes of the era about adolescent cliques and really struggling to do anything to question these judgments. There is such an emphasis on looking cool and being attractive, which is not surprising, but the show's refusal to treat anyone outside of those qualifiers as being equal is what's really problematic. Even in its after-school-special episodes, "Saved by the Bell" labored to include other characters in ways that didn't label them as others, whether it was a girl who weighed more or a girl who was in a wheelchair. The only goal was to teach Zack that they were dateable, but we still didn't see them having any serious relationship together. Once again, there was an opportunity for a positive message, and the show blew it.

Overall, this sort of re-examination of "Saved by the Bell" revealed that certain things were better than I remembered, while others were much, much worse than I could have imagined. A lot changes culturally as years become decades, and just because a lot of material looks awful in hindsight doesn't mean we should forget about the pieces that hold up. But we also shouldn't turn away from what should never have been in the first place. Hopefully anyone who watches "Saved by the Bell" in the future, either for the first time or returning to something they used to know and love/like/hate, will make those distinctions and find a lot to either be entertained or infuriated by, with much to be gained from conversations about how these seemingly innocuous storylines between absurd characters shape how we view relationships, friendships, education and, hey, lizard funerals.

Now let's dive into "The New Class" and count the number of times Screech said, I don't know, "Zoinks!" Nah, let's not.

Interviews

Ed Alonzo aka Max (21 episodes)

He may not have had a lot of lines or been given an opportunity to contribute much to the plot. But outside of the core six kids and their principal, no one appeared more on "Saved by the Bell" than Max (Ed Alonzo), the owner of the Max who also waited tables, performed illusions and occasionally provided life advice. He's even in the opening credits!

Considering Alonzo – who currently works on Justin Willman's "Magic for Humans" on Netflix, "Masters of Illusion" on the CW and will be appearing on the "Saved by the Bell" reboot – was such an important part of the series' beginnings, also performed for/with Michael Jackson, Britney Spears and Katy Perry, and, you know, is best friends with Neil Patrick Harris, it's to be expected that he'd have a story or two. So let's just dive in.

How did you get involved with "Saved by the Bell"? Was the role written for you?

Originally, I was hanging out at a new restaurant that opened up in Los Angeles called Ed Debevic's, which is a Chicago chain, a '50s diner. They have all their waiters and waitresses and cooks and everybody dress up in different characters, like tape on the glasses and funny T's and big hairdos and that kind of a thing. They were all very character-y in there, so I loved going into this place, and I got to know a lot of the people who worked at Ed Debevic's, and it was just a fun place to hang out. And then a few months later my agent said that in the breakdown services they were looking for an owner of a diner character for a new Saturday morning series, so they submitted me for the part, and I already looked the way that I did on the show. I already had the big hair and the glasses, and I got the part to look at, and as I started to read the thing I had a feeling that these characters that were in the Max were going to be just like Ed Debevic's. They were going to be fun and a little outrageous, and I thought, "I'm perfect for that." So I ran out and I got a paper hat from a hamburger place, got my audition prepared and put a couple tricks together that I added to the [lines] that they had given me, and went in and did the audition. I auditioned originally for Robin Lippin, who was the casting director, and it didn't seem like she really got it. It didn't seem to really go over great, but she said, "I'm going to bring you back so you can read for the producers next week. There's something about you. I'm just not sure if you're right." So I went back home and I practiced and I got the lines down better and the timing, and a few days later I went and read for Peter Engel and the other producers, and I killed. I nailed it, and they were cracking up. I even flubbed one of the lines; there was a line that said something like, "I hope Screech will be there!" And I forgot the name Screech and I said Scorch, which is like a slang word for the devil. I said, "I hope Scorch will be there!" And they started rolling out, and I didn't realize the mistake I made. I think they thought that I did it on purpose. [Laughs] So then they kept bringing me back, grooming me now to be chosen by Brandon Tartikoff. They were going to narrow it down to two actors for the part of Max and let Brandon Tartikoff decide. That's kind of how it happened. They looked at a few hundred guys to play the part of Max, and it came down to two, and I was the lucky winner that day. NBC and Brandon liked my audition, and the next few days I got to meet all the other kids on the show, and it wasn't long before we were in the studios at NBC and we started shooting.

So was the magic aspect part of what they were looking for, or you had those talents so it became part of him?

I did happen to have the talents – they were looking for somebody who could just kind of be a trickster. They didn't really know if it needed to be a full magician or like a jokey guy. I think they didn't quite know. And the tricks that I added into the original audition were very simple, jokey things, and I think it fit just right. It wasn't big, spectacular magic, yet it was more fun, like "I gotcha" magic. I think they liked that aspect because they already saw that they needed Max to be the big brother to the kids and be the shoulder to lean on. Max could solve the problem or bring a smile with a magic trick, so I think it all came together. They weren't quite sure what they wanted until it walked in, and when I went in for the audition, I had an apron on and a tuxedo jacket [Laughs]. If I had only known ahead of time, I would have probably printed a red T-shirt with a gigantic M on it, with Max. I was just very, very lucky, and good timing.

How disappointed were you when we never ended up meeting Screech's evil twin Scorch?

I wish they had thought of that. Boy, if they had just remembered. Hey, maybe there's still hope in the future. I guess the real evil twin Scorch came out muuuch later after the series was done. [Laughs]

When you think of the earliest beginnings, what stories or episodes jump out most in your mind?

Well, the main memories that I remember are not even really related to being on the show but kind of behind the scenes. Mark-Paul was just turning 16, and he was getting his learner's permit so he could drive, so we'd go out in the parking lot at NBC and I'd let him drive my car around so he could practice. [Laughs] Then there were times when the whole gang would go out and go over to grab a bite to eat at a nearby restaurant across the street from NBC. Just hanging out, those were really fun times. But as far as episodes, the ones that are my favorites, for me, obviously are the ones that I had the larger parts because Max was always the smallest part on the show. So "Dancing to the Max" of course was one of my favorites because of Casey Kasem. And I was really able to stretch my wings as an actor a little bit because when they had Max introduce Casey Kasem, the line just said, "All right, here he is, Casey Kasem." And that was it. And over the weekend when I was looking at the script, I thought, "When I go to the table reading, I want to do the intro to Casey Kasem, and I want to do a Casey Kasem impression." And I want to say "Casey Kasem" in kind of the Casey voice. So I started practicing over the weekend, and I did the table reading, and we got to the line where Max says, "Here he is, [Casey Kasem voice] *Casey Kasem.*" And they just started laughing, everyone at the table. And I remember Dennis Haskins looked around and said, "Is that in?" They go, "That's in!" So that's the way it rolled out that I was able to do that impression. So that's probably one of my favorite episodes. The second one would be "The Mamas and the Papas," where they are in the Max and the Max is all maxed out like a formal restaurant. Mr. Belding is the maître d' there. I see the kids at the table in their formalwear and they say, "What's the best thing on the menu?" And I open up the menu and then fold it up into a little triangle and a duck pops out. And I say, "Oh, the duck; that's the best thing on the menu." It's a real duck. So that was one of my favorites because that got a huge response from the live audience that was there as well, applauding like it was a real magic show. So that was one of the first real strong tricks that I had done on the show to where then they said, "You know what, maybe we need to have you do some other things that are even bigger and produce some of the characters out of boxes and things." So it kind of grew, and it became that every time I would walk on camera, about 99% of the time I'd be doing magic tricks.

Since Max so utilizes your own skills, was there anything you had to do to get into character?

The thing is once I get my hair all pushed up tall and I put the glasses on and get the apron and the whole thing, you just become that character. And it's so closely related to what I was doing prior to that on other talk shows with magic like "The Arsenio Hall Show" and" The Smothers Brothers Comedy Hour." I was doing a lot of those at the time, and I was that character with the spiky hair and the glasses and kind of nerdy and using kind of a high voice. So the Max thing was really just an extension of that; he was maybe just a little more friendly than the magician character that I do on other shows, which has little edgy sections to it. And the Max character, he was always just a friendly, nice guy trying to get everyone to smile and be happy. So, yeah, it was nice and easy. Once I had the costume on, it was easy. But even sitting at a table reading for me, once I'm into it, it just goes. It's pretty natural.

If we imagine Max's interactions with other students throughout the years, did he bond with a group of kids like the gang every year, or was there something special about this group?

I think that the Max character was the kind of guy that would have been that friendly and just a great guy to hang out with in his restaurant and just watch the magic for anyone. I think if there was a prequel to "Saved by the Bell" that the character would still be the same. It certainly is the same on the pilot episode for the reboot. They have me come in, and it's really no different: I say one line, I produce some food and then they're back into the storyline. So that hasn't changed too much.

How much have you ever imagined what Max was doing when he wasn't working at the Max?

Hmm. I always just assumed that Max was out doing shows. Doing charity events or whatever because he's a magician and put this restaurant together to have a platform to do his show. I always assumed that the Max character would be out doing what the Ed Alonzo character was doing.

Is he single? Is he married with kids? What's his personal life like?

Hmm. I never really looked that far into it. I always kind of considered him like a Pee-wee Herman type of character to where he didn't really think about that too much. Like Mr. Rogers – you just watch and learn from his teaching and his examples. Max was an extension of that kind of a character.

I never made that connection to Mr. Rogers. I like that.

I also think that's part of the same reason that the Max character didn't have the longevity of the other characters because they saw this was better for a younger audience, where the original show was meant to be for a younger audience on Saturday morning, and then it just blossomed into something that was more for teenagers and college students. And that's when they decided, "Well, we really don't need Max around for that; he's the trickster." So then they would just bring me in for an episode here or there to try and tie the loose ends together to make it make sense.

So you feel like the personality of the show changed?

Oh, absolutely. I think in the beginning they had no idea that it was going to be the success that it was and the camaraderie of the kids was going to be – when you look at that, it's the same kind of camaraderie that they had on "Friends," but just in a different generation. That's really what made the thing work, and they realized that at the network and that's what made the thing go for years and years.

On that note, so many sitcoms have a core hangout, whether The Max or Central Perk or MacLaren's or Monk's Diner, but there's an inequality where the location is central to the show yet the proprietor is rarely involved in the plot.

Yeah. The only thing I can relate it to is back when I was a kid and I would watch "Happy Days," and I would always certainly like the Mel character from Mel's Diner, which then changed later to Pat Morita, but that was the same kind of thing. And, wow, what a huge part that character had on the show, right? If only Max could have had that much involvement with the storyline.

Were there ever any Max-related plotlines that didn't make it on the screen?

There was a time I heard the writers were talking about having Max in a dream sequence where he was going to be the parole officer or maybe the sergeant or something looking at a lineup – this was in the Artie episode where Mario's lizard dies. And they were talking about bringing the Max character in to play this sergeant to have the kids look at the lineup, like "Which one of these guys did it?" That scene. Just days before, they decided that they needed to give that to Belding since he was more the authoritative figure on the show. So I think there were times when they tried to pop me into places and didn't quite know how. There's one episode, the only episode where I'm out of the Max uniform, and I have been hired to be the school photographer and I'm taking pictures all throughout the episode. And then the final scene is me getting the group together in Belding's office and I say, "Smile! Watch the birdie," and a bird appears on the top of the camera and the flash goes off and we get the final picture. So I think it was just a matter of they didn't quite know what to do with me as the series went on and it evolved.

Since the book looks so much at Zack's character, how would you describe Zack Morris as a person?

Well, Max of course liked all the kids that came into the diner, but he especially liked Zack because he saw that Zack was a little bit of a prankster and he liked to put little tricks together and he would come to Max and have him put things together for Screech. If you remember "Close Encounters of the Nerd Kind," Max intervenes and helps teach Screech how to be an alien through Zack's request. So, yeah, I think the Max character thought that Zack was kind of the coolest of the kids because he was using mind over muscle.

What goes through your head when you hear that he lied 329 times throughout the series?

That is like the perfect analogy of the Zack Morris character, being the trickster and the huckster and telling all these white lies to make his world better. I think a lot of kids can relate to that. I think it's an interesting concept that he does do that. It's almost like the "Catch Me If You Can" character. [Zack] was in and out of disguises, and he was "Screech's woman," and it just reminds me of a lot of those kind of things where it seems like maybe he could be a magician himself one day. Who knows.

I guess when I think of that movie, Frank's deceptions seemed somewhat on the harmless side, where we root for him to get away with it because no one is being hurt. But so many times when Zack is deceiving people it does come at the expense of family or friends, at least in terms of breaking their trust. If not worse.

Right, right. I think that's a great concept. It's certainly a great analogy. I'd have to look at specific instances where those lies actually hurt other people. I think it always turned out in the end where the gang was happy by the end of the episode no matter what.

Part of what's been fun about this examination is figuring out if people took that as a lesson of what not to do, or if because of the nature of sitcom television at the time and Zack's continued lies did that take something away from people seeing him as anything but a cool liar.

Right. Well, the Zack character is strongly based on the Ferris Bueller character from "Ferris Bueller's Day Off." And that's even where they got the idea to have Zack look into the camera and speak directly to the audience with an aside or a "Hey, this is how I'm going to try and solve this situation." So I think that Zack is made up of a lot of different characters that are so familiar to us over the years, and I think that's why he's got such an appeal to a certain amount of guys, [just] as Mario's character has a certain amount of appeal to the more jock-type person.

Does anything jump to mind from those early episodes that would have to be done differently now in terms of the way that character is created or behaves?

I think certainly in the last three or four years that the Zack Morris character is in many ways politically incorrect. [Laughs] So I think there would have to be some changes made to that. But I think for the most part even in the new series I think we're going to see that Zack Morris' son might have some of these same kind of tendencies. That's just something we're going to have to look out for.

I know you did some work with big pop stars like Katy Perry, Britney Spears and Michael Jackson. Do you have any stories of a time when you were working with those folks and it overlapped with the "Saved by the Bell" world?

Early on, when I had just landed the role, it was 1989 and we just started to shoot "Saved by the Bell." During one of the hiatuses that we had, I got a call that they wanted me to come out and do a show for Michael Jackson at his house. And at that time, he had just opened Neverland. In fact, it wasn't even really completed yet. He had all the land out there, he had some of the houses on the property, but all the rides and stuff it was really early in the development. But he did have a gigantic house out there that had a theater – a full-blown movie theater with a snack bar in the front, with a dance studio to the side, with the best sound system that you could afford at that time, and then behind the snack bar you went through these big double doors like you would in a regular movie theater and there was a full theater in there with several theater seats and a full stage. And we were able to do a show on the stage, and then afterwards the idea was he would show a movie for him and his guests. It was pretty unbelievable that we even got the job. And I went out with my crew and set up, rehearsed, and we did the show later that evening, and sure enough it was Michael and just a small group of people. A couple parents and some kids. It must have been five people total, including Michael. I did a whole, 45-minute show for him. That was the first time I got to meet with him, and he liked what I did, seemed to enjoy it. I talked to him after the show for a little bit. And then we went back to do "Saved by the Bell," and I had mentioned this to Peter Engel: "I was just out at Michael Jackson's Neverland. It was unbelievable. We did a show for him." And then they were like, "Do you think you can get him on the show?" [Laughs] Of course, I thought that was an impossibility. So that's the only time where the two sort of linked together where if I had maybe done more shows for Michael or had a better relationship with him at that time – like I did much later working with him on "This Is It," where I worked with him for a couple of months getting ready. If I had had that kind of rapport with him, maybe we could've gotten him on the show, possibly, some strange cameo. And the main reason was because Lark Voorhies was so infatuated with Michael, and Peter thought that would be a great episode if Lark's character who's in love with Michael Jackson – and I think that even in Lark's bedroom in a couple of those episodes you see that she has a Michael Jackson poster in her bedroom. They wanted to try and see if that was a possibility. Of course, it never happened. I had just done the one show for Michael. [Laughs] It wasn't a friendship enough where I could call him up and say, "Hey, would you like to do a cameo on a little Saturday morning show?" But that would have been nice.

Do you remember if he said anything about "Saved by the Bell" that first time or later?

Well, the first time when I did the show for him, "Saved by the Bell" was really new. And it was on Saturday morning, where very few people saw it unless you were a kid. And I don't think Michael even saw the thing. Michael had seen me on "The Arsenio Hall Show" and said, "That would be a great guy to have come in here." That would have been pretty crazy if we could've got him in [the show]. No, he was more focused on he just knew me from being a magician at that time.

How would you assess the perception of magic now compared to when the Max character first debuted?

Well, the kind of magic I was doing on the show, like I said before, was pretty simple stuff you'd see a birthday party magician do. They had little different themes; we'd try to keep them themed to the show with food or making the buddy bands appear or whatever. Tried to keep it all themed. But for the most part it was kind of birthday-party magic. I have even mentioned this to them for the reboot. I said, "I think if we're going to do some tricks, I think we should really do some things that seem unbelievable." And they really didn't want to go that route. They wanted [Laughs] to go the old route that was successful before and just do that again. I think it would be interesting to do some powerful magic on there. There's so much magic on TV now that I think people just don't know what's real and what isn't. They're bombarded with so many things and so many special effects and so many things that are divulged on YouTube. If you want to learn how the Statue of Liberty disappeared or how to saw a lady in half, you can go on YouTube and see different versions of their theories of how these things work. So that has really changed the game a lot. And so now even when I'm doing a magic illusion on television or helping someone behind the scenes like Justin Willman – I work with his show "Magic for Humans" on Netflix – or I'm working for someone else behind the scenes, you really have to focus on making the stuff bulletproof. Because now people can rewind and shovel through and watch frame by frame. Back when "Saved by the Bell" was on, everything was all videotape, so it was a lot harder to do that. And I don't know that people were sitting around taping "Saved by the Bell" episodes [Laughs] and watching them back to figure out the tricks. I think it was more about the fun, lighthearted character that was Max and not so much, "Let's see if Max does something that can fool us." I think he was more of just the fun guy.

That would be pretty startling if the first moment of the reboot was Max doing a David Blaine-esque stunt.

I agree! I should've been frozen in ice or standing on one foot on a flagpole 50 feet in the air. I thought that would have been great! But it's back to the same old Max, and that's what people are familiar with. But who knows, it could change. Maybe after this first round of episodes for the reboot go they're going to want to do more and he'll be able to get back in there again.

That would've set quite a tone to start out that way.

[Laughs] Right. I used to work behind the scenes for "How I Met Your Mother," and the Barney character, Neil Patrick Harris, he was an amateur magician on that show. So every time he did magic, I was always there helping to make it happen, and I had always suggested to them, "Put some unbelievable, big things." And one of the episodes they wanted the Houdini water torture tank and Neil to be locked up inside. Even though we were only going to see him in there for a few seconds as a flashback to an episode, but that's the kind of stuff I really like to do is put together magic and illusions for other artists.

Do you think Zack Morris is an ancestor to Barney Stinson? Do you see any overlap there?

Um, a little bit. You see the womanizing character and the smarminess, and the Barney character is very much the same as a lot of white lies and stories to help him get through. So, yeah, there's another character that we absolutely love as an audience that's very Zack Morris-like.

I know you and Neil are best friends. Did he ever come to the "Saved by the Bell" set?

You know what, he may have come down there on one occasion, but mostly during times when I was off I was going over to 20th Century Fox and hanging out with him while he was shooting "Doogie Howser." Because at that time he said to the writers, "Hey, I'd like Doogie Howser to maybe do a couple tricks now and then. He's a nerdy intellectual, and if he does a card trick or something now and then that could be pretty cool." So he'd bring me over and I would just hang out and he'd say, "What's something I could do on the show, just something easy, simple, visual?" And I'd show him things, and he would then show them. And sure enough there'd be little pieces of magic on "Doogie Howser" spread throughout the series. That's when I really got interested in creating magic for other people. Like you said, I was able to work with Katy Perry and the Britney Spears tour in 2009, where I actually did the show with her every night. And then later when she went to Vegas for her "All Eyes on Me," I put together the opening illusion she appears in. I really like working behind the scenes on shows. That's really more fun for me as time goes on.

Do you have any good stories about Saved by the Max in Chicago or L.A. that showed how much people cared about the restaurant or the character?

Well, I was absolutely blown away by the entire concept. First how I heard about it was I was in Malaysia in a big production show every night in a big casino show with dancers and magic, and one of the days I was looking at, it might've been Facebook, and it showed an ad that said "'Saved by the Bell'-themed restaurant to open in Chicago." And I hit "Like." Well, about two days later I got a Facebook [message] from the guy who was [doing] PR for the Saved by the Max restaurant, and he said, "Are you the same Ed Alonzo who was the actor on the show?" Of course, I responded to him and said, "Yes, I think this is such a great idea what you guys are doing." He said, "Would you be interested in being our mascot and doing some promos and then eventually coming to Chicago to do the grand opening?" I said, "Of course, absolutely! I would love to do it." So I got out the old costume and went into a little tiny studio and cut these promos about Saved by the Max, and they started airing those in different locations, and then it was time to open it. So they flew me to Chicago, and I got all dressed up in my Max outfit in the hotel and went over to the restaurant, and there was a gigantic line around the block to the next street to the entrance. I got out of the car fully dressed as Max, and the people started cheering, and I've never experienced that before. I thought, "Wow, this is really cool." Some of the people were like, "Oh my god, that's the real guy!" Some people didn't know if I was just a walk-around character. So now I go into the restaurant for the first time, and there's tons of people sitting at all the tables and booths and they see me walk in, and the place just goes nuts. It was so touching. That's the kind of thing that I know all the other actors from the show experienced all the time no matter where they went. But because I don't look like that all the time – I don't have my hair popped up and I don't even wear glasses – so unless I'm in uniform and in that specific look, I could be sitting next to you in a restaurant or the subway and you wouldn't even notice. [Laughs] So to get all dressed up and then walk in and get that kind of response was really, really amazing. And it's been a huge success for these guys. They moved it from Chicago after it was there for a year to Los Angeles, and then it stayed here for about six months. They're going to bop 'em around to other locations; eventually it'll come back to L.A. Maybe in the future there could be one in a Vegas casino. Who knows. It just shows you the strength of that show and the Max in particular. The strong connection that people have to that that would make them want to go out and spend money on a hamburger and fries at the real Max and sit in a booth and go, "Wow, I feel like I'm on the set of the Max on 'Saved by the Bell.'" It's really incredible.

Anne Tremko aka Leslie Burke (all 19 episodes of "The College Years")

The history of "Saved by the Bell" is filled with relationships that almost were but never quite got a chance, despite the possibility that they would have been better and healthier than the ones to which they received a backseat. One of these is between Zack and Leslie (Anne Tremko), suitemates at CalU who begin the series as bickering romantic possibilities for each other but quickly transition out of that dynamic after Kelly joins the suite and Zack has to decide where to focus his attention (and we all know how that turned out).

It's a shame because Leslie really had his number; in the pilot, she says one of the most psychologically astute things anyone ever said to Zack Morris:

"You're immature and selfish. You didn't throw that party to make me happy; you did it to impress me and make yourself look good. I guess it doesn't matter if somebody else has to pay the price."

Tremko (who went to the University of Illinois at Urbana-Champaign, as did I, and is now a sales executive for a French IT company) is extremely forthcoming about how much she does not remember about the series – she says she's never watched the episodes – but couldn't be more agreeable in talking about what she does remember and ultimately debating the merits of Zack vs. Screech:

When you think of your time on "The College Years," what do you think of?

It was great. It was pretty magical to get to be part of that whole group. That show is so well-loved by people, I felt like I was really lucky to get in. [Laughs]

Do you remember where you were in your career when you found out "The College Years" existed and what they were looking for in Leslie?

Oh, yeah! I had just moved to Los Angeles, and I got an agent. I had done a show at Steppenwolf, and I tested for a few things from Chicago because I went to Chicago after college and got a lead in a Steppenwolf play and tested for a few soap operas and one series out in L.A. And got all my cards in Chicago, [including] SAG and AFTRA. I decided it was time to go because I had enough going on and got an agent and drove my shitty little car out to Los Angeles. My agent got me a roommate, so I moved out there. I didn't know the person, and he had an extra room, and I drove out in January with one of my best friends who had just had the lead in the movie "Rudy." She also went to [U of I], and we were in the same kabuki "Othello" show together. So Greta Lind, she said she would drive with me so I could bring my car out there. I went on a bunch of auditions; I got a recurring role in "[The Adventures of] Brisco County [Jr.]" in February. I moved in January, I got "Brisco County," and then in May I got the audition for "Saved by the Bell." My agent had put me up for the part of Alex, and when I got there the casting director was like, "You know, you look more like a Leslie; why don't you read these Leslie sides?" Then I had a callback, and then I had a callback with the producers, and then I went to the test. And then I found out I got the role. So that was that.

Were you familiar with the other seasons? Did you have any sense of how "The College Years" would or wouldn't be different?

No, because I was in college when all that was going on and in high school, and I was really, really busy. I don't think I had ever really watched it. I knew it existed, but I wasn't like a fan. I wasn't really watching it, but I knew that it had been on a long time, so I was excited to get to be a part of that. I was busy.

It's a TV show, not a documentary, but can you think of a time during filming or reading a script or anything that something memorable went through your head about this portrait of college? You mentioned that you thought you were the only cast member to have actually just come from being in college.

It was kind of a sweeter version of college. [Laughs] It was more innocent. I don't think they were trying to make it really like college; I think they were trying to make it like a sweet little bubble of these people and what it would be like if these kids and their sweetness were in college.

If anyone treated their friends the way Zack did, where every single day it was like the lesson from the previous day never happened, how long would you expect that a real person would put up with that?

But that's a sitcom, right? Archie Bunker, good god, how many seasons was he on? He was a racist jackass. You're laughing at people doing things that people don't do. All of them are like that. I think it's a really interesting premise what you're doing, and I think it's really worthwhile to point out that he's in fact a scoundrel. And why do we make sitcoms about scoundrels? I don't know; people think it's funny.

Do you get the sense that if Kelly wasn't there, Zack and Leslie would have gotten married? Do you know what the arc was supposed to be?

I don't think the arc was supposed to be they got married; I think that was just because it didn't get picked up for the next season. If it would have gotten picked up, I don't think they would have written it that direction.

Even Zack and Kelly?

Yeah, I don't think anyone would have gotten married. I think they would have stayed in college and just gone on and had years and years of being in college. But they knew it was going to end, so they wanted to tie it off for all the fans.

You're right that Zack is far from the only flawed main character in sitcoms. But if you look at "Arrested Development," Jason Bateman is such an everyman. Even though his character makes a ton of mistakes, his intentions are good and people like him as a person. On "Friends," everyone makes mistakes and is a cartoon sometimes but never so much that you feel like they're trying to screw each other over. I mention all that to say that in terms of "Saved by the Bell," do you feel like Zack is a hero or a villain?

You know, anybody that can live in a dorm room with Screech is a hero in my opinion.

But Screech really came into his own in college! He finally met a woman that liked him for him, he stood up for himself, he joined the fraternity by himself. I feel like Screech's best moments are in college.

Yeah, but he also had his buddies. He lived in the room with them. They gave him a hard time, but they were really there for him, even though he was one of the most bizarre characters outside of that guy on "Seinfeld," what's his name?

Kramer.

Kramer, right. Screech was, like, talk about an odd person. [Laughs] So I think that kind of is a little bit endearing about [Zack]. That he's trying to be a ladies' man, but he ends up marrying Kelly even though she has an affair with her own teacher. He still is with her and he still has his friends and he's there for Screech even though Screech is a wacko. I don't think [Zack] is a villain.

I am not here to defend the honor of Screech Powers by any means, but what do you have in mind when you describe Screech as a wacko and Zack being good for tolerating him?

How do I define a wacko? I mean he was not functioning, not interacting with reality a lot of the time. He was off in his own world and not really understanding how the world operated. He was definitely an outsider. Wacko probably isn't the right word; that's fairly derogatory. I guess just that he was an outsider and didn't understand how the world worked. He didn't understand women, although he did have a date, which was great. And actually Hillary [Danner, who played Linda Addington] and I are still friends from that episode; I really like her. I still talk to her, she's very cool. But it's difficult to stay friends with somebody that's not really living in the same reality that everyone else is.

I think you're right; he was definitely out of his emotional depth in college. In the high school years his friends often suppressed him, so maybe that's why he was a little behind. In terms of it being hard to stay friends with someone who's not living in the same reality, that makes me think of Zack. For someone to lie every day and create his own world in which he is a ladies' man and he can get away with anything and doesn't have to be loyal to anyone and doesn't expect any consequences and no matter what happened yesterday he's still going to do the same thing today ... it's a different challenge to be friends with someone who's emotionally stunted, and especially in college might be "holding you back." But if you had to choose between those two types of people, emotionally underdeveloped and totally delusional, dishonest and selfish, which one would most people choose?

That's a great question. That's a great question. I think in college people are attracted to – I guess it depends on who you are. If you're an extrovert, you're probably going to be attracted to someone like Zack, who is a good-looking, charismatic person. If you're a guy in college, there's a good-looking, charismatic person that has women following him around. And you've got an unattractive introvert who doesn't understand how the world works. Different people are going to be attracted to different types of people, so I don't think you can unilaterally say people would more likely be attracted to Zack. But there's certain types of people that would be. And there's certain types of people that are more introverted and they don't want to run around and party and go to social functions, and they probably want to hang out with Screech.

So why do you think Zack has been such an enduring character despite often treating people so badly? Is that Sitcom 101, or is something else going on?

Well, I think one of the greatest sitcoms of all time is "Seinfeld," and everybody on there was lying and mean, right? I didn't watch it that much, but the things that I remember, wasn't it the whole thing that they were trying to pull one over on each other?

Yeah, both "Seinfeld" and "It's Always Sunny in Philadelphia" are meant to call out how horrible they are. I'm not sure "Saved by the Bell" has that same perspective. I feel like we're still supposed to like him anyway. In "Seinfeld" and "It's Always Sunny," we're supposed to think these people suck.

Oh, OK. I see what you're saying. I've obviously been taking a contrarian view of your contrarian view [Laughs], but I think you've got a fantastic point, and probably if I went back and looked at it I would start to see all the things that you're seeing. Do I think it's good to idolize a lying, cheating scoundrel just because he's good-looking and funny? Probably not. [Laughs] Probably not a good idea.

Troy Fromin aka Scud aka Ox (9 episodes)

It's astonishing how few recurring characters "Saved by the Bell" had. And it's equally astonishing that, aside from restaurant owner-magician Max (Ed Alonzo, 21 episodes) and best-friend-who-vanishes Tori (Leanna Creel, 10 episodes), the next most prominent supporting player is, yes, eight appearances of lovable doofus football player Ox (Troy Fromin, who also played drug-abstaining biker Scud in one episode before Ox existed).

While Zack always seemed to be out for himself, Fromin said, the actor doesn't remember any time Zack gave Ox a reason to be mad at him – or a moment the show laughed at him rather than with him. "I was usually behind the antics, like when Zack exchanged the oven knob [in 'The Will']," he said. "I was in with the gang when they showed me. I felt like I was part of them."

That said, Fromin recognizes how Zack saw people outside his core friend group as "lesser than him." "He looked down at the nerds," he said. "He was very pompous and sarcastic … He always got off the hook."

Fromin, who also appeared on "The Wonder Years" and recently popped up in an Iggy Azalea video ("Started"), is more than happy to talk for this book and continue exposure from his most memorable role. He's still a bit bummed that a promised role in "Saved by the Bell: Hawaiian Style" never materialized and that Ox never returned for "The College Years." These days Fromin still works at Fromin's Deli, his family's restaurant in Santa Monica, working the deli counter and on deliveries. (His wife is the manager, and no, there's no sandwich called The Ox. "No, but we got lox!" Fromin said. "I don't think anyone wants to eat ox on a bagel with cream cheese.") He's also auditioned for shows like "Euphoria" and notes that he got lucky in his younger days as an actor.

"I did a lot [then]," he said. "It's really tough now when you're older. I don't think I've lost any of my acting skill."

In fact, he spent months promoting the (self-created) hashtag #bringbackox in hopes of appearing on the "Saved by the Bell" reboot. (You'll have to watch to see if Fromin got his wish.)

Recently he joined several other supporting actors at the Saved by the Max restaurant in Los Angeles. There, Fromin was like royalty as fans lined up around the block. "They had a full bar there, so I was doing a few shots and getting in a really good mood," he said. "And they're coming up one at a time for signatures and photos. I felt like I was at a convention or something."

It was support from fans, actually, after Fromin joined Facebook seven years ago, that motivated him to get back into acting. It's clear he cherishes the experience that sparked the fandom.

"I wouldn't give it up for anything. I got friends out there that have done a lot more work than I have, been in a lot more things, but you just don't remember them," he said. "But people remember me because of Ox, and I appreciate Ox."

Some more spare takeaways from our interview:

- Ox has no real name. It's just Ox.
- How Fromin describes Ox: "Fun-loving, idiotic student of Bayside. He's a dimwit. Everybody loves him."
- What Ox might be doing now: "Some people have brought this to my attention that they pictured me as an assistant football coach or something involved in the school, but as an older person. I could have remained a dumbass and been a janitor at the school and been happy about it. The gardener, I don't know. Just somewhere in the school working. If you wanted to go total stupidity, I'd still be a student there."
- The only Ox moment cut from "Saved by the Bell" was from "School Song," in which Ox's entry involved him singing a tribute to his elementary school and telling Belding that his loyalty was because he went there 14 years. The video is on Fromin's YouTube channel.
- Some comedies he likes: "Kingpin," "Pootie Tang," "Van Wilder."
- No interviewer had ever previously asked him about playing a character also named Ox in a movie called "Time Burst: The Final Alliance." ("Bingo!" he exclaimed. "You get bonus points.") However, by the time he was Ox on "Saved by the Bell," Fromin had forgotten about the movie role and only realized the commonality when looking at his credits one day.

Edward Blatchford aka Rod Belding in "The Fabulous Belding Boys"

I have to preface this by identifying the surreal process of setting up this interview.

First, context: Mr. Belding's brother Rod (Edward Blatchford) is a symbol of unreliability, creating an elusive charm and then letting people down when they need him most (specifically, ditching the kids' rafting trip for a stewardess named Inga). While that exact scenario didn't happen in real life, through Facebook Blatchford responded in exclusively short phrases only to not be there by phone at our agreed-upon time. Then when we rescheduled for later that night, he still wasn't there. Was I being Rod Belding'd over and over again?

Number one, no hard feelings. This was happening during coronavirus quarantine, and this is not meant to point a finger at Blatchford, who now works in real estate and directs theater and by the way MADE A SHORT FILM CALLED "SAVED BY THE BELDING." Especially because, number two, we eventually did connect to discuss his classic character and episode (FWIW he said he was running late because he was finishing watching "Uncut Gems"), simultaneously giving me the extra-unique experience of being blown off by Rod Belding and then, at last, fulfilled by his presence.

As I mentioned, the book is a statistical analysis of Zack Morris' behavior.

I think this is funny, but I can't remember – what bad stuff did Zack do? I can't remember anything.

Did you watch the rest of the series beyond the one you were in?

Yeah, I saw 'em off and on. 'Cause I worked with what's his name, the producer a few times on his shows.

And you don't remember anything bad he did?

Not really, to tell you the truth. I mean, I didn't watch it religiously, but I can't remember. I always thought he was kind of a clean-cut kid who was a little sneaky, but just a teenager.

That is a perspective that I haven't heard before. So when you think about the episode you did as Rod Belding, which has become one of the iconic one-episode characters –

It's unbelievable. I've done lots of movies and TV shows and everything, but I can't shake that. It was just one episode.

Why do you think it had that kind of impact?

I have no idea. Why do you think it does?

I think it's because there weren't a lot of episodes like that. Wait, I have a better answer: I think it's because Zack was very unreliable the entire series, and this was one of the few times where he saw someone else treating him not so great and had to get a taste of his own medicine.

Oh. OK. Yeah. So that's why it became iconic?

Maybe. And also because you were really memorable in the role. What do you remember from the episode?

I don't remember much. It was the first job I got leaving the Chicago theater community. I graduated from the Goodman School of Drama, I did a bunch of shows in Chicago, I went out there and I got that part. It was the first television gig I got out there, and I didn't think two cents about it. I was a very good actor, and I think that had something to do with it – they had somebody who was more of a good actor than just a goofy person to cast. I just think that my long hair looked different, and it was funny too. I think the biggest thing is a guy who you really enjoy watching lets everybody down. How somebody you like so much can let you down; that's what I got out of it. That's what his lesson is. 'Cause Zack loves Rod, as I recall. And he let him down. So that's a big thing: How could someone you like so much and put so much faith in just blow you off like you're nothing? I think that resonated with people.

Yeah, because Zack gets so invested in Rod so quickly. That's a good point; I think people relate to jumping in on someone too quickly.

And people put too much on certain people as heroes. 'Cause really Rod didn't give a shit about the kids; he just wanted to go get laid. Which is a normal thing for a guy like him. He didn't care about being a substitute teacher, he was just doing a favor for a weekend. He didn't care about the kids. And Zack [thought that he did]. So it was a misconception.

Did you ever have a teacher like that growing up? Or were you like that as a student?

No, no, I just drew it from my own personal experiences of being a guy with wanderlust who wanted to have a good time. Kind of a guy from the hippie era, more interested in his self-pleasures than anybody else. He's a selfish guy but a good guy. A rolling stone.

I was going to ask how you thought Rod compared to Zack, but it sounds like you think there is no comparison.

No, there's not a comparison. Rod is the elder and he's living his life, and maybe the kid, Zack, thought this was a really cool guy. Haven't you had that experience in your life, some older person like, "God, this guy's cool"? And he wanted to create a relationship with him and looked past some things because you just think he's cool. And kind of a mentor situation, or maybe more of a big brother/mentor thing. That's why I think it was so successful because of that. He acted like everybody's big brother, ripping up the test.

Do you get recognized for the role?

I used to all the time. I don't so much anymore because I'm 63 now and look a little older. But up to maybe eight years ago I got recognized all the time from people about your age.

Did you feel like they expected certain things of you because of the character? What did they say?

It's like anything when you're in movies or plays or TV – when people see you in person, they recognize you and they have an intuition of who you are based on that character more than who you really are as a person. I think people are always happy to see me when they know who I am. They always love it. I still have people call me all the time on Facebook, they get my number somehow. I get [prank] calls sometimes on this phone number, and they'll call and say stuff like, "Is Rod Belding there?" I go, "Who?" "Rod Belding." And they'll hang up. This could be one too, I have no idea.

No, I assure you this book is real. Do you feel like the episode influenced you in any way outside of people recognizing you?

Yeah, it did, it got me hooked up with – I'm so stupid, I can't remember the producer's name now. Who is the producer? Engels?

Peter Engel.

I was cast in that, and then I didn't hear from him for four or five years, and all of a sudden he called and offered me a part in "Malibu, CA." Do you remember "Malibu, CA"?

That doesn't ring a bell.

What?! That was a show he produced and was on for a couple years. It was really good. You should YouTube it. Then I did all the other shows of his ["Hang Time," "City Guys"] as guest stars. The one about the basketball players. He had all these Saturday morning shows. I did guest stars on all of them. It was great. He kept me going, put money in my pocket, [helped] my family, and I'm really appreciative of Peter.

What would you recommend to people if they encounter someone like Rod, who is really charismatic and you fall for them instantly? Do you have any advice for people who find themselves in a situation like Zack and everyone did?

I'd do exactly what they would do: Go for it, love 'em and that's the way the chips fall.

So just hope for the best even though it could go wrong?

Yeah. Yeah. I think that's what was appealing. Rod's a free spirit, and I think that's what all the kids loved about him. He didn't do things the way that everyone wanted him to do. He's not like the principal, Dennis Haskins, who was stiff and by the book. And this guy came in as a free spirit on the wind, and they loved it and he swept everybody away with him, but then he left. And that's kind of how things happen in life. But they all had a good experience for it.

I guess for me it felt like the lesson was maybe not to buy into someone so much so fast, not that it was a beautiful whirlwind. How are we supposed to feel about Rod at the end?

It's so funny because people always say to me, "Oh, god, why'd you leave the kids for Inga?" But no one ever says, "You're a jerk." They always just think it's funny. It's a comedy.

If Rod's story continued, what happened to him? Is he married to Inga now?

No. No. It's a fling, definitely a fling. I think he eventually got married and settled down, had a family, chilled out a little bit. Maybe a surfboard maker, mountain climber guide or a ski guide, parasailer. Raft guide. Explorer.

That's an optimistic view. I didn't know if you'd say world traveler or dead in an alley somewhere.

No, no. There was nothing negative about that guy. He was on his own trip. He was just doing his thing, moving forward.

I feel like I got the best of both worlds in pursuing this interview because I thought you might be blowing me off, but you came back and here we are. Zack wasn't so lucky. I got the full Rod Belding experience.

There you go. That's right, you did. That's probably what he would have done too. He probably would have come back to school eventually and been a substitute teacher again for his brother.

I never thought about what would have happened if they did another episode with him.

They're making a remake of it right now, and there was some talk about me coming onto it, but I don't know what ever came of it. I didn't pursue it. I have a family and do really well what I do right now, and we're happy so we're good.

If there had been another episode with him later in the season, how do you think the kids would have welcomed him back?

There'd probably be a big apology, and I'd have to get their trust back again and make all these promises. And then blow them off again.

[A few days after our interview, I email him follow-up questions. He sends the responses that night.]

You mentioned not remembering Zack doing anything that was too bad. Does it surprise you to hear that he lied 329 times throughout the series? To what extent does that make you think any differently of him, or does it not?

Never thought twice about his character.

With "Last of the Mohicans" following your "Saved by the Bell" episode by a couple years, any chance you have a memory/story of talking about Rod Belding with Daniel Day-Lewis? Do you think playing Rod Belding was helpful at all in you landing and/or playing the "Mohicans" role?

Daniel Day-Lewis is a huge fan of "Saved by the Bell." In fact, he didn't leave me alone until I made him a paper airplane.

Nancy Valen aka Nurse Jennifer in "From Nurse to Worse"

Considering Zack Morris' reach always exceeded his grasp, perhaps it was inevitable that he would fall for an older woman and never consider that he wasn't ready for the sophisticated relationship he imagined having with her.

In "From Nurse to Worse," Zack's desire to go steady with Kelly disintegrates at the sight of Jennifer (Nancy Valen), the new school nurse who tells Zack he's cute and wonders "what's going on in that body of yours" but otherwise is not interested in an examination beyond what's professional (and legal). It leads to a quintessential, prank-driven reversal in which Jennifer, with support from the gang, pretends to be in love with Zack and wants to leave her (imaginary) wrestler husband for him, causing Zack to freak out and meekly shut down the crush that previously had him ignoring Kelly and rehearsing hellos ("Hey, Jen babe") in his bedroom mirror.

You couldn't watch TV in the '90s without seeing Valen ("Baywatch," "Friends," "Boy Meets World," "Full House," "Walker: Texas Ranger"), and after more than a decade favoring producing over acting, Valen has recently returned to the screen, including an appearance on the Fox drama "9-1-1." As with almost everyone interviewed for this book, Valen says her "Saved by the Bell" role is the one she is most recognized for, and it was a blast talking to her about Nurse Jennifer's integrity and Zack's teen fantasy.

When you think about your "Saved by the Bell" experience, what do you remember? Is there a specific story that comes to mind?

I'm out of my comfort zone doing three-camera sitcoms. I remember the cast being so sweet and so helpful. They would talk to me about their experience and their process, and of all the shows that I worked on, I would say that that cast was the most ingratiating, the nicest, the warmest. I felt like I was a part of the cast from day one. And often when you do a guest spot, you're the guest star. You don't feel like a cast member. Everyone's usually very nice, but they were above and beyond. Really wonderful.

When you say helpful, is there an example that comes to mind?

I remember Elizabeth Berkley and maybe Tiffani-Amber Thiessen – is that her name? She was on that show, right? OK, sorry, going back a long way – I just remember them telling me, "We all feel [uneasy], and on the day of the shoot we punch it up a little bit more." Stuff like that. Just in general, they were very supportive. I'd have to say that that was the word. They were also just friendly and open. They talked to me like I was their friend for a million years. Maybe it had to do with the fact that they were so young possibly, but they weren't at all closed off. They just were warm and open. Lovely, lovely people.

If you had to describe Nurse Jennifer, how would you assess what makes her tick?

I think I just wanted to do a good job as a teacher, and a teacher that has a sense of humor and that would go the extra mile to help the kids out and learn a lesson.

I like that: "the extra mile." One of my favorite parts of the episode is the notion that a new employee on her first or second day can team up with the students to pull one over on someone.

Yeah, like one of the crowd. I liked that, that she would do that with the students.

She seems like such a sweet person the entire time, and that's a testament to you. There are some amusing innuendos that cause Zack to look at the camera and give corresponding expressions. On a scale of 1 to 10, how appropriate do you think it was for Jennifer to say, "I wonder what's going on in that body of yours"?

Gosh, you know what, it was a different time. I don't remember that line specifically. I would imagine that it was a double entendre, and I played it probably very innocently. I think I would play it out of curiosity, very generally. Not at all in a flirtatious way, I don't think. I don't think that Jennifer had that in her head at all. She wasn't flirting with him. The writers obviously did that as a double entendre to make it more fun and so he could maybe interpret something different, but I don't think Jennifer had anything else in her mind except for the wellbeing of how he was feeling.

Absolutely. It sounds like you believe in her integrity as a nurse.

Yeah! Jennifer at that time was not that much older than the kids at the school. How old was I when I did that? Maybe I was 25 or something. It's not like I was a 40-year-old. [Laughs] I wasn't like Anne Bancroft in "The Graduate." [Laughs] She was still young, but she seems much older. I think that Jennifer was like fun-loving and casual, cool.

I never thought about that; it seems like she got through nursing school pretty fast.

Yeah, maybe. I don't know; maybe I was a bit older. I just saw it as she wasn't the uptight, older authority figure. Just more fun and cool, that's all.

How would you describe Zack's behavior, and what do you think the episode is saying about temptation?

I never thought that it was saying anything about temptation. [Laughs] I just saw his behavior as the typical teenage boy. I think that no matter boy or girl, we've all felt that in the past. When we're young we've idolized somebody that was older and we thought that we were in love, and really it was just an infatuation and we don't understand anything about an adult relationship. So you don't understand that difference yet. So I thought he was a typical teenage kid, and that's why I think so many people related to him. And what I liked about it is they didn't make it that he should be ashamed that he was thinking those things. It's just normal.

Did you ever have a personal experience that you can relate to this episode in any way?

I don't know. I just think that as a young girl, I remember being in love with my boyfriend, and actually the feelings are very intense if you're in a serious relationship. But having a crush on somebody – I have to say I more agree with you in terms of I felt like teachers who were 25, they seemed old. But I wasn't the girl that ever had a crush on a teacher or an adult. That wasn't me. But maybe I just justified it in my mind. [Laughs] I can see how a teenage boy would have a crush on somebody older. There are movies I've seen where young kids have crushes on somebody older, right? What's the movie I just watched recently with Charlize Theron, did you see that movie? It was funny. And they actually end up getting together later, [years after] she babysat him.

"Long Shot." I did see that.

Funny comedian, what's his name?

Seth Rogen.

Yes! Seth Rogen. I don't know what the age difference was there, probably not even that much. But even if you're in that type of situation where someone's supposed to be the authority figure – no, I never had that, but I could see a lot of boys feeling that way. Or even girls. I remember having a girlfriend that thought she was in love with this guy, and he was 35 years old, and I remember being aghast, like "What?!" And I think he did actually hang out with her for a bit. I don't really think anything went on there, maybe a kiss though or something, which is statutory right now! [Laughs] But I don't think back then we looked on it as harshly as we do now. Should've. But didn't. I still think there are plenty of kids walking around high school who have crushes on a cute teacher.

Despite Nurse Jennifer's innocent intentions, if a nurse were to say the innuendos that were written for her nowadays, do you think that would get an authority figure in trouble?

Yes, I do. I think that times have changed. Definitely changed for the better. I just remember at that time, shortly thereafter, I did a show called "Hull High," directed by Kenny Ortega, who did "High School Musical" and so many other great projects. I remember at the time we were Sunday at 7, so it was family night time-slot. They thought that my character – because I had this sexy dance that this teacher imagined I was doing, and all the kids were in love with me at the school. Kind of [like] Nurse Jennifer but not. This character was more just insecure, normal teacher, but I guess … kids had a crush on me. They completely came down on that at standards and practices, and I got a lot of questions I remember from the press about, "Do you think this is responsible? Isn't this irresponsible programming for Sunday at 7?" Now jump forward to today. I don't believe that that would have been a problem because I never had any flirtation with the students at all. So with Nurse Jennifer, some of those double entendres, yes, I think that they would have a problem with that today. However, on the other hand, I don't think that today there would have been any problem with my teacher character. I think that sex in general has become more open, what we accept; there's nudity on TV now. Not on the networks but on cable and curse words and all that, profanity. But in terms of protection of children, we've definitely evolved. And protection of all people, just being more respectful and drawing those lines and understanding what it could lead to. I think we've become more responsible in a better way. We've become more open and free, and at the same time we're protecting the people who need to be protected. Does that make sense?

It does; that's a good way to put it. There were a couple other "Saved by the Bell" episodes that featured nurses. Did you ever see any of those?

No, did they do other sexy nurses?

They did. At the hospital where Lisa's mom works, when Zack goes in for knee surgery, there's a nurse named Monique who gives flirty waves and tells Zack "You're dangerous" and gives neck massages. In terms of this being a show for kids, it's curious to watch this stuff back now and see the presentation of female nurses as steamier and more easily misinterpreted than you'd think it would be.

Here's what I think: The creators and writers did an incredible job bringing to life a fantasy that a young kid would have. That a 16-year-old would have. So that is from the mind of that character. I think there's something to be said about our perceptions. If it's a 16-year-old kid, maybe he's seeing everything sexually. Maybe the way that they did the show, the characters came to life through his perception. He is the protagonist, right; he is the lead. So you're really seeing everything through his eyes. Could they get away with it now? Maybe not. However, I think they did a great job because it's true today. Sixteen-years-old, a boy is going to have those type of fantasies, and he is going to be feeling like he's the man if a pretty girl is flirting with him.

That's an interesting theory that in these moments that seem surprisingly adult, you think that we're seeing the fantasy through his eyes.

I think that the writers intended to bring the fantasy to life. They wanted a 14-, 15-, 16-, 17-year-old boy to see himself as, "Yeah, I'm that cool, I'm that good-looking," that these gorgeous women are after me. That's a fantasy I'd imagine of most guys coming of age. I think that that's why they wrote it, for that to be relatable for kids because it's normal. I think we could be seeing his perception of them too.

At the risk of turning you into an armchair psychologist, how would you interpret the direction the show goes then? If it's his vision but it still winds up with Nurse Jennifer calling him out and Zack walking away with his tail between his legs?

Because he really wants to be with somebody his own age. That's what he shows; it may sound great, but he's not ready for all that yet. I think that's actually good to make that 15-, 16-year-old boy that's thinking he's ready for all that back up a minute. And say, "Oh, OK, I may be thinking these things and feeling these things, but I'm not really going to act on these things because I'm not ready for it." Just like he's not.

You're mildly blowing my mind as I now consider if this entire series was a dream.

[Laughs] I don't know about that. I don't know what the writers intended, but I know that obviously kids related to it, and that's so important as you're growing up to feel that we're not alone to feel that the things we're feeling are normal. There are so many different types of characters in that show. It didn't matter who you were; you identified with one of them. They're universal. I've heard someone said the more personal something is, the more universal it is. I think they really did a great job of relating to kids, and it's important. It's a hard time.

If Nurse Jennifer had been in more episodes, how would her character arc have developed?

Wasn't there some young, cool teacher, or was that a totally different show I'm thinking of? There was a young, cool teacher, right, on "Saved by the Bell"?

Are you thinking of "Boy Meets World"?

Yes, I am. Because I did that. He was a young, cool teacher. That's what I think I would have been, even though I was the nurse. I think that it would have been fun to have Nurse Jennifer come back, and she could be the one that maybe the girls went to for advice or that they could talk to when maybe they wouldn't feel comfortable either bringing this to their regular teacher or to their parent. In a perfect world, they'd go to their parents, but sometimes that doesn't happen.

And over time it wouldn't have felt like it was just a reason to objectify her. She would have just been one of the people on the show.

You know what, though? Everyone objectifies everybody, and that's just the way it is. We can try to control all we want, but it's just going to happen. At some point, somebody's objectifying you in their head, [Laughs] and you don't have control over it, right?

Eddie Garcia aka Johnny Dakota in "No Hope with Dope"

Eddie Garcia has appeared in music videos and toured with no less than Michael and Janet Jackson. Content cut from this interview for space includes Garcia talking about going on "It's a Small World" alone at Tokyo Disneyland when the park opened just for the Michael Jackson tour and getting to hang out with Pink Floyd after seeing them at the Palace of Versailles.

Yet he appreciates that he will forever be followed by his role as Johnny Dakota, an undeniable part of "Saved by the Bell" lore. Johnny, an actor who goes from adored hotshot to discarded hypocrite after shrugging off smoking pot while preparing to shoot an anti-drug commercial, represents the extremely rare opportunity for Zack to make a moral decision and take the high road. (No pun intended, really.) It gives the show a different balance (along with its after-school-special message) and has led to Johnny, who also dates Kelly and calls most people "guy" instead of learning their names, becoming somewhat of a cult figure. (See the intro to this book.)

Garcia, who was dating Tiffani-Amber Thiessen at the time – they dated for four-and-a-half years, starting when he was a junior and she was a freshman in high school – and got the role on short notice to fill in for the actor originally cast, is now a choreographer/dance educator and also runs the week-long Camp ME.

What do you make of Zack's character? In this episode, he has uncharacteristic integrity and doesn't give into peer pressure either.

I think the series is very much a story of the time period. Any kid that's going through high school, you try to be the best kid you can, but sometimes you do and say dumb things. For the most part on the series, you saw him always trying to do things for himself, but then you would see these occasional places where he realized that that's not necessarily the best thing to do, and it's not necessarily the nicest thing to do. They were always trying to teach lessons. It's hard when you're doing a sitcom because part of the humor is when he was selfish because it's funny. You go, "Oh, wow. He's being so selfish." But a lot of times he would figure it out, or someone would teach him: "You can't do that. That's not nice." And be like, "Ohhh." I think that's what it was trying to get across to the kids that were watching it is, "Yeah, sometimes you want to do this or cheat on this, but it doesn't necessarily make it the right thing to do."

And you could argue that the two most memorable one-episode characters were Johnny Dakota and Rod Belding, Mr. Belding's sleazy brother who lets the gang down. Those are two episodes in which Zack proved to be the better person, which happened almost never.

Right, right. It's the weirdest thing to me that people would remember the character I played out of all the characters throughout the [show]. I think it was the whole "Say no to drugs" campaign at the time. Also it's funny, like anything, when you see that particular time capsule of what was important, of what they were trying to get across to kids at that time. The nostalgia – some of those people grew up and are like, "Oh my gosh, you were, like, my hero." I was like, "Hero? How was I your hero?" For whatever reason, they could relate to my character, and I don't know why. Probably the pot side of it, and maybe how people perceive that particular drug now as opposed to then. It is a little funny to me. I think for Zack's character, because he was always fighting the selfishness, to see him not do that and actually go, "I don't want to be that." I think he saw a piece of himself in my character, and maybe that's what it was that he was fighting. Like, "You're fake." Because at the beginning, I'm kind of a hero to him. That's why he gives me my jacket back. [Laughs]

I wonder what would have happened if there were more episodes where he stood up for what was right and didn't just sheepishly say, "Sorry I was a jackass."

[Laughs] I think it was of its time. It's kind of like "Family Ties." Seeing Michael J. Fox's character. He became the favorite character even though sometimes his viewpoints were very selfish. I think we all see a piece of ourselves in people like that, and then I think we see the fact that maybe we can better ourselves by seeing their mistakes, and I think we learn from that. I think by having a character that has those flaws and makes those mistakes, it teaches us not to make those mistakes the same way.

What goes through your head when you hear he lied 329 times throughout the series?

[Laughs] I [thought] he lied even more! That's what's crazy to me. When kids are caught doing something or being mischievous or trying to put something together that they're trying to stand up for their independence and their own say and their own thoughts, they lie. So it doesn't surprise me. I teach teenagers now, and it's funny: You can tell when they're totally lying to you. But you kind of want them to figure it out and talk to you and say, "I messed up." From a teacher's point of view, you go, "That's cool. The fact that you stepped up and owned up to what you did is huge." Because I've had that happen with some of the kids, and for them to know that there's forgiveness … I think as he got older, it changed, maybe. I never watched the later shows; maybe he didn't. I don't know what they're doing in the new show. That will be interesting to hear about.

I know the Johnny Dakota storyline was inspired by Corey Haim and Corey Feldman supposedly filming an anti-drug commercial when they were doing drugs at the time. Your episode makes Johnny out to be a terrible guy and a hypocrite. I think it's worth considering: If Johnny's a big star and an anti-drug commercial would make a big impact on kids, does it matter what he's doing behind the scenes?

For me, in theory, it does matter. Because I think if I were a kid and I'm looking up to somebody and you find out that person is straight-up lying to you … I remember being around the Coreys, either from people I knew at the time or working on something, it was interesting to see their personality differences. And the fact that they were so close was interesting because they were so different. Feldman was more standoffish, and Haim was very sweet. Very open and sweet and always saying hi to people. Feldman was a little more to himself. I couldn't even imagine being in their situation, where they're kids and have all this pressure put on them. The behind-the-scenes part is to escape into a different world. Like "Alice in Wonderland": "Take this pill, and you'll do this." They just wanted, I think, to feel, because everything was so – you never knew who was being real or fake to you. Being around some of the kids I knew that had hit shows. Once the show was done, no one talked to them anymore. All the people they hung out with didn't hang out with them, and they were freaking out because a lot of how they were built up was through those shows. Fortunately I got more into my dance side of stuff. It was crazy to me, being on tour, how many people were super nice to you because you could get them backstage. You're like, "Whoa, that's weird." I had people showing up at my door. We had twins show up once, like, "We want to be with you." I'm like, "No, I'm good. It's cool. Try down the hall. Peace out." It was weird! And it's all because they want to be that much closer to something famous. I wish I would've had more time to sit with the character because I think you would have seen a little bit more of a deeper take on it. Knowing a little more of what I know about the Coreys now and some of the turmoil and things that happened to them as young people is something else that you can also bring to the table. Later in my life I learned how to be a better actor because I learned how to be more vulnerable with stuff and understand. Then again, you're doing a sitcom, so you don't want to get that deep, so there's a balancing act of what is it that you're going for? If you're going for the laugh, sometimes you gotta play the straight bad guy. If you're going for the real, then you get a little deeper, and you make it more of, "What causes this to happen?" They used pot as the drug, but it's not necessarily what it was really about.

And certainly I'm playing devil's advocate a little. I recognize that hypocrisy is terrible and certainly a bad look when pushing a message to kids. I guess I wonder if you could make an argument that if Johnny is on any level putting out the message to try to keep kids away from the emotional cycle he's involved in and needs to escape from, you could justify that he doesn't practice what he preaches.

Yeah. I don't know. Maybe for Johnny the character, pot's not a big deal. It's like having a beer or taking a shot, so he doesn't see what the big deal is. He doesn't see it as the drug that was being portrayed, so he doesn't see the bad in it. But it doesn't necessarily make it the right. At the time I had a very close friend, one of the sweetest people you'd ever meet, who was a Calvin Klein model. He was an actor; he was doing all these awesome things. He got into a heroin thing, and it was crazy because I never knew. At all. I hung out with him and had no idea. He kept it really quiet. Later in life, he kicked it. He got completely sober, he was with somebody, they had a kid together, he was in the best place in his life. And for whatever reason, they broke up, and within a week he had died from a heroin overdose. He just went right back to it. I was like, "That's crazy." It shook me. Here is a person that I thought I knew, but I didn't really know. This emptiness that he felt he had to fill with that particular drug. And I've seen people party on drugs and they're fine. They go out, and everybody's cool. And I've seen people, and it's the worst thing that ever could have happened to them. It's like, "Whoa." I think you have to really understand, especially from a kid's perspective, if you glamorize stuff too much, you don't know how that particular kid is going to take it. And literally take it. I think it's important to put out there and put forth the person you want them to see you as and not necessarily the image. Dean Martin, from what I understand, wasn't drinking when he always had the drink in his hand. It was water. It was an act. It was for the funny. That's crazy to me that it was part of an act because that was part of the persona he was trying to create at one point. Someone like Johnny, they were straight-up with me when they said, "We want you to be like the Coreys. We heard they did a PSA and were high as kites." I was like, "That's crazy. How did people not know? How did people not know they were altered?" But then I go to my friend, and I didn't know what he had been on. And I've had instances where I've run into people and I had no idea, and then I found out later and was like, "Get out." "Saved by the Bell" was very safe with how they tried to portray certain messages. It was Saturday morning, and you still are dealing with censorship and how much you can say on a kids' show. The caffeine pills episode was another one. They were trying to do the best they could, and I think the writers would try to pick, "This one's not too hard-core, but we can say the same thing." If you plug and play a certain drug in there, it changes the perspective of the person. If you found out Johnny was more of a person who was taking heroin, you would have a whole different look at him as opposed to pot.

That would have been a memorable moment on a Saturday morning if he came in to shoot the commercial with a needle sticking out of his arm.

[Laughs] Right? "Is he shooting up?!" That would've been crazy. I think the idea was, "Ooh, we shouldn't do this because it can lead to worse things."

And now we can say that more kids these days are familiar with Johnny Dakota than with the Coreys.

That's hilarious. [Laughs] That's so weird to me.

Do you imagine that Johnny's movies were good?

No. I don't. I think they were probably very formulaic. I think he was an OK, just-gets-by kind of actor. And kind of a thing of the time: There were so many actors that were around, and because they relied more on the image and less on the talent, even though they were probably all talented, but the image became bigger than the talent. I think a lot of his movies were probably the ones that were like, "Hey, do this movie. It's going to get you a lot of magazine covers."

Do you think Johnny Dakota was his real name?

No. No. I remember this from experience. I remember when I was younger, I had an agent who was like, "You have to change your name. There aren't enough roles for Latin kids." Kind of like Charlie Sheen – he's really Estevez, but he changed it to Sheen because they were going to get more roles. His dad had done the same. Whereas Emilio embraced it: "No, I'm an Estevez; that's what I'm going to embrace." It's probably Johnny Garcia and they just changed it, trying to be more middle America, get along with everybody, be anything. 'Cause I got that talk.

So you think it was still Johnny, just not Dakota.

Yeah. Because that happened a lot. Or if you had a first name that was similar to Johnny, they would change it to make it seem like you could be anything from anywhere. For me they were like, "You could be Italian, you could be Spanish, you could be a white kid, but if you tell them what you are, then that's what they're going to think you are." I was like, "That's weird." Nowadays it's a little different. I embrace my Garcia name. It's part of who I am. I understood what was going on. I remember I made a conscious decision. I think [the idea at the time] was Eddie Gray. I was like, "What?" They're like, "Yes! It's cool." I was like, "No, it's not. It's weird."

What is the biggest difference in terms of dancing for Michael Jackson vs. Janet Jackson?

Ooh, that's a good one. There's probably more similarities than there are differences. At the time, he was the biggest superstar in the world. So the difference was I walked out on the stage with her – we did a performance at Madison Square Garden for a hockey game, and I thought that was the craziest thing I had ever experienced because it was so loud and it was New York. I was like, "Whoa." I was 16 years old. Flash forward, my first show with him, we walked out and there's 85,000 people. I was like, "OK. Yeah." She would eventually get there and have those stadium things, but for him we played stadiums more than once, which was unheard of. Most people do arena tours; he did stadium tours. Before people did stadium tours as solo acts, and that was pretty spectacular and crazy. People like to see the similarities in the two of them, but you have different energies. She may be a little more laid-back. He put a little more staccato into certain things. He hit certain things a little harder. But they both had that drive and that want to be better at everything every single time and just get better and better. They were both really nice to me and very kind. He knew of me because of her. So the first time I met him, he brought her up and he goes, "Hey, you danced for my sister." I was like, "I did. How do you know that?" He goes, "You did all the turns in her video." I was like, "I did." He was asking me if that was a camera trick. I was like, "No, I actually did it." He's like, "Yeah, that's what she said." That was our first conversation ever. I was like, "Wow, that was cool." I literally just met him.

Do you have a guess of who the bigger "Saved by the Bell" fan was between the two of them?

I would probably say Michael. He liked cartoons. He was a kid at heart. We went to Tokyo Disneyland when we were on tour, and they closed the whole park for us one night, so we had the whole park all to ourselves. It was crazy. "I'm walking around Disneyland all by myself. That's weird." I could see Michael watching it. I could totally see that.

It wasn't just you two, right?

It was the whole tour: The crew guys, us, the band, the singers, everybody, and their families, the people that had their families there. So we had the whole park just for our tour group. We all went over to Space Mountain, and they did it three times in a row. It didn't stop. We would pull up and he'd be like (in a Michael Jackson voice), "Let's do it again!" And we would do it again, and I would be like, "Make it stop!" It was fun ... I think some people from Bon Jovi's group also came with us because they also had invited them.

Regarding the episode title "No Hope with Dope": Do you think that's A. true and B. effective messaging for kids?

I don't think it's effective messaging for kids because I think any time you tell a kid not to do something, they're going to try to do it first so they can experience it. I think you have to educate them and let them understand consequences that can happen by doing something. And then through those things, they can make decisions that will be good instead of being told not to do something. It's just inherently in us that if we're told not to do something, we're going to want to try to do it because we want to know why we shouldn't do it ... I think the whole idea of "There's no hope with dope" is if you get caught up in a lifestyle and it damages you and your brain cells, you're not going to come out OK, regardless of how rich or popular you are. And we've seen that over and over. We've seen people spiral, regardless of how famous they are ... I think with kids you have to let them have a voice. You have to let them speak to you, and you can't speak at them. If you speak at them, it doesn't turn out well. I learned that from teaching. I can offer advice, but if I tell kids stuff that I know, they don't want to know. Whereas if I encourage them to seek out the knowledge, they feel empowered when they find it.

And this is a relic from the era. Nothing would come out now equating pot and cocaine.

Correct. [Laughs] Like I said, they picked the safest thing they could for Saturday morning. I even think they went back and forth with NBC and the censors about, "This is what we're trying to do, and this is why we're trying to do it." And I don't think it was subject matter that was easy for them. They made a conscious choice as a Saturday morning show to deal with it.

As a viewer, I think I would've gotten more out of it if they'd called it "Some Hope with Dope."

[Laughs] That's hilarious. I don't judge people for anything. From experiences of being around people, I've seen the good and bad in all of it. I've seen the good and bad in drinking. I've seen people who I'm like, "You should not drink. Ever. Ever!" Other people are fine. It's like, "Hey, they're cool." And like you said, the way we perceive pot now, it's not the same as it was thought of then. If you saw my episode now, your perception of me and the person and the character may be different than if you had seen my episode then.

Did NBC ask if you did any drugs to make sure they weren't perpetuating the same thing they were trying to expose?

It's funny. They gave me a joint to smoke. But it was like a fake little rolled-up cigarette thing. I didn't smoke because I'm allergic to smoke. So the crew guys are trying to teach me. [Laughs] I was like, "Wait, what do you do?" "You gotta hold it in, bro." Because I would like smoke it and push the smoke out as quickly as possible because it was freaking me out. I didn't drink then; I was just pretty straight-laced. But what's hilarious is the crew guys were being super helpful. Like, "Oh, dude, let me teach you. You gotta do this, hold it this way." I was like, "I don't know what I'm doing!" [Laughs] It tasted awful. It was nasty.

But before you were confirmed in the role, did someone make sure you didn't do them in real life?

You know what's funny, I'm sure they asked Tiffani. I'm sure they did. I'm sure they checked, but they never asked me. And they knew – especially when I was on the set, and I didn't know what I was doing. There were a couple times where I tried to take the hit off the little ciggy thing, and I was choking. I was like (coughs). "We gotta do that again." "This thing's nasty!" I forget what they put in it. It was something weird. It wasn't tobacco because that wasn't cool either. It was gross. It was nasty.

That would've been funny if Johnny is dying while saying, "Come on, it's just a little pot."

For real, though, in rehearsal I totally did. They're like, "No, you have to hold it in longer." The director was really nice. I was like, "I'm trying. I'm trying. I'm sorry. It burns. It hurts."

Dion Zamora aka Alan Fairbanks (4 episodes)

It goes without saying that nerd culture has come a long way. Now it's arguably the majority; when "Saved by the Bell" was around, nerds were relegated to the sidelines, and the show was determined to separate students by social class without nuance or anything (at least, anything lasting) challenging Zack to respect people he saw as being unworthy of him.

One of the few "nerd" characters given a chance to stick around and have any identifying characteristic was Alan Fairbanks (Dion Zamora of "Encyclopedia Brown"), who was probably best known as the student most concerned about the availability of cake. Appearing in "The Friendship Business," "The Zack Tapes," "The Prom" and "Zack's War," Alan wasn't allowed to be much more than a punchline, but he registered quickly as a memorable and endearing fringe character.

Zamora, now working as a financial advisor (his manager recently popped a slide of Alan Fairbanks into a presentation as a joke) with a son (12) and daughter (11) close to the age he was when he appeared on the show, says his kids get a kick out of their dad's episodes. "The way that my character was treated on the show isn't the way that we treat people in my family," he said. "I think it's a great way to point out what's right and what's wrong, and it's all in a fictional setting. As you watch the show it's campy and hokey sometimes, but there are lessons to be learned there …

"If you look at our social media today, what do people thrive on? They thrive on watching other people. Whether it's fights on social media, someone pulling a practical joke, it's always someone getting something over on someone else. And that's what Zack did. People love to watch that."

What do you think about when you look back on your time with "Saved by the Bell"?

When we started shooting, the first two episodes I filmed were on the NBC lot, which was nice because I'd worked on the NBC lot a couple times before, so it was nice to be there, like an at-home feeling when I was there. The second two episodes I filmed were at Raleigh Studios, which was across town in Hollywood. It's pretty much the same set moved from one studio to the next. It was a good time in my life; I was young, 12-, 13-years-old. Going through puberty myself and going through it on the show at the same time. I did film four episodes. The first episode I just had a few lines, it wasn't much, and then they brought me back and elaborated from there on my character a little bit. I did receive a notification about three-and-a-half weeks ago that they're doing a reboot, and they invited me to come back to revive my character. So when all this madness ends I'll get ahold of the casting director and talk about me flying out to California for a few days to film. And I'd like to reignite my acting career as well. I'm a financial advisor with New York Life insurance. I work with life insurance and annuities and retirement planning and all that fun stuff. But it gives me a lot of spare time, and if there's something I'm passionate about I'm able to really dive into [it] and investigate. Acting's always been something that's kind of sat on my shoulder and been a driver for me. I'm looking forward to really getting back into it.

I'm so glad they'll bring you back. What do you remember of what they were looking for in terms of Alan's character? If it were me at that age, if someone said, "We'd like to bring you in to play someone who's awkward and gets made fun of," I don't know if that would've made me feel awesome.

As a child, I began acting when I was 7. I've been working solid my whole life. When you go in to play a character, you're not really playing yourself. You pretend to be someone you're not. It's got its advantages and its disadvantages, but it seems that over the years Alan Fairbanks, this character on "Saved by the Bell" that was only on four episodes, has really developed a following, and people really enjoy "Saved by the Bell." When everyone in my office found out, and they didn't know until about a month ago – I've worked for New York Life for almost two years now. I kept it very quiet. I don't share this part of my life with many people, and someone in the office found out, and it seems like I get blown up more about that, that people want to talk about "Saved by the Bell" or refer to me as going to Bayside High and what was it like going to Bayside. It's pretty interesting. But that's the character people seem to love. When I was a kid and acting on the show, for me it was an opportunity to play something that I'm not. They put me in a little bit of a fat suit, so I wore a shirt that had a big pad on the front because I wasn't as heavy as they wanted me to be. If you notice my character always revolves around food, so Alan's always eating. He's always talking about food. Zack says "halt." "I thought you said malt." It's that sort of thing. The way they wrote shows back then and the way they write shows now are completely different. Zack was kind of a bully in the show; he bullied people into things, and he was a wisecracker and trying to make things happen. If you watch shows now, the people who do things like that are viewed as more of a negative connotation, whereas when I was a kid and you were filming shows like "Saved by the Bell," playing the nerd was the bad thing. Being the sly, cool kid was the good thing, and those roles have definitely reversed over the last 30 years.

To what extent did you find yourself thinking about Zack's treatment of outsiders and if Alan is being laughed with or at?

The nerds, obviously, they're definitely being laughed at. It wasn't a laughed-with situation. It was definitely being laughed at and made fun of, put in that light. You really don't stop when you're filming it as a kid. It's all make-believe. Because you're wrapped up in it, and you know that this isn't what they're really like. When you're on set you have to have school three to three-and-a-half hours a day, so I was in a classroom with Mark-Paul and Mario and Tiffani and Elizabeth and Dustin. We sat very close together, we were sharing tapes and earphones, and it was a really nice experience. These are super-nice people that I had a chance to work with, and I had a really good time working with all of them, so when the shows aired and I saw the shows, it never really hit home as to what the public was seeing. It wasn't until later on, in my 30s, and someone was like, "Oh, you were that nerd," and they kept telling me, "You were that nerd," "You were that nerd," and it started setting in: "Wait a minute: Maybe the character I played was made fun of a lot." But it didn't really affect me. I have nothing but positive things to say about "Saved by the Bell." It was a really good experience.

Do you have any sense of why that was the norm at the time?

I don't know if I would call that the norm. Let me ask you this: How old are you, Matt?

I'm 37.

I'm 44. I've got about seven years on you. Growing up in the '80s, things were a lot different in the acting industry, in the entertainment industry. A lot of things have come to surface since then, so there's a lot more sensitivity out there. There's a lot more sensitivity with human beings right now. With the way that social media has really stepped up in the last 10 years, you're seeing a lot of online bullying, you're seeing a lot of things that are going down while people are able to step back and they're thinking about their past experiences, shows they've watched, things they've gone through, and at any point in time they're relating things that are going on now that they've seen on TV in the past. For instance, things that Zack did on the show that's really going to develop a negative connotation. Now when the show was written and the show came out, it's all fictional, and there's definitely some comedy in there. Zack is written as a wise-cracking, fly-by-the-seat-of-your-pants, there's always a gimmick – that's just the nature of that character. The way that television was written back then, it's a lot different than it's written now. I worked with one of the writers on that show on a few different things he had worked on, and some of the things I had worked on with him, the characters were all kind of written the same way. You can look at a movie in the '80s and know that anybody who's got a little bit of weight to him is going to be eating. There's always going to be a nerdy character in there somewhere. They always try to fit in the stereotypes, whereas now those stereotypes have really been bled out. Even if the stereotypes show up or people that might represent that stereotype, whatever's on TV now definitely breaks those boundaries and allows us to dig deeper. It's more than looking at the surface of somebody; we're really getting into who that person is now, and that's something they really didn't explore back then. It's just the nature of Hollywood.

You played a bully in "Beethoven's 2nd," the voice of the bully in "Why, Charlie Brown, Why?" and Bugs Meany in "Encyclopedia Brown," who I believe was a strong character too. Did you feel like you were trying to reverse the perception of you by pursuing parts that were the opposite of Alan?

No, if you look at the characters I played … at a very young age I wasn't at the level in the industry where I could go out and request parts. The parts I was sent out on were best friends, bullies, nerds. Never the leading guy because I was always a little overweight. That's different now; now someone that's carrying some extra poundage can be the leading man. They didn't do that back then. So I was always the friend or the nerd or the bully. I got used to playing those characters, and it became easy. It's not hard to be a jerk if you're getting paid to do it. [Laughs.]

Why do you think Alan has become such a beloved character?

I think Alan just strikes a chord with everybody's subconscious. Alan loves to eat. Everybody loves to eat, so when you see someone not afraid to dig in and they got a big ol' belly on them, it kind of makes you feel comfortable with yourself too.

If someone doesn't speak up about cake, maybe there won't be cake, and everyone will be unhappy.

That's right! See, someone's gotta say something about it. It'll just be me.

Sometimes people are cast to play versions of themselves. When you say that wasn't you, were you unusually confident at 12 and 13 in real life, like the Stefan Urkel to Alan's Steve Urkel?

Never afraid to embarrass myself. That's the best way to put it. My whole life I've never been afraid to embarrass myself. I don't mind getting on stage. I don't mind singing a song. I don't mind dancing. I like being in front of people. I like that reaction that I get. In high school I was on a dance crew; there were 30 girls and two guys on the crew. It wasn't a real popular thing for guys to do, but it was something that I did. I've always been used to being on stage. I've always been a performer. Even with my career now, when I'm sitting with a client, it's definitely a dance that we do. It's not a one-off sale. So it's nice to be able to work with people and be able to engage. Being in front of people drives me. So this whole quarantine is murder on my soul.

Jennifer Blanc-Biehn aka Melissa in "Teen Line"

"Saved by the Bell" periodically attempted to make statements about important issues, and the show usually bungled these messages partially or entirely. An exception, though, is "Teen Line," in which Zack feels extremely uncomfortable around Melissa (Jennifer Blanc-Biehn), a fellow Bayside student who uses a wheelchair. Thanks to Blanc-Biehn's strong performance and lines like, "Don't treat me like I'm broken," the episode makes effective strides in helping young viewers understand that just because someone's circumstances may be different, it doesn't mean they should be treated differently.

Blanc-Biehn ("Party of Five," "It's Always Sunny in Philadelphia") and I spoke for close to an hour while her husband, Michael Biehn ("The Terminator," "Aliens," "Tombstone"), watched their five-year-old son and eventually yelled that our interview was longer than his wife's "Saved by the Bell" episode. (Accurate.) Oh, and a side note that Blanc-Biehn talked about sometimes going out and doing karaoke with Dennis Haskins, which is a fun image. And Leah Remini taking her to the Scientology Celebrity Center, an image that's somewhat less enjoyable. And the idea of a "Saved by the Bell"-only convention featuring both main and supporting characters, which is a great idea and needs to happen.

What do you remember about your episode? What stories come to mind when you think about it?

First of all, I knew it was a popular show, but at the time it was a daytime show. Right now, there's not any stigma that separates shows from anything; back then there were TV actors [and] movie actors. They hadn't quite started to blend yet. So while I knew it was really popular and I was excited, it was just a different kind of show for me than I had ever experienced before. I don't think it had the respect that it should've had back then, that it has now, oddly. Then when I got there, what struck me the most was everybody there was so nice. So fun. So friendly. I was just really excited to be guest-starring on a show that popular because when I got there, I started realizing it was really popular even back then. I don't think any of us at that time really thought this was really politically incorrect. We thought exactly what it was supposed to be: that Zack was just making mistake after mistake. But I think as it ages it gets funnier and funnier. The wheelchair thing wasn't really something that was popping out in my head at that point. I was just really excited to be there. I really liked my dressing room at NBC. [Laughs] I was so young, and I moved here from New York to do a Kenny Ortega series called "Hull High" that I had gotten when I was here for pilot season. Then I got this shortly after that was canceled, so it was a big deal. I had come from theater in New York, so all of it was overwhelming and a big deal for me at that time.

You mentioned how nice everyone seemed. Without suggesting it wasn't that way on anything you'd done before then, compared to "Married with Children" or "Beverly Hills, 90210," did "Saved by the Bell" feel different because it skewed younger?

Well, until I did "Friends 'Til the End" later with Shannon [Doherty], then I had a very different experience with all the "90210" people. I'd done five movies with them. I ended up friends with so many people from that show, and I knew Gabrielle [Carteris] from New York, and she used to work at my manager's and all this stuff. "90210" was for me a traumatizing experience. I guest-starred, and I went home crying in hysterics because the director at the time – I came from theater and I had to learn to pull it back, and I guess I was pulling it back too much. And instead of taking me aside and trying to help me, she would yell things at me in front of all the extras and the entire cast. I was just horrified and traumatized and went more inside myself. The "90210" experience was so traumatizing for me. I know you would never know it by the little [guest-starring role]. So that was that, and anything was going to be better than that. And then "Married with Children," I had a great time. I got along with everyone really well; Christina Applegate and I went out for lunch, and everybody was welcoming. But they were more established, and they were so famous at that time that there definitely was this feeling of, "Well, you're the guest star, and we are a family." Even though they were very welcoming on that show, so it was not an issue at all, but I knew I was going after that. With regard to "Saved by the Bell," I literally have no other memory but feeling so comfortable there. Like I could've stayed. It would've been nice if Melissa was back in some sort of wrap-up episode. But I really could've stayed there and had that be my family. They were really, really great. And maybe I wasn't getting all of it, I have no idea. I ended up knowing Elizabeth outside of there later on and was there when she met her husband. We took some dance classes together and have a mutual friend that did a movie with her. I was literally there the day she met her husband. Mark-Paul, we've had a couple of run-ins with each other at events, and he's just a sweetheart of a person. And Mario and I were in acting class together for quite a while, so we're friendly. But it was all separate from what I had done on the show. But I found the people involved with that show to have been really nice and welcoming and loving. If there was other stuff that went on, I certainly didn't feel it when I was there. A lot of times when you're a guest star, you go there and you feel like, "This is their show, and I'm just here." It sort of feeds into every insecurity an actor might have at that time in your life. I've gotten better at that as an adult, coming into situations. As a 17-, 18-year-old, it's a lot harder to deal with of course. They certainly made me feel comfortable. Back then, I was so involved with doing my homework on projects. I probably also stayed in my room obsessively making sure I knew my lines so I was not the one to mess up. [Laughs] Whereas later on I got a little more comfortable with messing up here and there. If that happens you can always come back from that. Especially now with digital.

The episode stands out in that it's one of the few aiming to teach a lesson that actually strikes the right tone, like when Melissa says things like, "Don't treat me

like I'm broken" and Tori tells Zack, "Maybe she'd rather be your friend than your cause."

I'm glad that you think that. I thought that too because on the other side of whatever he's doing that's inappropriate, there are people that are seeing that and saying, "Hey, I'm just a teenage girl with the same feelings." And what I liked was every time he did something that was a little bit like, "Really?" that was her reaction. Instead of curling up in a ball and crying, she got exasperated. It was more like "What? Why would you do that?" And finally a confrontation and the victory. But I think that when they made that Funny or Die thing, "Zack Morris is Trash," where they pinpointed a lot of the complete inappropriateness of it, I was on the floor hysterically laughing when I was [watching] it. And it made me think, "Oh yeah, it was really inappropriate." I hadn't until that time really thought that. So it's nice to hear the other side of it and that you think it was a little bit more appropriate with getting their message across than some of the other episodes.

How would you describe Zack's behavior in this episode, and how much more informed would an obnoxious, 18-year-old kid be now?

With the Me Too movement going on now, I think there might have been a bigger problem with him setting up a date with somebody that he met on a help line. So that probably wouldn't fly. Or it would have to be addressed a little bit more than it was, instead of like, "Oh, Zack, you shouldn't have done that, you silly guy." I don't know – because I'm so far removed from high school times, but this is such a different environment, especially in the last year – how that would've worked. With Donald Trump as president, we've got a president who has now made fun of people with disabilities. So I'm not sure where this would fit in. Would it be appropriate or not be appropriate? [Zack] clearly still went on dates with her, and once he realized she was in the wheelchair he was totally uncomfortable with it. I think that addressing that uncomfortability was good because it made us all realize that we're all really the same. I'm not sure. It might even work nowadays because we've got such a weird thing going on out there where we've got the Me Too movement and a president that can pretty much do anything in my opinion, and there's no shame at all. This episode, I kind of think it could work still [Laughs], especially with the environment that's going on now. Maybe a few more things touching on, because it was for kids, matters like respect.

Yeah – there's definitely value in helping break through discomfort that comes from lack of experience. It's also been notable to identify that when Zack dates someone who is different from who he expects or is comfortable with – like Melissa or Wendy, who was larger than his usual dates, or Laura, who was homeless – he doesn't kiss those girls. Whereas he kisses every single other girl he dates who gives him the time of day. Did you shoot any more romantic connection, or was anything else ever talked about?

I think that's a really, really great [point] – you're obviously a good reporter. [Laughs] I didn't ever really think about it. I don't remember that being in the script, so that was probably more of a network choice, which is my guess. It's a total guess because you're bringing it up. That's interesting. That anything that was normal and streamlined for him was OK to be romantic, but the others were not. No, we didn't shoot anything like that, and I never thought of that or knew that. There was a part of me that thought maybe once he realized Melissa was in a wheelchair it was going to be too hard for somebody like Zack to really be in a relationship even though he was trying to date her, but that was just specific to that episode for me. That's interesting that if somebody's not the perfect – what about, did he date Leah Remini's character on there, were they dating?

Yes, he did.

They dated, OK. Leah and I also did a play together after we had both been on there, so we had talked about it, but I didn't know much about that. Leah's kind of an offbeat sort of girl, kind of tough cookie, but I don't know if she played that; I don't think she did on that show. [Editor's note: She did.] But, no, I never knew that, and I never thought about it. The romantic part never came up on our episode. It was all seemingly like he was into it, then he met her and was happy for a second, and then when he realized she was in a wheelchair it all spiraled into more of a cause for him than a real relationship.

That is one thing I think maybe would be different if it were made now.

Right. I think as a network I think they would make that choice now. If you look at shows like "This is Us," where the lead in the show who is now a very big star is very heavy. Still very beautiful but very heavy. And whatever the situation is, something different than the quote-unquote norm. And mixed couples and so many things are different now than when we did that. I guess there was kind of a mixed couple in a sense because there was Jessie and [Slater], but not really mixed. [Laughs]

And he treated her so badly.

[Laughs] Right. So it was a stereotype in itself. [Laughs] Oh, god. "Saved by the Bell," it's so interesting to me. I have a lot of credits. I was on "Party of Five," my stuff was written by Susannah Grant – she was the one who wrote "Erin Brockovich." I was on "Dark Angel." I was on so many different things over the years. I had a movie ["Everly"] that came out a couple years ago with Salma Hayek. But the thing I get asked about the most and stopped for the most is my one episode on "Saved by the Bell." I've been stopped at airports with my husband, who was the star of "The Terminator" and "Aliens," and we think they're stopping us for him, and it's about "Saved by the Bell." It's sort of a mind-boggling show because the popularity is insane. [Laughs] That's one episode. Imagine what Mark-Paul is going through his entire life. [Laughs]

What's the airport story?

I was ready to be like, "Yep, Michael from 'Aliens.'" We both were ready. "Hi, do you want a picture?" Just because we had come from something where we had been bombarded, so we were just ready for it. And they turn, "No, we know you from 'Saved by the Bell,' you were Melissa. Can we take a picture with you?" And Michael just said, "Oh, OK," and walked away. We were both dumbfounded, but I think he more than I was like, "What?!" And it's happened a few times, so he's gotten used to it. But the first time, he was a little like "Huh?" I don't think he ever watched "Saved by the Bell," so he was really confused. Then I ended up finding pieces of the episode to show him. It was one of those moments where we started, "Yeah, this is Michael," and they're like, "No, no no. No, no. You. You're Melissa from 'Saved by the Bell.'" I'm like, "What?!" [Laughs] This is not an uncommon thing. He knew my other credits and stuff we had done together. We had never even talked about that credit. So for that to be the thing that gets pinpointed when we're out in a public place together and my hair is a different color now, everything about it was like, "Wow, this really just sticks with you."

Were you ever contacted by an individual with disabilities or an organization representing people with disabilities about the episode?

Shockingly, not that I know of. A lot of times things don't get to me. I think I have been contacted, like fan letters here and there from people who either felt less-than or had something that was maybe not as big a disability as being confined to a wheelchair, and it made them feel better. I've definitely heard that, that the interaction and her being so confident made them feel more normalized. But, no, not as much as I thought I would have. I would have thought at that time, how popular the show was, that they would have wanted me to come out and talk to people. But I might not have been reachable. I might have been doing that show "The Mommies" by then. Who knows? It's so many years ago. But not as much as I thought I would. And I would love even to this day to donate pictures to an organization like that, if I could find some Melissa pictures and sign 'em and donate 'em to an auction that would go to help people with those kinds of disabilities that needed equipment or whatever. I think that's a great idea. But, no, for sure not enough.

Patrick Thomas O'Brien aka Mr. Dewey (4 episodes)

It's almost unthinkable that Patrick O'Brien only appeared in so few episodes of "Saved by the Bell." Mr. Dewey, the hilariously deadpan math teacher who seemed like he wanted to be absolutely anywhere else but Bayside, featured in "The Election," "King of the Hill," "Jessie's Song" and "Screech's Birthday," yet he remains one of the show's most iconic educators. And we're in luck: He's already filmed two episodes of the reboot, while also being written into another episode not yet filmed.

Besides for the "Saved by the Bell," O'Brien has worked with some impressive filmmakers (on the Coen brothers' "Intolerable Cruelty," David Fincher's "The Curious Case of Benjamin Button" and Steven Spielberg's "Catch Me If You Can"), though only on "Win a Date with Tad Hamilton!" did co-stars (such as Topher Grace and Kate Bosworth) show excitement for working alongside Mr. Dewey. Now producing some theater and creating his own one-man show in Minneapolis, O'Brien is a wild ride in conversation, and also noted this about Zack Morris: "It was odd for a protagonist of a show to be that much of an asshole."

Do you remember what they were looking for in terms of Mr. Dewey's character?

Well, from the script I thought it was pretty obvious it was a take-off from what's his name in "Ferris Bueller's Day Off." I'm blanking on the guy's name. You know who I mean, the boring teacher in "Ferris Bueller"?

Ben Stein.

Ben Stein, thank you. And I had done characters like that before – boring, lackluster people, so I said, "Yeah, that's in my wheelhouse." I don't know if in the breakdown, in the character description, it actually said a "Ben Stein type." Because it's kind of interesting: He's kind of a dick. Or he was really a big dick, actually. There was a time that they'd put a "Ben Stein type" or a "Wally Cox type," and [Ben Stein] didn't like that. And he actually sued some casting director to get them to stop using "Ben Stein type." He wanted to be paid for it or something. So there's just a little side note.

I didn't know you could sue someone for being inspired by your work.

[Laughs] Why would they want to? It's an honor! It shows you have reached a certain level of notoriety. He's an attorney. So actually maybe he's looking for more notoriety or more attention or something by attempting to sue someone for it.

Of your four episodes, "Jessie's Song" is the one that's become legendary. Why do you think that happened?

The most famous – or infamous, as the case may be, depending on your point of view. I don't know that much about the whole series, but wasn't it their first attempt at the "very special episode" where a comedy takes on a serious subject? I think it was the first try at that, so I think that's why it probably sticks out quite a bit. And I don't know if it was successful or not. [Laughs] I'm sure it probably went a little too far in the "I'm so excited!" scene. I assume that's why it's the most memorable.

What do you mean "went too far"?

A little too melodramatic. I don't know. Isn't that how it's looked upon in retrospect?

It's definitely the moment that stands out the most for people. Do you think the caffeine pill addiction that Jessie experienced said more about her as a student or Mr. Dewey as a teacher?

[Laughs] I think considering the level of the backlash, I'd have to put it on Jessie as more of a reflection of her obsession than Mr. Dewey's cracking the whip. I don't think he was too much of an overbearing teacher.

Do you think if he had been more emotionally available Jessie would have made any different decisions?

[Laughs] Analyzing this as if it were Shakespeare. If I had been more open to having my classroom door open to after-hours tutoring … that just didn't come up in the script. I don't know if that backstory would be essential for consideration. [Laughs] Very possible though.

Part of what makes that episode interesting also is that Jessie, Kelly and Lisa form a pop singing group called Hot Sundae and seem to have the inside track to a long career in music that gets derailed because of the caffeine pills. Do you think the episode is a more accurate portrait of the music industry or addiction?

Well, I'd have to think neither. [Laughs] And another thing about the episode would be that they chose caffeine pills – probably the most innocuous thing to get addicted to – is in and of itself kind of humorous. They wanted to tread gently in their first attempt at tackling a serious subject. Although they did have smoking weed in various episodes, didn't they? Or at least one. Who was it, some singer who came to school and tried to get the gang to smoke?

It was an actor.

The only reason I know about that episode is I'm living in Minneapolis now. I've been back here for 13 years, and when I came back here there's a website where you check for auditions, and [I saw] "Holy shit, they're auditioning for 'Saved by the Bell.'" They were doing a staged version of "Saved by the Bell" at this little theater, and they were looking for a Mr. Dewey, it just so happened. Because they'd been doing it for years, and their Mr. Dewey left for Los Angeles. We crossed paths, I guess, when I came back here. And they would always do "Jessie's Song" for one show, and they would intersperse commercials from the era – it was a loving spoof of the show – but then also do one other episode that had particular appeal. And that episode with the smoking weed ("No Hope with Dope") was also used on one of the runs that they had.

So did you audition for Mr. Dewey again?

Sort of, yeah. I showed up. Of course there were a lot of dropped jaws when I walked in. I was just going to do it as a joke. I wasn't really thinking about actually doing it. But they were such nice people; they really were. And they loved the show, and I was like, "Oh, hell, how can I refuse?" And we tried to fly under the radar. They didn't have a budget, so wouldn't have to get actors' equity involved. But it was fun. It was a really nice group of people … They would do it for a couple weeks and then take off for a year and come back and do it again later. It was five or six different little runs they had. Always doing "Jessie's Song" and then one other episode. There were always two different episodes for each run that they did.

Did the audience go crazy when the real Mr. Dewey showed up?

Yes, they did. [Laughs] Definitely an ego trip. And the other ego trip [was going to Saved by the Max in Chicago]. I was down there three different times, I guess. Made the old appearance, and it's an ego trip to have these 30-somethings oohing and aahing and wanting to have their picture taken with the Dew-man.

Do you remember anything someone did or said?

There was another incident. Dennis Haskins came to town once. There was this bar downtown that was doing a '90s night. He came in to MC it. They had a "Saved by the Bell" look-alike [contest]. It was Halloween, as a matter of fact, so it tied in with the costumes and Halloween and the '90s. We happened to be running one of the shows for the staged "Saved by the Bell" thing, so we all went down there, so I hobnobbed with Dennis. We played cards a couple times; I'd see him at auditions in L.A., so we got to know each other a little bit outside of doing "Saved by the Bell." People are getting drunk, and one gal, she wanted me to autograph her ass, which I did. There's a picture on the internet of me doing that. You can probably Google that and come up with it. The one of me autographing the top of her breast, I don't think that ever made it to the internet. So there's that.

When you think about Zack's behavior, what do you make of him as a person?

[Laughs] Well, yeah, there's a lot of really good-looking guys that get away with a lot of shit. You gotta put him in that category … I mean, he's not always an asshole, obviously. Sometimes he's a wonderful guy. Am I correct, or am I wrong about that?

Well, there's the cliché about the broken clock.

Yeah. I remember when I was a kid, I was into pro wrestling. And there was this bad guy, the Crusher. And for the longest time, he was the ultimate bad guy. And then all of a sudden, I can't remember what the thing was, but he turned into a good guy. And then he was more popular after that transition than the ultimate good guy was. Everybody just loved the Crusher then, being the bad guy going to the good guy. I guess there's something about that parable – I'm not religious, but the parable of the prodigal son, of the bad guy coming back and turning his life around, that really resonates with humanity. I don't know if that applies. Like I said, I don't know the series very well. Does that sound plausible to you that that could be something going on in people's heads?

In the sense that when someone does bad things it oddly makes people want to root for them to get better?

No, that once they do get better, they are really, really adored. More so than just the guy who is always a nice guy. Someone who can transform their life is revered sometimes more than the person who has led a good life from the beginning.

Then by having each episode be a mini version of that it hooks people in, even though he goes back to being a bad person at the beginning of the next episode?

Does that work? I don't know. You know "Saved by the Bell" better than I do, but that's what I'm going for. It's just a hypothesis. I can't give you any supporting evidence there.

What do you think Mr. Dewey's "American Gladiators" name would have been if he got the job after his tryout?

[Laughs] Do you know Wally Cox? How old are you?

37.

You're too young for Wally Cox. OK, this kind of ties in with Ben Stein. When I was just starting off in the biz, I'd get calls from my agent saying they were looking for a "Wally Cox type." And whenever they'd say that, I'd go "ch-ching." Because I look a lot like Wally Cox. He was an actor back in the '50s. He was a teacher; he had this series called "Mister Peepers," and he was a junior high or high school teacher. We look alike. Look him up on the internet. He was one of the regulars on ["Hollywood Squares"]. He was a little wimpy, milquetoast guy, but he was roommates in New York, when they were in acting school, with

Marlon Brando. And oddly enough, Wally Cox rode a motorcycle and wore leather, whereas Brando would dress in cardigan sweaters. So they had this off-stage persona that was opposite of their onscreen persona. Anyway, Wally Cox. How did we get onto Wally Cox?

Are you suggesting Mr. Dewey's gladiator name would be Wally Cox?

I was thinking "Wally Cock" or something. That was going to be my porn name, Wally Cock.

Do you think math gets a bad rap as being boring?

I have to admit I did not excel in math. I did OK until calculus, and then I was just lost. I don't think it gets a bad rap, but it definitely has that rap. You have to have the right kind of mind to appreciate math. One of the reasons I went into the arts, I think, was I was not strong at science. But I have a 15-year-old who, just today with his distance learning, announced that he got 100 on his math test. He was pretty thrilled at that. He said that bumps him up to a strong B+, so he's shooting for an A- with the final coming up next week. Maybe it's not too genetic.

He hasn't been looking for help from you because of your role?

No. Interestingly enough, my wife was really bad at math. She just had this blockage. But she loves to go to school, and she was going for her nursing degree, and you had to have good, solid math. And finally she had this breakthrough. She had this one teacher who helped her and broke through that blockage that she had, and now she's pretty damn good at math. She's the go-to person in the house if our son has a math problem. But now he's pretty much gone past where she left off or what she can remember of her math classes. You can get through that blockage if you work at it. Or some people can, anyway.

So if I need someone to check the math on my statistical analysis I'd be better off talking to Mr. Dewey's wife than Mr. Dewey?

Yes, yes. Most definitely.

George McDaniel aka David Spano in the two-part "Palm Springs Weekend"

"Saved by the Bell" loved to spend an episode here and there with the main characters' family members and then go back to ignoring their existence entirely. That is certainly the case with David Spano (George McDaniel), Jessie's father who's suddenly getting married to a much-younger aerobics instructor named Leslie (Barbra Brighton), leading to a two-part episode in which the gang attends the wedding while Jessie tries to break it up, Kelly and Zack rekindle their relationship and Slater dates a princess (Eva Loseth).

McDaniel, a veteran theater and TV actor ("All My Children," "Three's Company," "Law and Order," "Beverly Hills, 90210") who is now mostly focusing on theater and also recently auditioned for "The Young and the Restless," says he doesn't think David knew that Zack initially tried to pick up Leslie – but even if he did, he wouldn't have minded. "Obviously, his fiancée is a very attractive younger woman, and he's not surprised a younger person would want to approach her," he said. "I think he's a bit wiser than that. I don't think he'd bother saying anything to Zack about it."

Also, McDaniel was the right choice for David Spano for reasons it seems producers didn't even know: At the time he was married to a woman 13 years his junior.

When you think about the episodes that you did, what do you think about? What stories come to mind?

I remember Elizabeth most of all. We developed a lovely relationship in that week we shot it in Palm Desert at that beautiful hotel out there. Zack and everybody else, we hung out quite a bit together. Hot tubs and things like that because we were all there for a week. One of my favorite memories was that scene between Elizabeth and I where we confront one another. I don't know what I was expecting, but she was terrific in the scene, and I thought that it went really well.

Do you remember your audition or what they were looking for?

[Laughs] It was a very interesting situation. A year before I had done a production of "A Funny Thing Happened on the Way to the Forum" with Ernie Sabella playing Pseudolous, and I played Gloriosus. And we became good friends, hung out, had dinners together and stuff. I was up for this show, and I was waiting to hear about it, and I called my agent and I said, "What's going on with this? Am I doing this?" He said, "They're just a little uncertain." I said, "OK. Let me see if I can do something on this end." Ernie had done a six-episode [arc for the Malibu Sands Beach club episodes as Leon Carosi]. I called up Ernie and said, "What's the deal over there? They're kind of dragging their feet on whether they're going to hire me or not." He said, "Let me call you back." And so he called me back about 15 minutes later and said, "I talked to them and told them how good you were, and I think everything's going to be fine." So I owe that job to Ernie Sabella.

Do you have any sense of why they were waffling about you before that?

I don't know exactly. At that point most of my television work had been playing bad guys. The bad guy was always the second-best part on the series. I'd done a lot of that, and I think that was their reluctance because it was an afternoon show for kids, and there I was playing a guy selling babies and stuff. I did a lot of bad.

Meanwhile, Zack is usually terrible, but during your two episodes he only lied once.

I remember that! I'd watched it a little bit before I did it and thought, "He's awfully nice in this. He hasn't done anything that might be taken as disturbing." [Mark-Paul Gosselaar] was a terrific kid and has had success since then because he's a wonderful actor.

So you were aware this wasn't the Zack Morris people were used to?

Well, I wasn't that aware. Everyone on the show had their own take on everything that was going on, and they weren't reluctant to share it with you. I think one of the gals said, "Watch out for Zack; you never know what he's going to do." And in [those] particular [episodes], he was just fine.

How would you characterize the way David deals with Jessie? He's happy to have her there, but the kids are still in high school, and David and Leslie lay it on pretty thick. There's the moment Leslie tells David, "I think older men are very sexy." Do you think David is respectful to Jessie? Is there anything he shouldn't have done?

That's a really good question. Because they're all there for this wedding they're about to have, I think that's the biggest concern on his mind. I think he's surprised to learn Jessie's so upset about it. That's when he starts trying to reason with her. Although he knows it's thin ice he's on anyway because of the big age difference. I know this from having been married to two women who were considerably younger than I. So I have experience in this regard, and a daughter as well.

Did that happen before making this episode or after?

I was living with my second wife at the time in Topanga. I met her in '74 I believe. That would have made me 32 at the time, and she was 19. There were a lot of my friends saying, "George, the cradle is empty now." We were together 20-some-odd-years and married for 14. It was something that I was aware of, and she was very funny about it. She said, "You don't have to even do any research. You know what it's like marrying a woman considerably younger."

So from your own experience, what would you advise to David and Leslie?

Just listen to one another. And understand that these things can be potential problems and work hard to meet them head-on. At the time, because Elizabeth and I were getting to know one another and we were talking quite a bit, I let her know early on. I said, "Look, I know something about this because my wife is considerably younger than I. So I know there can be problems, but they're all surmountable problems." I let it go at that, and a few days later Elizabeth came to me and said, "I've been thinking about what you said, and I have a boyfriend who's considerably older than I am. Is it OK if I tell my mom and dad about your experience with your wife?" I said, "Please do. If it'll help you, if it'll relax things. But you're young; you may make other choices in the next year or so." So we really had kind of a father/daughter relationship during that period.

Susan Beaubian aka Dr. Judy Turtle in "Operation Zack" and "Drinking and Driving"

In just two episodes, we feel like we know Dr. Judy Turtle (Susan Beaubian). In "Operation Zack," the surgeon is both authoritative and comforting at the hospital, helping Zack calm down about his impending knee surgery while ensuring that her daughter, Lisa, actually works in her role as a candy striper. In "Drinking and Driving," she's incredibly supportive toward Lisa's bid for homecoming queen and even more disappointed when she finds out about the gang's lies and poor judgment. Though this is all we ever see of Dr. Turtle, she really does seem like Lisa's mom (even if her daughter still has much to learn).

A lot of credit for this should go to Beaubian ("American Crime Story," "Insecure," "The Naked Gun"), who in fact found out she was pregnant with her daughter just before shooting "Operation Zack." "It was really a double layer of an acting exercise," said the actress, who still auditions and acts periodically while also working on screenwriting. "Having that energy, those hormones and that knowledge that I'm soon to be a mother myself, it stimulated my imagination, I think, and my willingness to reach out toward Lark and go for it a little more. With all the kids it heightened my sensitivity and sensibilities about interpersonal relationships and parent-child relationships. And in the second episode my daughter had been born, so I actually was a mother."

[P.S. Beaubian also told me that she wore the same wig to play O.J. Simpson's character's wife in "The Naked Gun" and to play the foreman of the jury for O.J.'s murder trial in "American Crime Story," which is awesome: "I went and auditioned, and I mentioned to the casting director, I said, 'Fun fact: This wig has actually met O.J. Simpson.' They said, 'Really?!' I said, 'Yes, actually, when I played his wife in 'The Naked Gun,' I wore this wig.' And they were like, 'Oh, if you get the job you've gotta tell everybody!' … Well, my wig became a celebrity on the set. When I would be in the hair and makeup trailer, people would come in and they would go, 'Oh, is this the wig?' [Laughs] I'd be like, 'This is the wig.' 'O.J. knows this wig, huh?' 'Yeah, this wig has met O.J. Simpson.'"]

When you think about doing these two episodes, what sticks out in your memory most strongly?

It was eye-opening for me. The first episode I did of "Saved by the Bell" was very early on in my career of doing television. I had just recently, within a year or so, moved to Los Angeles from New York, where I was doing mostly theater. So being on a soundstage for television, it wasn't exactly my comfort zone. If you put me in a theater, I'm good to go. But on a soundstage at that time, I didn't really have my bearings. I remember walking in the first day for the table read to meet everyone, and I really didn't know anything about the show. When I walked in and there were all these young people sitting around the table, I felt like I had walked into a clubhouse. Everybody was so relaxed, and everybody was so beautiful to look at [Laughs] and so professional, and they just welcomed me with open arms. I was totally struck by Lark, how beautiful she was. I was like, "They hired me to play her mother?!" [Laughs] It was like, "Wow." And everybody was so inclusive and welcoming and kind and professional. It was just like, "Wow, if this is what TV is like, give me more." I was very happy to do it. It was the professionalism of the kids and how relaxed they were with the table read that set the tone for me. So I knew it wasn't the same kind of energy that it was in theater … It was kind of a quick study in television acting for me, and I had the most amazing, young, talented kids to teach me. So it was really fun.

Lisa's being raised in a great household with two doctor parents, and Judy seems like an excellent mom. I hope it won't offend you as her TV mom to say that Lisa isn't a great person. She's extremely shallow, superficial and self-involved.

Oh, she's a little princess, yeah.

What do you make of how much Lisa seems not to have gotten from her parents yet, in that she's such a princess and needs to be pushed in the direction of helping people?

Well, I chalk it up to high school. I chalk it up to her age. I chalk it up to her privilege. I can't tell you in real life how many – because now, as a matter of fact, in the last 20 years or so, I've taught voice to high school kids, and I've had a lot of kids who have come through my lessons who are beautiful young high school girls with talent that, you know, may be a little bit shallow. [Laughs] And they want what they want, and I would just chalk it up to her being immature. As Lisa's mom, I would say that I would have faith in her that as she grows up, as she matures, that all those qualities that we tried to instill in her will come to the front. But right now, she's a little bit selfish, a little bit shallow, a little bit spoiled.

That's a very positive, supportive, parental perspective.

That was good, huh? [Laughs]

Yeah, you're modeling the behavior you want to see in your daughter.

Right, right. You asked me as Dr. Turtle, I'm answering as Dr. Turtle. [Laughs]

In the two episodes you did, Zack is a scared kid in very different ways. How would you describe what Zack Morris does and the person he is?

I think in the first episode, it was really part of my character's job to expose the vulnerable side of Zack. Because he was trying to play it off, but as his doctor and having had many patients come through there, I knew what they were going through, even if he was trying to play it off as if he wasn't scared. I think my character was able, without embarrassing him, just to sensitively handle and let him know, "It's going to be OK. I'm here for you. I know you're scared, but it's going to be OK." ... We had that moment in his room where he was really afraid, and I helped him out there. I think for the audience maybe – I didn't watch the entire series, so I don't know if Zack had other moments previous to that in other episodes where this side of him was exposed, but that's kind of what we were working on, just showing his vulnerable side. And in the second episode, I feel like everybody was back to their old tricks.

What do you mean?

Well, what they did with the car and everything and trying to pull off the scam with the car. I just felt like that was not about exposing Zack's vulnerability. That was them just being back up to their old tricks again, trying to pull one over on the parents.

But that's one of the few episodes where – when I watched the series growing up, he seemed like a confident, swaggering guy. Rewatching for the book, and your two episodes being good examples, especially "Drinking and Driving," he just seems like a kid in over his head and not actually confident. Most of the episodes don't teach a good lesson because there aren't big consequences, and Zack isn't that remorseful. But in "Drinking and Driving," the parents are furious, and it's clear the kids were being extremely reckless. I feel like it's one of the few episodes that really lands.

Yeah. Yes. I didn't have a lot of experience in TV comedy at that point. I had a little more by the time I got to the second episode, but I really took the parents being furious in my own interpretation of it. I remember that I was like, "This is serious. This is real." And in some of the takes there were points where I almost took it to the point of drama. [Laughs] Rather than comedy. Forgetting that this was a sitcom. I discussed it with the director, or he discussed it with me, I should say. It was like, "You can pull back. You're angry, but we have to walk that fine line." Because maybe again this is where being a new parent informed my performance in a way that there were a couple of takes where it was like, "OK, let's fine-tune this a little bit because it's getting a little too real." Too demonstrative or too harsh. "Let's pull it back a little bit and remember this is TV. This is a sitcom. We have to walk that fine line."

Can you explain how that was different, those takes that felt too intense?

Well, just that. It's not real complicated. But maybe I was too intense, maybe a little too angry, maybe too much of the anger was on the surface, was showing. It's kind of a fine line between comedy acting and drama acting. It has to be grounded in reality, but there has to be sort of a cap on it in comedy. You have to leave room for the story to move ahead and not get bogged down in the anger of the moment. You have to be willing to let the story move on and pull itself out of that confrontational moment. I don't know if I'm explaining it very well.

Sure. Because even though it's a message episode, it's still a Saturday morning sitcom. It would be different in an hour-long drama where the gang drove drunk and killed someone.

Exactly. It's still a Saturday morning kids' show.

"Saved by the Bell" did a lot of things well, but casting non-white actors wasn't one of them. I don't mean to make you the mouthpiece for race, but the fact is that most of the people on the show were white. Because you've also been on "Insecure," which obviously deals with race, I wanted to ask if you think it was good that "Saved by the Bell" didn't really address race in terms of Lisa being part of the crew, and nothing was ever said about anyone's experience being different. Or in theory would you have liked to see them address the different challenges these friends might have experienced?

I would say that because we're talking about a Saturday morning kids' show, I don't think it really would have been the platform for politicizing or making grave social commentary on the state of racism in the U.S. You've gotta remember this is a totally different time. I always saw the show more like pop culture. And because of that, I think it was a good thing that Lisa was a regular on the show, she had plenty to do, she was very visible, she was very much a part of the crowd, part of the group. That in itself is a commentary on the state of race relations. As a black actor and a black woman in America, I always wish that there were more roles and more role models in television and film for African Americans. But I think that's a cultural thing, and I don't really feel like it was a responsibility of a Saturday morning, silly show about high school kids to take up the mantle of the civil rights movement, so to speak. It would've been a whole different show. I have to give you the caveat of I did not watch the series. I tuned in once or twice, three or four times in between – I watched it one or two times before I did the first show, and then I watched it again a couple of times to see where everybody was before I did the second show, but I didn't follow the series, so I don't know what their over-arching story arc was. There may have been episodes having to do with race that I don't know anything about, so I'm not really that knowledgeable about how they handled issues of race. But I will say that at that time, back in the early '90s, I was glad to see a beautiful, young, black actress in a series regular [role] who wasn't treated with kid gloves or specially or like she was so different because she was black. I was happy to see that. That's the kid that I was when I grew up. I was a minority in a largely white situation, but my parents raised us to just fit in. It's not like, "Oh, you're special, and you have special problems because you're black." That's not the way I was raised. So it wasn't an issue for me seeing Lisa Turtle portrayed that way. And the fact that both of her parents were doctors, positive role models, that's all good to me.

I think those are great points. Not that relationship status was the biggest issue, especially in the context of race, but the fact that they never established a romantic partner for Lisa besides for the guy in the "Wedding in Las Vegas" movie seemed to reinforce her place on the totem pole with the characters. But as you said, it was a different time.

Yeah, yeah. And I understand what you're saying. Let's say if hypothetically they brought in a young, black man who comes to the school and he's the new guy and Lisa falls for him and they become a couple. Then you've got the issue of, "Well, why does he have to be black?" Or, "Did they just bring this guy on just so Lisa Turtle wouldn't be left out?" Then it's like you're sequestering the two black people off, and they have to be a couple. Or you bring a Hispanic guy or an Asian guy or a Caucasian guy and she pairs up with him, then you've got all the flack of an interracial couple on TV. We're still talking the early '90s. Then "Saved by the Bell" becomes groundbreaking. It's a Saturday morning children's show, but it's also groundbreaking in showing an interracial couple. Those are issues I have a feeling the producers probably didn't want to have to deal with.

And there were a few episodes where she dated guys, both of whom were black, and then it just becomes the issue of no continuity, with no one ever sticking around if they weren't part of the main cast, no matter how good the relationship. So at least they tried.

Yeah. They tried. And people can only write what they know. There weren't any black writers on the show, as far as I know. I won't say any more about that. [Laughs]

Andras Jones aka Deke Simmons in "The Showdown"

There is a scene in this "Good Morning, Miss Bliss" episode, the sixth of what became the first season of "Saved by the Bell," that I think stands up to possibly anything else in the entire series. Deke Simmons (Andras Jones) is so used to being mocked for not being able to read that he creates an intimidating persona for himself to reject people before they can reject him. After bringing Screech into the bathroom for a planned fight, Deke confesses his illiteracy, hoping that Screech will laugh and then bring the punishment on himself. But Screech doesn't laugh; he doesn't mock Deke at all. And the older (Jones was 20 when he filmed the episode), larger student no longer wants to fight.

When Deke later goes to Miss Bliss to accept her offer to help him learn to read, it's genuinely moving, and a moment the show didn't achieve particularly often as time went on.

It was fantastic in a much different way to speak with Jones ("A Nightmare on Elm Street 4: The Dream Master"), whose "musical tarot cards" radio show/podcast Radio8Ball has had a guest list that includes John C. Reilly, Viggo Mortensen, Patricia Arquette and "Weird" Al Yankovic, about how impressed he was with Dustin Diamond's talents, his real-life inspirations for Deke and what might have become of the character in the long run. (He also expressed sympathy for Mills having the show taken away from her and how much it meant to him for her to see him as a peer.)

When you think about this experience, what specific memories come to mind?

I've done TV, but it was the only time I did a show that was shot on a soundstage, and it's much more theatrical than almost any other film work. People took it as a joke when they're like, "What's your favorite thing that you've been in?" and I was like, "The episode of 'Good Morning, Miss Bliss.'" It was more gratifying as an actor [than anything else], plus I got to work with Hayley Mills, who's a legend, and this insanely talented kid, playing Screech. I thought he was going to be Haley Joel Osment. Or – why am I forgetting his name? "American Psycho."

Christian Bale.

Yeah. I thought he had the talent to grow up to be one of those people. Obviously things didn't go that way, but the experience of being in the middle – an actor who is trained and knows what he's doing and is working with this very young, untrained but supremely talented actor and getting to work with someone like Hayley Mills, who comes from that lineage, was amazing. And getting to play kind of a fun role. Not funny; the punchline is just sort of how much bigger I am than the kids. But it was a really great experience, honestly … It's just funny that it became one of the things that I'm most recognized for because it's so popular. I grew up on "The Brady Bunch," and I remember people who did one guest star on "The Brady Bunch," but to me, I saw them so many times and I watched that show every day after school for so long, that when I would run into people like that, I'd be like, "Oh my god, you're so and so from 'The Brady Bunch.'" And they're like, "I've done like 50 things since then that are way better than that." [Laughs] But when you get people when they're kids, it lodges in there.

When people recognize you from this, do you have a sense that they expect you to be intimidating like Deke?

I wouldn't say so. It's usually not people recognizing me from being in it. When I work in jobs that are not in the entertainment business – there was like eight years where I was working as a bartender at different bars, and when people who I would work with would find out that I was an actor and they'd look stuff up, the thing that they would always be like "Oh my god!" was "Saved by the Bell." I wonder if I could find the video – I have a friend who's a filmmaker who did a film about me where I'm playing the bartender and I correct him. He's like, "You were in 'Saved by the Bell.'" I'm like, "Actually, it was 'Good Morning Bliss,' which was the first season." And he's like, "None of us care." For the people I'm talking about it's probably more jokey and kitschy, but you can tell it's such a cultural thing that a whole generation grew up on.

Do you remember your audition or what they wanted for Deke?

I met with the director, Gary Shimokawa, and I was sort of on a little roll as far as booking a bunch of stuff. I guess I probably auditioned, but I remember I just came in and he was like, "We really like you, and the joke of it is you're bigger than all of them. I really like the intensity you brought to the thing." I felt very respected as an actor by the way I was brought into it, particularly by the director. If I'd met more guys like him, I would have had a whole different career.

Was there anything from your own life that you pulled from for the character?

I was bullied terribly. So I definitely was channeling guys that I don't particularly like. Maybe that's why those scenes have a little bit more bite because I was definitely Screech a lot more than I was Deke.

Was that from around the same time, the junior high years, that you were drawing from?

Yeah, definitely junior high. Sort of between fifth grade and tenth grade. Yeah, right in that time period.

When you read the script, did that personal connection prompt any thoughts in your mind?

Again, it's a long time ago, so anything I would say I'd be making up. I know how I approach playing a role, and it's a combination of not judging the character and also totally personalizing it. People think I'm joking when I tell them that my favorite work that I did as an actor on film is that, but maybe that's one of the reasons, too. I always say it's because it was pretty much live and I was working with two phenomenally talented people, in my mind. Most of my scenes are with Screech or with Hayley Mills. I call him Screech – Dustin. But on the set, I just called him Screech. Not 100% method actor-y, but that's just how we played. I think it also could be the schoolyard violence that I faced gave that an extra level of intensity that wouldn't be there for someone that was pretending more.

Did you follow the series before or after in any way to note the differences in how the junior high episodes were attuned to the psychology of the kids' experience in ways that didn't continue as time went on?

I must admit I am not a "Saved by the Bell" scholar. I don't know if I would have paid attention to it if I wasn't in it. There's something about where you're in something and then you're not in something – "A Nightmare on Elm Street," I think I may have caught a sneak peek of the fifth one after I got killed in the fourth, but I always tell people, "I'm a method actor, and after I'm dead I wouldn't know what was going on." I think there's something psychologically, like, "OK, I did my part on that show, and unless they ask me back, I'm not going to pay attention to it." [Laughs] Maybe there's something there, a little bit of sour grapes. Also, it was aimed at kids. The style of acting that they do on that show – and not just that show, those sorts of shows – really bugs me. Again, this is from only catching glimpses from other people's TVs because that's really not in my wheelhouse aesthetically. But I have to wonder, and maybe you can tell me this, I have always suspected that that style of acting and the success that the Screech character had, aside from all the other stuff – and I haven't really followed, I just sort of hear "Dustin Diamond's getting in trouble" or people making jokes – I just feel bad because I feel like that style of acting and maybe fame at that age warped something at the time. I mean, I've worked as a manager for actors, and I've encountered a lot of really talented people on their way up. I'm not going to drop names here, but if I was, they're big names of people who I'd see them in acting class or I'd be in an open mic with them and I'd be like, "Holy shit; that's going to be someone." And a lot of times, it has been. And I really thought that was going to be the case for him.

So when you ask about continuing the show, that's one of those things I have had a question about: What if that kid had ended up in Spielberg world instead of the "Saved by the Bell" world? I'm not saying he would have been Christian Bale, but he could have been a Drew Barrymore. He could've been one of those kids that transitioned better to adulthood. There's a part of me that loves acting so much that wonders if that "bad," very demonstrative kind of acting, just has bad mojo. The fake-style acting I think is just bad for the soul, and you don't want to do things that are bad for the soul to young, talented people. You want to give them a little bit better. Maybe you can tell me. I don't know what the story is there. But I will always remember that week as getting to work with two supremely talented actors. One on one side of the career, and one on the other. I was surprised, I guess, that it didn't go that way for him. He acted like an adult. His instrument was strong. He had great timing and was a very sensitive young actor.

That's a big question. The lore of the show is he was much younger than the other stars, and allegedly that had negative psychological impacts of being left out as the years went on. In another interview for this book, someone talked about, as simple and shallow as it may be, that the other actors had physical attributes to rely on that he arguably didn't, and he wound up getting left behind in that way too. [Editor's note: See the Sean Masterson interview toward the end of the book.] You're right, though; when it comes to being a gawky kid, if "Stand By Me" or something had come out a few years later and he found himself in that, maybe things are different.

Yeah, just the kind of people you work with changes the trajectory of your career. And maybe he evolves into being one of those really interesting character actors. A lot of those people have longer, better careers than the good-looking person who has a short run of leading roles and then is associated with a particular time period. I think it would be interesting for you making this book – the thing I'd be interested in reading is something about that. Maybe understanding a little bit about what happened there. I was there before anyone knew anything. It's a great time to be on the show. You're there in that first couple of weeks when everyone's working really hard in the hopes that they get picked up. There's no star egos, everyone has a great attitude and is excited to be there. I just thought, "That kid's going to be a star."

While I wish I could get to the bottom of that, there are a lot of moments in the book where I point out things that were made funny by his good comic timing and instincts as they matched the material. Which isn't necessarily something you hear people raving about a lot when it comes to the series.

Yeah, well, people are bullies. That's also true. He played a character who gets picked on a lot. The show, when I would see it, he ends up being the butt of the joke, which is good for comedy sometimes but ultimately – the week that I was on the set, people did treat me like I was more intimidating because people treat you like what you pretend you are. And if you pretend you are a nerd that people pick on for that many years, I think there are people that just like to pick on Screech. I can't imagine that Deke was such a charismatic character that that's what inspires it, but to the extent that the role would seem like a justification of that, it's the opposite. If it's good, it's because this guy's sort of pathetic and lashing out, and I guess he's a victim too. But none of it's like, "Yay, he terrorized a fellow classmate, that's wonderful!" It's not good. Bullying is bad. I know I'm stepping out on a limb here, but, yeah. Deke Simmons says, "Bullying is very bad. It's my least-favorite thing in the world."

Do you remember anything specific in terms of people treating you like you were intimidating?

No, it's more like just a general thing. I've also played nerds, and when you're on the set and you're playing a nerd, people treat you like a nerd. And when you're playing the romantic lead, people are more likely to treat you like boyfriend material. It's one of those weird things on a set. And also, again, I was much older, and I was taking my role really seriously, so I was sort of standoffish with everyone, kind of, I guess, but Screech. Again, it's trying to remember a long, long time ago, so anything I say I'd probably be just making up.

If you had to speculate about what happened to Deke after the episode ended and in the years that followed, what would you imagine?

Oh, I'm sure he got a job in the Trump administration. He's not very smart, but he knows how to push people around. I guess what I imagine is that he got enough help to get him to the next rung, but – I was going to say for a second, "Oh, he could become president of the United States," but he didn't have the financial backing and the money that Trump has. But I could see him bullying his way into that stratosphere and being the kind of guy who – I don't know. I'm just being flippant. I've never thought about where Deke would end up. [Laughs] I hope he learned to read.

Obviously we're being goofy to speculate about the future of a fictional character, but for what it's worth, my response to that potential trajectory of his life is that part of what I love about the episode is the idea that he just needed a teacher to take interest in him and a kid to not make him a target. Corny or not, I think you come away feeling like Deke is a vulnerable kid, and maybe he won't be such a bully anymore.

Let's game-play this out a little bit because this is a fun game. OK, I'm with you, except that he finally finds one teacher who is going to stand by him, and what happens? They just fire her! And then he's back where he was, and that kid, Screech, he never says hi to me in the hall. I'm invisible. From then on, none of those kids give a fuck about me. I have a feeling he ends up getting his hopes up a little bit but then being brokenhearted and going back to his old ways because once again the system has failed him. Sorry, I know. This is why I'm not a Disney guy. I spent the morning listening to a podcast about Ingmar Bergman's "The Seventh Seal," and that's definitely more my speed.

It's funny because I feel like the result of a show that has so little continuity of characters outside the stars is that I don't imagine the people we no longer see at the school are even there anymore. If Deke was still there but we never see him, that probably would unravel the progress.

Plus, it's even more than that: He's too old to be hanging out with those kids anyway. But they fired the one teacher who made a connection with this kid. I guess she just went back to England? I don't know. "Good Night, Miss Bliss."

I think it was just that Zack, Lisa, Screech and Belding went to California, and Miss Bliss stayed back to help Deke in Indiana.

Oh! OK. You know what? You may have turned me around on this. Let's take it a little bit further just for fun: I can see Miss Bliss and Deke getting together.

Oh, wow!

He was 20 years old. They're studying, she's tutoring him, she misses all the kids that left, I don't know. Sparks fly. I was a good-looking young guy. I could see that happening. Now that's a movie I'd like to [see].

I can't understand why people weren't on board with a kids' show about that.

Yeah, come on! That might've flown in the early '80s, but not by the late '80s.

Julie St. Claire aka Danielle in "Fake IDs"

For an 8-year-old kid watching this episode, no place could look cooler than The Attic, the over-18 club that Zack and co. sneak into using fake IDs, mostly so he can keep up the ruse that he attends USC and is therefore eligible to date fellow Trojan Danielle (Julie St. Claire). And no one could have seemed more worldly than Danielle, what with her being a couple years older and her carefree attitude toward college sweatshirt placement on shoulders.

Via email, St. Claire answered the following while declining to identify what she's doing now or what she'd recommend to people who encounter someone who is charming but full of excuses like Zack. Because what can you do?

What do you remember about this episode? When you think about this experience, what stories come to mind?

The episode was filmed in front of a live audience, and those are the most fun to shoot because of the energy the audience brings. Young girls had made "I [heart] Zack" signs and T-shirts. It was sweet.

Do you remember your audition and what they were looking for in Danielle? Was there anything in particular that stood out, or that changed by the time the episode was shot?

Robin Lippin, the casting director, was a fan and told my agent she was thrilled to have an older role and thought of me. She brought me in to read with the producers and director.

How would you describe Zack's behavior in this episode?

For the time, what seemed like a typical teenage boy.

What do you think Danielle feels about Zack when he makes excuses about why she never sees him on campus? Is she just enamored with him, or do you think she suspects he is deceitful early on?

She is also young, so I don't think she put too much thought into it. I don't recall his exact response, but I assume it made sense to her ... Enamored is a strong word. I'd say that she thought he was cute.

In this episode Zack lies 11 times, which is tied for third-most in the entire series. Does that surprise you, and how, if at all, does that impact your perception of him?

Doesn't surprise me at all. That was his character. There have been many characters who have been/done the same. He's a tad scheme-y, like Eddie Haskell in "Leave it to Beaver" or Jason Bateman's Derek from NBC's "Silver Spoons."

What do you see as the message of this episode?

Don't lie to your parents. They are smart and they will figure it out. OR, like the phone call [Zack's mom] intercepted, karma will get you!

Did you watch the rest of the series? If so, can you name anything you especially liked (and why)? And anything you especially didn't like (and why)?

I didn't. I was much older than the targeted demographic. I was on the NBC soap opera "Santa Barbara" when the show was on the air. From my dressing room at the studio, I could watch the camera feed from their set and would occasionally do that on my down time between scenes. I had no idea what I was watching or what the show was until I booked the episode. So other than "Fake IDs" and the run-throughs I saw from that feed, I didn't see much more.

When was the last time you watched this episode? Has anything changed about the way you perceive anything that happens in it, or the way you look at the Attic? (When I was a kid the Attic looked extremely cool. Now, of course, not as much.)

I haven't seen the episode in at least 20 years. The Attic then seemed like a cool place for college students to hang out. It was the early '90s, so yes, not as cool now.

What do you think would have happened between Zack and Danielle if Zack's mom hadn't shown up? Do you think Jeff and Danielle went on to get together?

They would have danced and had fun for sure! Jeff and Danielle, no.

Greg Kean aka Adam Trask in "Model Students"

"Model Students" is a strange episode. Zack takes over managing the failing school store, hires Screech to secretly photograph the girls in their bathing suits for the purposes of selling a calendar at the store, the no-longer-upset girls are tabbed by photographer Adam Trask (Greg Kean) for a high school fashion spread, and eventually Zack again shows how controlling and selfish he can be by doing any deceitful thing he can to prevent Kelly from acting on the professional modeling opportunity in Paris that Adam presents to her.

The storyline also includes a pivotal scene of Adam firmly identifying how terrible Zack has been, and Kean laughs at the idea that the photographer would take it upon himself to play this role with a high school kid. The actor ("Dead Like Me"), who was 27 when he filmed the episode and has been teaching high school drama and overseeing homeroom in the Vancouver area for the last 10 years while doing some acting here and there, also shared thought-provoking ideas about what Adam might have done differently then and definitely would now in a similar situation.

Do you feel like we're supposed to see Adam as a good guy or a bad guy? How should we feel about this person?

Honest to god, I don't know. I rewatched it maybe four years ago. I teach high school now, and I showed it to my grade-nine homeroom. And they were taken aback [wondering] who is this guy, who he worked for, why he approached them, why he was taking these pictures of girls in bathing suits. The character seemed – certainly I was trying to play him not in any way creepy, but there was something creepy about it. It seems kind of exploitive to be taking pictures of high school girls and having them published. And that they had me play that scene with the Zack character and being the moral conscience or reflecting some kind of moral consciousness that you can't lie to people and expect that your relationships are going to do well. Maybe he was supposed to be a good character. I don't really know.

I do think in that scene he's representing the audience because Zack is being so selfish and dishonest, and when Adam sets him straight viewers probably all say, "Finally."

Yeah, I can understand that. I think there had to be some self-interest. I may be thinking about it from an acting point of view: Why do I care that this kid lied to this other kid? Am I the moral conscience of the community, or is he messing with me? There must have been self-interest. I'm sure I was playing it as, "You did something wrong, but it must have affected me somehow" or something my character had expected to gain from this. But maybe he was the voice of the audience.

To your point about the creepiness, obviously it was a different time, but when your character says "Check out these hot-looking girls," was there ever a point where you cringed while reading or shooting that? Or when you showed it to the students?

Yeah, I think some of my grade-nine female students were looking at it and thinking there was some impropriety in this guy 10 years older than these kids asking them to pose in this way. I think he said, "Make it hot," or I don't know what I was saying. Honest to god, Matt, I do not remember. There are things I've shot that I do not remember entirely having shot them. This one I remember the experience much more so. The guy who produced this, I forget his name, I think he was Christian and came at this from a Christian point of view, or maybe I understood that at the time there was that component to it. I remember the one girl, Lark, did not want to pose in a bathing suit. I think she was a Seventh-day Adventist, and her family was quite – I know there was some rigamarole about that. I think I remember on the set that she was not comfortable with doing it. I understood there was some sensitivity to that as there should have been, but it was a different time. So I don't know. High school girls in bathing suits, would that [happen] now? Taking a calendar? I think it was supposed to have some allure to it. These girls were all 17 years old at the time if I remember correctly. Having met them, they were all not yet 18. Yeah, there was something precarious about it, I guess. But did I think about it much back then? Honestly, I don't know. [Editor's note: The episode aired in late 1990, at which point Berkley was 18, and Thiessen and Voorhies were both 16. I don't know when the episode was filmed.]

Do you think it was ethical for Adam to move forward with the photo shoot with the girls after he found out the calendar was made against their will, even if they're in favor of being shot by him?

That's a good question, Matt. Probably not. Probably not. Certainly now one would say, oh my goodness, the kid should be punished, the guy should walk away. And say, "Listen, I'm so sorry to have bothered you; I did not understand that these were taken surreptitiously. I thought that everybody was on board, and now that I've discovered that this has happened this way, this is not something I can be party to," and walk away. And then of course there would be no episode. [Laughs] But I think you're absolutely right. If you think about it in context of what we know now or perhaps what we should have known then, moral behavior, then this guy should not in any way have ever been party to that.

How would you describe Zack's behavior in this episode, the way he's conniving to stand in the way of Kelly's opportunity?

My recollection of that, and again I don't think I did a deep text analysis of the work, but the character seemed like he was acting like a jerk. He was acting selfish, narcissistic. He wasn't trusting; he was untrustworthy. I guess the one thing I remember about the tone of that scene at the end was I felt I had to play it from righteous moral ground. That I had perceived something that definitely was shitty behavior, and I had the capacity to correct it in a way. I think I probably borrowed from my dad, which I did a lot as a younger actor, how he might've addressed a certain situation from a high moral ground. So I guess that if I think back to the acting choices I made in that scene, it was based on the fact that Zack Morris was acting like a dick.

Can I ask what you did that prompted your dad to talk to you in that manner?

Oh my gosh, what didn't I do. Uh, I can't think of anything specific about growing up, but I know frankly that my dad showed up a lot in my early work as an actor because he had a pretty strong personality, and I felt more paternal in that [scene]. If I'm thinking about the choices I made too, it probably wasn't as much to punish but as to teach. Like, "Hey, buddy, you fucked up, so listen here's what I'm going to share with you and maybe you can do better next time." [That] was more along the lines of what I played rather than just, "You fucked up, and you need to know that you're morally compromised."

That's a good distinction.

Yeah. You want to be as specific as possible. And my recollection would be that, given what I perceived to be the tenor of the show at the time, that was probably the more appropriate choice. If in fact that's what I did; I have no idea.

When you showed it to your students, you alluded to female students sensing impropriety. Do you remember anything specific anyone said?

This is a fairly insulated school. It's a smaller, private school, so these kids, it's not like a public-school situation where you might expect people to be less conservative, more worldly. I think they really sensed the character was kind of creepy and this was inappropriate for me to be telling the girls to be posing in these particular ways. I can't remember the specific things they said, Matt, but I remember my defense was, "This was meant for kids to watch on Saturday morning, so if you find it inappropriate, I get it. I'm watching it now too going, 'Yeah, maybe it is inappropriate.'"

You're right, but there's an irony to that defense. Did they say, "Now that you mention it was for kids, now I feel better"?

No, no, they didn't. They questioned the world around them more than my defense about it. [Laughs] Watching it through their eyes, I'm going – times certainly have changed. This was put on Saturday morning television, and there were no special interest groups taking particular umbrage. And like I said, it was produced by somebody who I understood to have been a fundamentalist Christian. [The students] were completely right. I don't even know what my decision was to show it to them. I was just bored; I had nothing else to do in homeroom, and I was like, "Hey, look what I was doing 30 years ago. This is interesting; have you guys ever seen or heard of this particular show?" I always think maybe they'd be interested in some of my work over the course of my 25-year career, but, honestly, they're not. [Laughs] They never have been. Once in a while I'll go, "Take a look at this stuff that I did," and then they're just back on their phone. They moralized about it, it didn't seem too impressive to them, they thought it was a little creepy, and then they were moving on to their first-block class. So I think that that generation is not under the influence of "Saved by the Bell" as previous generations have been.

Larry Cedar aka Steven Jameson in "Mystery Weekend"

In this unique and classic episode, the gang's excursion into a murder mystery game (thanks to Lisa winning the outing in a radio contest) exists completely outside of Bayside, one of very few times the gang is seen hanging out together separately from anything happening at school, the beach club or a family-related event. It's also notable because Zack doesn't lie at all, even when he is wrongly accused of murder, and because the episode is fun and silly in a way that a lot of the others struggled to achieve.

Larry Cedar, who plays mansion host Steven Jameson, is an anomaly as well in that he hasn't been recognized for his role at all – which he thinks could be because he has a mustache in the first part of the episode and (spoiler alert, I guess) dresses up as a woman in the second half as Jameson, the actual killer in the game, pretends to be a female detective. It could also be because Cedar ("Deadwood," "Trial & Error," "Mad Men," "Grey's Anatomy") has had a long and varied career, including a recent appearance in the new "The Call of the Wild" with Harrison Ford.

Do you remember how you got involved with this episode?

When was that shot – it was 1991, wow. That was almost 30 years ago. It was probably just an audition like any other audition. A lot of auditions I remember; this one I don't really remember. I remember them being super nice. The first thing I think when I go back on this job, because you remember every job a little differently, everybody involved, from the director to the producers to the cast, was so freaking friendly. It was like a party. I didn't know anything about the show at all. I was not aware of it. I'd heard something about it vaguely, and I knew it was kind of popular, but I had no idea that it had almost like a cult status. When I came onto the show, I was aware that they hadn't been shooting for a while. It had been on hiatus, and this was the first episode back. So at the first rehearsal, everyone was talking about how they were, what they had been doing, super friendly, super nice. I'm trying to look up the director – Don Barnhart, who I think had done a lot of the episodes. So he was talking about getting back into the vibe of the show and the importance of the relationships, and I remember thinking, "This is a little comedy sitcom thing. Look how seriously he takes this." Because the dynamic between the characters for him and the cast was super important. They had established these characters and their relationships, and each of them had their unique personality. And that was one of the first things he talked about was, "Let's get back to that dynamic." And I thought that was pretty cool. He wasn't just like block and shoot. It was like, "Let's get back into who these people are." And I'm a serious actor, and to see someone treat it like real characters and relationships, I thought, was great. So my initial impression of the whole set-up was very, very positive. The kids were really, really nice. I spent probably most of my time during the rehearsal week talking to Screech. [Laughs] He's kind of different now. At the time, Dustin Diamond was this super sweet, kind of naive kid and super friendly and wanted to talk to me and tell me all about the show and the things they'd done. He was kind of innocent and just a sweet kid. So he'd come over and hang out with me and tell me a little bit about everybody. It was just great; it was like being invited to Disneyland. Then just skipping ahead for a second because I'm trying to remember what my main impressions were. The main thing I remember was when we shot the show, which was probably a Thursday or Friday night – which is what you do; you rehearse for the week, and then you have your audience in – and they introduce the cast. And at that point, I had done a lot of sitcoms, and I knew they introduced the cast before the show, and I remember everyone in the cast was brought out before the show started and got some nice applause. And then Mark-Paul Gosselaar was introduced, and the audience went nuts. They went nuts! And I said, "Who is this guy? Why do I not know who this guy is?" And they went crazy. I remember at that point thinking, "Jeez, this show is an even bigger deal than I realized. This has got a real fanbase." He was also really nice, really level-headed. He wasn't walking around like he had a huge ego or anything. He was just super famous. I remember that making a real impression. That without even knowing it, I was about to participate in this big-deal show. [Laughs] So I was pretty excited to be there.

Do you remember anything specific that Dustin Diamond said when you guys spoke?

I just remember his face. I haven't paid a lot of attention to him as an adult, although I hear he's gotten himself in some difficult situations, but I remember talking to him and thinking, "What a sweet kid." He had this wide-eyed wonder, like, "Isn't life great? Isn't this fun? Aren't these people terrific? We're so glad to have you here." And I was like, "Jeez. Here's a kid who's really enjoying this opportunity." He was a little geeky, a little dorky, like he is on the show. But he had a lot of natural talent. He had a lot of personality. I remember feeling a little sad for him because the other kids were so cool, and he was the butt of a lot of jokes, so I felt like, "That must be rough." But he didn't seem to mind it. He seemed to really enjoy the role. There was a part of him that was very professional. He didn't seem the least bit overwhelmed or thrown by the magnitude of the show. Later, who knows, it might've got to him, and that might've been part of the reason he took a weird turn. But at the time, he seemed like a total pro. As did everybody.

I still think his line, "Ah, then the dog lied!" is one of the best jokes of the series.

[Laughs] Yeah, there's all kinds of acting out there. I love acting; it's still my passion after 40-some years. And people say, "How can you go from doing heavy drama to doing a sitcom like 'Saved by the Bell'?" I look at every acting challenge as a puzzle, and how do we make this one work? How do we make this one fly? How do we make this one live and breathe and come alive so people are interested in it? Dustin was the kind of guy that was totally plugged in to how do we make this work; how do we make this funny. They all were. I was honored to be a part of that. If it works in the end, if the thing comes together and has the desired effect, everybody wins. What you don't want is a situation where the actors aren't connecting, the script's not really taking off, there's not a lot of passion behind it, and then it just lies there, and nobody wants that. So this show, and this episode, everything was going in its favor. You had the cast, you had the chemistry, you had the script, you had the fan base. So it was great to be a part of that even just for one episode. I still remember having a great time.

Were there any scenes that took the most work or were particularly memorable to you?

Well, of course, I had to come back disguised as a woman. [Laughs] I do remember – vague recollections because it's 30 years ago – but I do remember them doing me up with really nice makeup and hair and nails and high heels, and I remember having to walk around in this character and make it as un-obvious as possible that I was my previous character. So that was kind of interesting. I think of course most people knew who I was, but I think a lot of the audience may not have known because it was a pretty cool reveal, so that was kind of fun and challenging. I just remember the nails and hair and everything, suddenly feeling like, "I've gotta take on this character. I've gotta really be into this thing." Looking at the credits now, there's a guy in the show – it's so funny, it's coming back to me now – who played piano in the show. I haven't seen the episode in a while, but do you remember what I'm talking about? This guy and I became friends from that point forward because we had a lot of time off-screen to chat, and he's a very talented pianist and great actor. I can't find his name now. And then of course I'm looking at the credits and see Dennis Haskins; he and I worked on a stage production [together], so I know him and he's a great guy. The thing that amazed me was the audience enthusiasm. They were nuts for this show. It didn't take much to get a real applause or cheers out of them because they really loved these characters. Unbeknownst to me, they were really well-established by the time I came to the show.

So you became friends with the piano player, even though you murdered him.

[Laughs] Yeah, that's not atypical. It's just acting. But he's a great guy, and he and I both do a lot of stage work, so we have that in common and see each other's shows and stuff. I run into Dennis occasionally out and about town. Another terrific guy. All really great people, so friendly. Every one of them took a moment to come up to me and introduce themselves. It was kind of astounding. There was just a great chemistry between them. I'm assuming that's a big part of why the show did so well is because the chemistry between them was natural. There was a genuine love between them. They kind of were all dialed into the vibe of the show. I did a show called "Deadwood" on HBO, and completely different type of show obviously, but that's so key to a show being a success: the chemistry between the characters and the actors being good and everyone being on board with what the show's about. It's a really beautiful thing; it really creates a solid energy, and everyone kind of plugs in.

How are you personally at mysteries like this, if you do a murder mystery event or escape room? If you're doing it with friends, are you the one who solves it, or are you the one who says, "I should've seen that, but I didn't"?

In real life, I don't involve myself in the least bit with murder mysteries or anything. Games like "Clue" and all that stuff, I never do it as a hobby. Not because I don't like it; it's just not something I'm drawn to. But as an actor, I'm really drawn to it. I like stuff that has kind of a dark edge to it, and mysteries are by nature dark-edged comedies usually. And I have a comedic sense, and I like also the dark-edged stuff, and mysteries tend to combine those two. It's light-hearted murder if you will [Laughs], and as an actor that appeals to me. I love that kind of stuff. I've never read murder mysteries or any of that stuff.

How would you describe Mr. Jameson, and was there any particular inspiration you took for the performance?

Well, I've always had a fascination with Englishmen. I don't think he's English, but that sort of officious sort of people that direct people and take charge and seem to know what's going on. I've always loved that kind of role: officious, I guess you could say. I have a natural affinity for those characters, I like them. So I immediately liked that character, and of course being the guy that has the secret, being the guy that's in control, being the guy that's pulling the strings, that's always fun. That's just really fun. Especially getting the power within the scene, within the episode. That appeals to me.

How would you describe Zack's behavior in this episode? On the one hand he doesn't lie, which is a rarity for him. On the other, his friends aren't that surprised he could be a murderer.

I'm trying to remember. I wish I could get it – if you got a way of sending a link to it, I'd love to watch it because it's been so long. [Editor's note: I tell him it's available on Hulu.] But I don't remember the specifics down to that level. It's been a long time, and I haven't seen it. So what you're saying kind of rings a bell. But I do feel that Zack's character – this is one of the reasons I think he went on to be a very successful adult, and when I say adult, I mean more adult, serial actor – he always had that dark side to him he could tap into. He wasn't just good-looking and adorable for the girls. He had a sense of that darkness, and I think for him to make that switch and to play that twist, I think was really natural for him. I think he liked it, and I think it played really well.

That's an interesting way to put it. The vast majority of the episodes revolved around him being deceptive to his family and friends. Usually not getting away with it but always being forgiven without any long-term consequences. What do you

make of the show and character still being so popular? You'd almost think people would think he was horrible.

Well, the standard answer to that is, "Girls like a bad boy." It's very appealing. He's good-looking and charming and gets away with stuff, but that's the appeal. He's kind of a dangerous – he's a mystery. Speaking of "Mystery Weekend." This guy is elusive, charming, can't quite pin him down. You never know exactly what he's thinking, what's he trying to do. Women love that. And I think that was his appeal. He wasn't just a sweet kid; he was a bad boy. Again, I think [Mark-Paul] had that part of his nature. I think it is part of him. He's capable of going to that darker, more dangerous place. Did not affect how he was as a person, as a professional. He was a sweet guy, really nice, very professional. But I think he was very conscious that he had that side to him, and he played it to his advantage, particularly in this role. He was extremely nice to me. I do remember a moment, I think it was that same moment I described to you, he would talk like a regular person and then he would become this star. We were standing up there, he's waiting to go up there for this introduction, and he's just chatting, and they said, "Now, we'd like to introduce to you, Mark-Paul Gosselaar!" And I remember seeing the shift. His eyebrow went up a little bit, he cocked his head to one side, and you could see him get into that movie-star [persona], that Zack character. I took that as a sign that, "This guy's a really good actor. This guy knows how to inhabit a character." Which to me is the key to being a great actor: to inhabit an alternate reality so convincingly that people believe that it's real. And he had that instinct. I think maybe more so than even some of the actors, who were very good at being themselves, but what they were playing on stage or off was themselves, basically. Whereas I think he could more deeply transform himself into something a little different. That to me is a sign of a really good actor. I admire the guy. I think he's a great actor, seriously.

Someone else I interviewed mentioned that during the curtain call, Mark-Paul turned to him and was like, "Yeah, that's right." But it didn't occur to me that he was in character at that time. [Editor's note: See the Sean Masterson interview toward the end of the book.]

[Laughs] Yeah, it could be. I think he was very aware of himself, of his power as an actor, of his power as an individual. He wasn't uncomfortable with it; he knew what to do with it. This is what I think makes really successful actors: They see themselves very clearly as the commodity that they are, and they're able to market themselves because they know what's them, what's their character. It's all clear to them, and they work it. That's not a bad thing; that's how you have a really successful career. You say, "This is what I have to offer. These are my strengths." And when it's working, yeah! You see it. So he's going, "Yeah, I'm working it. I'm Mark-Paul Gosselaar, and people love me, and that means I'm getting even more work and more money and even better choice of scripts." It's all good.

What goes through your head when you hear that Zack lied 329 times throughout the series?

[Laughs] Well, I think to myself, "That was Zack. That wasn't Mark, that was Zack, and that was Zack's character." And that was very much a crucial element to the show, having a character who lied a lot. The show had a lot of morality to it. There always seemed to be a lesson of sorts in every episode, as I recall. And I think having someone who misbehaves and having the audience see consequences and how that plays out, certainly for kids – I know my kids watched it a lot – was a gratifying lesson. So you've gotta have your bad guy. You've gotta have your antagonist. No story worth telling exists unless there's your bad guys and your good guys. Unless there's your conflict. So when you say he lied, I say two things. I say good for him as the character, staying true to his part, and also congratulations to the writers and producers for having a real consistent character. I don't know how many episodes, what did he do, 300-something episodes, is that what you said?

It was like 118 episodes.

Oh, 118. He lied 320. But I think it's very important, and I was aware of this when I was in "Deadwood," that your character remains consistent for the show to stay strong and for people who tune in every week to know what they're getting: "I'm going back to this because I know what the show does for me." It has to be consistent. And you say he lied 320 times; I say then they were very consistent.

And this is something I'm trying to get to the bottom of: the idea of trying to show right and wrong and if that is effective when he never had permanent consequences. If you had a friend like this who screwed you over every day, apologized, and then did the same thing tomorrow … is that a good way of teaching lessons?

Well, I haven't watched enough of the series to say how I would feel about that over the long haul. I will just say this: A character has to be true to who that character is. A lot of our most famous characters in art and movies, film, TV, theater, in general, are bad. We tune in to watch people behave badly. The appeal of it is that it's easier to deal with in TV than it is to deal with in life, and we can watch it unfold. Clearly there was enough good in him or fascinating enough in him or appealing enough in him that people weren't turned off by his behavior. If anything, they wanted to see more of it. They were fascinated by it. I don't know that the show ever claimed to be a moral standard for kids. "Tune in to watch 'Saved by the Bell' to learn how to be a good person in life." I don't think it ever claimed to be that. It claimed to be an entertaining show that you would always find interesting. And apparently people did. So they succeeded in that. I guess it's up to parents and individuals to say, "Well, that may be a hit, that may be a success, but to me that's teaching a bad lesson." That's up to the individual. I don't remember how much my kids watched it or didn't watch it. I don't remember them thinking about it particularly about Zack, if he was a good person or a bad person. We never said, "You shouldn't watch that show; Zack lies all the time." I don't remember thinking that. If I recall anything, it's, "That show's funny." We just watched to be entertained. It's a gray area.

And it's important to reiterate that he's not a bad guy in this episode. I interviewed the creator of "Zack Morris is Trash," and we agreed that Zack Morris is not trash in this one. [Editor's note: See the Dashiell Driscoll interview at the end of the book.]

Yeah, I saw an interesting study on "60 Minutes" like 20, 30 years ago, and it always stuck with me. They said, "Great leaders are always good liars." I thought, "That's a horrible thing to say." How cynical, how disillusioned to think that our great leaders are good liars. I think about that when I think about people who lie: These are people who will do whatever it takes to achieve their goals, for better or worse. You've gotta decide if he's doing it for worse, if he's really doing bad things as a result of these lies he tells, then, yeah, he's a bad person. But if he's doing it to achieve something else, maybe it's OK? I don't know. I personally don't like liars. I don't lie. I don't like being around liars. I don't trust them, obviously, and I tend to think if they lie it's a reflection on their character. Again, I want to make a distinction between that and watching the liars on television for entertainment value. [Laughs] Which can be fascinating. I guess that would take greater minds than myself to parse out.

I guess if great leaders are good liars, then bad liars must be horrendous leaders. Not that I have anyone in mind.

[Laughs] Yeah. Yeah! Yeah, yeah, I guess so. I gotta be honest with you: All I remember is liking the guy. When I go to a set, I really look at the character of the people I'm working with, and 99.9% of the time I've worked with good people who want to do good work and respect their fellow actors, producers, directors, writers. He was definitely one of those people. The character they play, I don't take that as a reflection on them at all. That's the character they're playing. So I think about the person. As an actor, my recollections are always more about the actor than the character. That's just the way I remember things. I remember the person I worked with much more than the character they played. And I just remember having a positive impression of him.

Is there anything you did or encountered afterwards that reminded you of this episode?

Well, think of it what you will, but I've done more than my handful of dressing up as women in shows, in television, in theater, for usually comedic situations. Whenever I do that, I think back to that episode. That was I think the first time I ever had to do that. I remember being a little uncomfortable, not quite sure. Of course, the solution for any of these types of roles is just go for it. Don't half do it; really try to become that woman or whatever. Since then if I've had to portray a woman on stage or anything like that, I always think about that episode. Because you get uncomfortable and it's like, "How do I do this?" Until you say, "I'm just going to be this character. I'm just going to be this woman." And then it's really fun.

I also came across a video of you dressed as a woman for a "Sonic the Hedgehog" commercial. Right? Was that you?

That's me. And that's one of those roles I did. I think I might've done that after I did "Saved by the Bell," I don't remember. Denita Stokes, a character that hates Sonic the Hedgehog. She's like this old bitty who's always trying to catch him.

That's a funny thing to come out of that episode, being typecast in this sort of role.

[Laughs] I'm not sure because it's been so many years – I can't remember the first time I actually was dressed up in drag as a woman. But I have done my share of it. Denita Stokes being one of my favorites. That was a lot of fun, that commercial. Acting is fun, man. If everyone's pushing for the same goal, which is to make whatever this piece is work, and you respect each other and you're having a good time, it's a blast, man. It's just a blast.

Are there any elements from the episode that have come true in your life? Do you have a secret passage in your house? Do you drink mango tonics with a kiwi twist?

Well, I will tell you this: The first thing that pops into my mind when you ask me that question is that I have a recurring dream – this happens a lot – that I find a door in my house that leads to an attic in which there is this massive collection of books. I have this dream a lot, and I always wake up convinced, just for a moment before I come to my wits, that there really is a wing of my house where there's just all this incredible, crazy stuff. I won't say it's because of that episode [Laughs], but I suppose it's referencing that part of my consciousness. I'm always fascinated by that idea that there are mysteries in your life you have yet to discover that will somehow open up a whole new area of consciousness. I think to a degree, like think about right now [during quarantine], the circumstances we're in, we all sometimes feel stuck in our own being: "These are my choices, I only have this many options, and this is who I am." When you're not happy with yourself, and "I'm just stuck with what I got." So the idea that there's a part of you that could open up a whole new set of options, it's always kind of fascinating.

And in that dream, you never walked into the room and Screech was there?

[Laughs] Screech! No, I've never had a dream where I walked in and there was Screech. No, that's never happened. I only have the one image of him. And it's more so than even being on the set with him. It's sitting in the bleachers with him. When I think of him, it's always him coming up and sitting down next to me and saying, [squeaky voice], "Hey, how's it going? Welcome to the show! So do you like the show?" And I'm thinking to myself, "This guy's really strange and wonderful." That's the image that always pops into my head when I think of him. That's why it was so strange when he started having these troubles, and I was trying to reconcile these two people, that this new troublemaker guy could be that same sweet kid. But that's what happens. That's life.

Melody Rogers aka Melanie Morris in "Fake IDs," "Home for Christmas" and "Saved by the Bell: Wedding in Las Vegas"

Perhaps it's not surprising that Melody Rogers doesn't recall her TV son as a pathological liar. The actress, a Broadway veteran seen recently in the affectionate documentary "Bathtubs Over Broadway," appeared in just a few episodes of "Saved by the Bell" – the two-part "Home for Christmas" saga (which totaled just one lie combined) and "Fake IDs" (which had a whopping 11 lies but ended with Melanie having the last laugh, catching Zack at the Attic).

Also, any parent, even a TV parent, is going to want to see the bright side of their child.

During our interview, Rogers, who also appeared in "Wedding in Las Vegas" and now works as a realtor, couldn't have been nicer while also being apologetic for not remembering more of her "Saved by the Bell" experience. She had a great time making it, though, and has been recognized for her role as far away as the Great Wall of China.

"It's just amazing the reach that this show has had. I thought it was a really good show for kids growing up," she said. "I'm not sure I understand exactly where you're coming from [with this project], but I'd like to know more."

The season where you appeared in multiple episodes was Zack's best behavior. Maybe it's because his mom was around sometimes.

That's absolutely the truth, Matt. I had a great influence on him. Who knows? But as characters and as actors, we had a really good relationship. I was not the strict, overbearing mom, as you know; you saw that. I was going to make sure that bad things weren't going on, but I was trying to be a friend too.

Is that how you would characterize the relationship between them?

I think we had a really great mother-son relationship. If I had a son, I would like to have that kind of a relationship. I didn't fool around, but my son knew what was right and what was wrong, at least in my eyes. And when I saw him, like with the nightclub, I would get him. But there was always a sense of, I would say, friendship too. I sort of based this a little bit on my relationship with my mother. I wasn't a boy, but she was a fantastic mom, but she didn't let me get away with anything. We always had a great relationship. I feel that Zack and Melanie had a really good relationship. Did that come across to you?

For sure. So many shows make it seem like parents are a different species and have no nuance as people. Melanie always seemed like a fun person with her own life but also, in theory, a stabilizing force. You mentioned Zack knowing the difference between right and wrong. What goes through your head when you hear that he lied 329 times throughout the series?

He lied 329 times?

He did.

[Laughs] Oh, Matt! I'm very disappointed with my son. I didn't know that! What did he lie about? What kind of things did he lie about?

I mean, you name it. In "Home for Christmas" he's pretty honest, but in "Fake IDs" he lies 11 times. It's one of the most dishonest episodes of the whole series.

I remember that. You know what, he was a teenage boy. What can I say, right? Does that make sense?

Can you elaborate on that as an explanation? Is rampant dishonesty with family and friends inherent to the teenage experience?

No, no, no, absolutely not. I was not aware of that, honestly. I was not. I think I was in three or four episodes and then did the movie, and I know in "Fake IDs" he did, but the other episodes it didn't hit me that way. But now that you mention it, maybe he did.

The average throughout the show is about three lies per episode, and for the most part each one involves him lying to family and friends and repeating the same mistake in the next episode. In addition to lying 329 times, I charted how often he treated women poorly, and that was in 50% of the episodes overall. And there wasn't ever a time he said something positive to Kelly that wasn't just about him liking her for her appearance. It sounds like you're surprised about this, though. Do you think Zack's mom had rose-colored glasses about what he was really like?

Well, you know, listening to you, I guess I did. I guess so. Again, I wasn't in every episode, and I didn't get up Saturday morning and watch "Saved by the Bell." I watched a lot of it, but probably she had rose-colored glasses because I don't remember in any filming, in any taping, that any director said to me, "You know, your son is a scoundrel." I just don't remember any of that. Obviously you have researched this and you saw – do you think that that was the purpose of a lot of the shows, to show him as a young guy getting away with a lot of crap?

Let me hear what you think about that first.

I as a person tend to see the best in everyone. I try to; it's just who I am. I don't know. I know [producer] Peter Engel, or I knew him. I know [writer] Jeffrey Sachs. I know [producer] Franco Bario. I know so many of those people. I know Jeffrey Sachs now; he's also a realtor. I'm a realtor now; my husband is very ill, and I've had to do that to take care of him. I'd be interested to talk to [Sachs] and see if when they were writing this if that was a through line. Obviously you've really researched this so obviously it was, but I guess I missed it. [Laughs] … I find it interesting because if you're saying that by not doing the right thing he didn't get what he wanted, I think Peter Engel's reason for doing the show was really to do a show for young kids with morals and to do the right thing. I've actually talked to him about that when we were there.

What do you remember about that conversation?

I remember him, I believe it was him, or someone telling me that he – this is going to sound really weird, and I could be wrong, but I believe he was very ill, and he's Jewish, and he said that he had a visitation from Jesus, who said, "You need to do a show for young kids to teach them what's right and wrong." And he did, and the rest is history. Now I don't know if that's true; I know that's what I heard.

In terms of "Wedding in Las Vegas," a line that stuck out to me in the beginning, when Zack and Kelly are trying to get the wedding off the ground, was Melanie telling Zack that she supports him but can't go against his dad, who thinks the kids are too young to get married. What do you make of that interaction between the two of them? It seems out of character from Melanie's previous independence and support.

You know, I don't know. I think oftentimes parents are not in agreement with what their children are going to do. I don't have children, but I've certainly been around enough with my friends with kids. I think that a woman does usually – this was a while back, this was 30 years ago – try to go along with her husband, and I think that if Melanie really thought that this was a horrible thing to do, she would have somehow not let it happen. I think. I don't know.

It's a TV movie, so there aren't any therapy sessions about the psychology of these relationships, but it seemed different from what we had seen from her before.

Yeah, well, it may have been. To be honest with you, I don't remember it; it's been so many years ago. But I do remember that I adored him, I loved him, I wanted the best for him, but I was always going to try and make sure that he stayed on the straight and narrow, even though he would deviate from it. Like most mothers of young boys, I think. But I just was never aware of all this.

You mentioned that the director never said anything to you like, "Zack has been acting terribly" or anything. Do you remember any guidance you were given about the way Melanie sees her son?

No, I don't, I really don't. We had a really good director, and I can remember other shows I've done where there was certainly direction about "This has gotta be this way or this way," but I really don't. I'm sorry; I wish I did.

The detail that's been released about the reboot is he's the governor of California and has closed a lot of low-income schools and continues to be a person that lacks empathy. To be perfectly honest, as absurd as it sounds, there are a lot of moments in the show in which Zack is not terribly unlike the president.

Oh, god. I'm going to throw up. [Laughs] Really?

He is delusional about his exploits with women, he is cocky but doesn't have anything to support it, his default setting is dishonesty and there are many episodes in which you would not be wrong to label him as a sexual predator.

Obviously you've done a lot more research on this than I have. Let me say this: I'm disappointed. But it worked for some reason, and maybe it's because it showed that you can't do it like that. Does that make sense?

And I should reiterate that this book is an appreciation of the show. I don't want to come off like I'm taking it to task. I still have a lot of fondness for it, and I'm so thankful to talk to people like you who made it and made it the success it was. I'm just trying to understand how and why we all love it so much despite Zack behaving this way. What role do you feel like Zack's parents played in his life, and how much responsibility do they deserve for the way he treated other people?

Hmm. Well, as the mom, as the character, I think the mom treated him really well. The dad, I never met the dad. There was never a dad on the show. Maybe there was, but not in any of my episodes, so maybe he was like his father. He wasn't like me; he wasn't like his mother. Maybe he was like his father.

That's a good point.

As I said, I didn't really know that character. Was he ever in the show?

Yeah, he was, a few times. Among other things, there's one where Zack's dad is always on the phone selling computers, and Zack is frustrated that he doesn't have his attention.

There's part of your answer right there.

Stephen Mendel aka Frank Benton in the two-part "Home for Christmas"

In no way am I likening being homeless to being an overlooked character actor. Yet there's no question that some people try not to take notice of people in need, and I definitely, though of course not intentionally, had no idea until preparing to interview Stephen Mendel what an extensive career he has had. He's always been here, even when I didn't see him.

All I knew was his "Saved by the Bell" role of Frank Benton, who Zack and Screech first see in the mall bathroom, shaving. Whether in that scene (which ends with Zack leaving money for Frank in the coin slot of a pay phone), or when Frank showcases his gift-wrapping skills to Slater (who doesn't possess those abilities), or when Frank explains the extremely, frighteningly ordinary progression of events that led to him and his daughter, Laura (Jennifer McComb), being homeless, Mendel gives Frank a remarkable kindness that's undercut by wounded resilience. In this book I write that the character seems saintlike, by which I guess I mean that the show seems so intent on reinforcing Frank and Laura as genial and innocent that any difficult emotions about their hardships have been sanded off.

That, obviously, is not Mendel's fault, and in fact the actor, who is so precise and warm in his two-part "Saved by the Bell" arc, has a remarkably wide-ranging filmography that stretches from "You're the Worst" to "Grey's Anatomy," "Mad Men" to "Power Rangers," "The West Wing" to "Ninja Turtles: The Next Mutation." When I ask him if any of Frank's scenes were especially difficult to get right, he explains that for him acting challenge comes from incorporating physicality into a performance, like having to act while syncing with a difficult blocking set-up for Steven Spielberg and Tom Hanks in "The Terminal." No such multi-tasking was needed in "Saved by the Bell," and Mendel seems to have accessed his character effortlessly.

"For me as a human being, to connect with a person who's been down on their luck is not a big stretch. Because unless you've been extraordinarily fortunate as an actor, sometimes there's long periods of time where you don't know if you're going to work again," he said. "So to be able to find in my own emotional history times when I felt, 'Jesus, oh my god, what am I going to do? When am I going to work again? What the hell do I have to do? I know I'm good at this, why can't I [catch a break]?' So finding the places of truth and reality in that situation for 99% of the actors in the world who are worth their stuff … that was not a difficult place for me to go to and to find reality, find truth within myself, find a way to connect that story to some real places of emotional truth within me, within my own personal history. Have I ever been homeless? No. Have I ever not had enough money for food? No. But I've been hungry. So I explore that, and I take that further."

These days Mendel is still a working actor along with recording audiobooks, doing other voiceover work and playing music, recently releasing an album called "Sing Me a Story." He says that no organization dealing with homelessness ever reached out to him about his "Saved by the Bell" episodes, and, when I ask if he thinks his calming voice contributed to him landing the role of Frank, that only in his off-screen vocal work does he separate his voice from the rest of him as a performer.

"As an actor, it's part of my toolbox. So my toolbox as an actor is my body, my face, and my voice. And to a certain extent what I dress myself in," he said. "When I went to audition for Frank, I wore my oldest, rattiest pants and a cardigan sweater and a plaid shirt that I buttoned up to the top button. I wouldn't separate those aspects out when I'm working on camera. It's part and parcel of who I am and what I bring to the table. And if they like it, they like it."

When I ask if he thinks the "Home for Christmas" episodes will hit people in a particular way during a period of so much unemployment, he tells me about his fiancée, who has long taught at the university level where previous adherence to tenure tracks and respect for/loyalty to adjunct professors has diminished in recent years. "She was kind of lamenting the fact that she didn't know whether she was going to have a job next semester or whether she was going to be able to have her health insurance, and I looked at her and said, 'Welcome to my world.' So in a sense as an actor and as that character, Frank, it's welcome to the world of uncertainty, of hunger, of being afraid," he said. "Would it resonate [now]? Wow … There might be some resonance there with somebody down on their luck and trying to figure out how to get back onto the merry-go-round that you've fallen off of."

Blake Boyd aka Derek Worthington in "Saved by the Bell: Hawaiian Style"

The first "Saved by the Bell" TV movie may be predictable, but interviewing Blake Boyd – who in "Hawaiian Style" plays cartoonishly lousy Derek Worthington, son of the evil hotel magnate and boyfriend to Andrea (Rena Sofer) until she leaves him for Zack – sure isn't.

He answers the phone by saying, "So you want to talk about 'Saved by the Bell'?" Soon his assessment of misogynistic behavior leads to a discussion on Trump's election sparking the Me Too movement, and he also speculates on parallels between Zack's behavior and Bill Clinton's behavior.

"Culturally men have not been held accountable," he said, later noting that this book is "socially responsible." "It seems like we used to be held more accountable, and then we weren't held accountable."

Besides for everyone involved being incredibly kind and professional, Boyd ("First Kid," "The Cable Guy") also remembers that Mark-Paul Gosselaar was really into lifting weights.

"He was really, really into fitness at the time, and he wanted to be as big as he could," Boyd said, with Gosselaar even quitting smoking because it was suppressing his appetite and preventing him from building muscle. Boyd initially auditioned to play Brian (Dan Gauthier), Kelly's boyfriend in the movie, and did not, in fact, go to Hawaii, filming his scenes in Laguna Beach, California, which passed for Hawaii on screen. (The main cast did film much of the movie on location, though.) He says he tested for the part that went to Andrew Shue on "Melrose Place" and laughs when I tell him he's one of the few people in "Saved by the Bell" history to lose a girl to Zack, who normally makes other guys look good by comparison.

Here are some other notable comments that came from our interview:

On vivid memories from filming:

"At LAX, the scene at the international terminal, that's real traffic and that's real people. There were extras walking around there, but that's outside the Bradley international terminal. It was underneath; I think we were shooting downstairs where the arrivals are. Or maybe the arrivals are upstairs, I can't remember which. But we would get into the limousine, when I'm picking [Andrea] up from the airport and she's with Zack and I take her luggage and I try to tip him and I realize he's not a bellman and I snatch the bill back away. And I get in the car, and we had to make the entire loop of the airport. We couldn't just stop and back up and do it again; we had to continue around the whole loop because that was real traffic. They can't stop traffic at LAX. Even though we quote-unquote owned the location, we didn't own the traffic. So Rena and I driving in the limo together had on body mics, and we would look at each other, and we'd start talking because actors tend to talk when you're not working, you chit-chat. And Rena looked at me and put her finger up to her mouth and was like, 'Be careful what you say.' I would never disparage another actor or director or whatever, but we were reminding each other, 'Don't talk because we're mic'd, and they can hear us.' [Laughs] I don't know if she was having any difficulty or not on the show, I don't think so. I remember sitting around and talking about Biblical history with Peter Engel, the producer of the show. He's a Biblical scholar. A friend of mine joined us one day; he was also very, very well-versed on Biblical references and scripture, and that was pretty interesting to talk to a Hollywood producer about the Bible."

On making Derek appealing:

"At the screening when everybody was there, I remember when Derek was told to get lost, or when Derek would get bad news and I would react to it and be sad, the entire audience would go, 'Awww.' I was kind of this likable loser. It's a compliment as an actor if you can do that. You want the villains to be likable. Particularly on a show like 'Saved by the Bell' or a Disney movie."

On rhythm being a major part of comedy, after he demonstrates a flat vs. funny delivery of his memorably absurd line "I've got sparkling water and hot snacks in the car":

"It's like Martin Luther King's 'I have a dream' speech, arguably one of the greatest speeches of all time. It's a great speech, but it's his delivery of it. The way Dr. King delivered it was so impactful. I've heard of other examples where people did it, and they didn't have the voice inflection, they didn't emphasize certain words, and it just felt flat. And I'm not comparing Derek Worthington with Dr. Martin Luther King in any way, shape or form. One is one of the greatest leaders of all time, and one is a cartoon character. But the point is the delivery. The number one job is when we're working and you have a line like, 'I've got sparkling water and hot snacks in the car,' don't judge it. Just do it and make it funny."

When he notes that the show was a good bridge between the '80s and '90s and I comment on how many times it referenced both Gorbachev and MC Hammer:

"Well, Gorbachev represented an enemy, and MC Hammer represented that cool older brother. What I tend to do that's helpful is look at the metaphoric issues. Look at the symbolisms in what that's saying. MC Hammer: hip, cool, young. What were his songs? '2 Legit 2 Quit.' That's about determination, integrity, not quitting. Gorbachev, who apparently was a very nice man. He and Reagan were great friends, and when Reagan died in 2004, Gorbachev went to the funeral. There were several shots [of him] at the funeral of Reagan. They developed a friendship."

On getting recognized for his role:

"I got recognized in 2005 in Jackson, Mississippi. I walked into a bed and breakfast in an old antebellum mansion. And the girl working at the front desk told her friend, who told me later, 'That guy was on 'Saved by the Bell: Hawaiian Style.' I remember him.' And I'm not a star by any means, but I was shocked at how many people saw that show and loved it."

Hillary Danner aka Linda Addington in "Screech Love"

You probably wouldn't think that one of the sweetest episodes in the history of "Saved by the Bell" involved a love triangle between Zack and Screech. (And not the one involving Lisa.) In fact, despite treating Screech as a complete doofus in the romance department – not including his relationship with Tori Spelling's Violet Bickerstaff, a pairing that was identified over and over again as nerd love, separated from the cool kids – "The College Years" finally gave him a chance to shine, and outshine, his best, sleaziest friend.

The rapport between Screech and tennis star Linda Addington (Hillary Danner, who, yes, is the niece of Blythe Danner and cousin of Gwyneth Paltrow), who is dating Zack and being tutored by the far more compatible Screech, has a kindness and innocence that "Saved by the Bell" often refused to let peek around its Zack-centric boulder of nasty. Danner now runs the successful Jenkins Jellies and an L.A.-based safari tent glamping operation, and by phone was just as kind and open as Linda.

What do you remember about your "Saved by the Bell" experience? What stories come to mind?

I had actually initially tested for one of the series regulars [for the role of Alex]. I didn't get it. When you do these jobs and then you don't get something and they actually call you back, they're like, "No, we really loved you, it just went to somebody else. But we brought you back for this role." So I was like, "Oh, wow, they really liked me!" [Laughs] It was a positive. "Oh, you brought me back, that's so nice." It was super early in my career. It might have been my first full guest role. I think it was. I remember it being very early in my career, so generally it was a very positive experience. And then I became friends with Anne [Editor's note: That's Anne Tremko, who played Leslie and who recommended I interview Danner] and we continued our friendship for quite a while until she left Los Angeles, and I got reunited with her again when they had the "Saved by the Bell" popup cafe or something. Do you know anything about this?

Yeah, Saved by the Max was in Chicago also.

OK, cool. So she called me, she's like, "I'm coming out there for this, and you need to come with me." That was really fun to be a part of that reunion and see her again and reconnect. So that was very positive. Also, we shot the show on my birthday, which was a Friday, I think. It was October 8 because that's my birthday. I remember my uncle who was a TV producer always said it was extra good luck if you were working on your birthday, doing something like your ideal job. I remember a lot about it. I remember where we went out after the party, I remember that Mario Lopez was sitting next to me, and they brought in a cake for both of us because I think his birthday is October 10. So in our dinner break before we went to shoot the show they brought in a shared cake for us, and of course I thought that was pretty cool at the time. So generally speaking, I have very fond memories of that whole experience.

What was going through your head as you became part of this franchise? Were you nervous?

I was totally, totally nervous. As I'm standing here thinking about it, I even remember certain moves at the end of what would close a scene. I remember this ridiculous tennis racket, and I think my name was Linda Addington. There is so much that is deeply imprinted in my brain because it was a lot of firsts. I remember the curtain call, and I remember I didn't know which side to run to afterwards, and I was totally mortified. I'm sure one person was telling me to go to one side, and the other one told me to go to the other side. [Laughs] I remember I was like, "Am I going to get through this?" You know, you're nervous. But I did. I remember my outfit. And I remember watching it with my friends when you had to be like, "It's airing!" And your friends come over, and you're just horrified. [Laughs] It's very hard to watch yourself on the screen. It was fun. It was a lot of fun. "The College Years" was a new show, but the history of it being on for so long, you're also nervous because you're walking onto a set of people who've been doing it a long time, and it's your first actual guest spot. I think I did another one before that. I think it was a pilot with Henry Winkler, and I had two lines or five lines or something. I just remember those early experiences. And I was working, actually, at Starbucks when I got both of those jobs. And I remember the phone call coming in – of course we didn't have cell phones, so they called my work, and my manager was like, "Hillary, it's your agent!" I just really started working a lot after that.

Well, you have a unique place in the show's history in that you were the only person who rejected Zack in favor of Screech.

[Laughs] That's awesome. No way. I was like, "Am I the only quote-unquote girlfriend he had?" And someone reminded me the only other one was [Tori] Spelling from the original show. So I thought that was funny. I did not know that – I did not know I was the only one who rejected his advances for Screech. That's pretty funny.

I think the episode really works. It's one of several times Screech's character comes alive in college, and you play Linda with such sweetness. I'm wondering what type of rehearsal was done – the notion of bringing in a one-episode guest star to establish as a romantic possibility for the person who never had any possibility like that seems like a big swing for the show. What was involved in building that dynamic?

That's interesting. That didn't really play in, but I see what you're saying. I can see now that maybe there could've been a little arc there. That could've been a two- or three-episode arc, and then Linda goes back to playing tennis or something. [Laughs] I don't remember that being a thing. From my standpoint, I came in and I did my lines, and my job is to make it work. Whatever it is, make it as believable [as possible]. So that's what I did. I was pretty young and excited to be in this space. That wasn't my job, really, the bigger picture that you came up with, which is interesting. Now that I'm at a different stage of my life, I see what you're talking about. No, I was just expected to hit the mark, say my lines, show up and get the work done.

Sure. I recognize that a chemistry read is something that might happen for a series regular or movie and not one isolated incident about Screech finding someone who sees that he's a nicer person than the worst guy on campus.

Right, for sure. I see what you're saying. It wasn't like, "Let me have you come in and read with [Dustin] Diamond." It wasn't like that where I can see that would be if you're going to be on for an arc or for a series regular, there would probably be an extra step in the audition process to bring you in to see if you actually get along with the person at all. That did not play any part of it. I just came in, I auditioned, I had a callback, I got the job ... Regardless of whatever the heck happened afterwards, I will tell you that he was a very nice guy to work with. And that experience, he was quite lovely. So that was nice.

How do you characterize Zack's behavior in terms of how he treats Linda, who he's only interested in for her appearance, wealth and success, and Screech, who he doesn't respect and sees as a non-threat?

I'm sure if I looked at it now my viewpoint would be very different than how I was looking at it at the time because I have such different outlooks on people who treat me poorly now than I did then. Because I've certainly had a lot more experience with that. And maybe this is too much information, but just for me what I do remember is I never had a very big ego, and I think part of my personal nervousness in that role was I didn't have an ego and personally, not as Linda but as Hillary, would never have thought that I would have the Zack. Which is maybe why this worked on screen – if it worked, if you're saying it worked. Do you understand what I'm saying, or am I not really making any sense? So in terms of doing the show and at the time, it seemed to me that this was just normal behavior. Being in Hollywood, you deal with those people all the time, so it didn't seem that strange to me. It seemed like it sucked, and I personally would not want to be friends with that person anyway. So it seemed just normal and normal that I wouldn't be with that person anyway. Am I making any sense or no?

Yeah. It sounds like the reasons are multi-faceted.

Yeah. I wonder – if you think there was a chemistry there – if you would have a different reaction if there was an actress who maybe had more self-confidence at the time. It maybe wouldn't have worked or been believable. I don't know. I remember feeling very comfortable in the scenes with Screech and less comfortable with Zack.

So how does your perspective on the way things play out in the episode change looking at it now?

I look back at this and I sort of go, "Oh, please." I think I have much more of an armor up about it. If I had to go do the [episode] over again, what I think would happen is I would be much stronger in my scenes with Zack and internally taken him to task a little bit more. I could see myself at least internally feeling less – I don't think I was googly-eyed. I don't think the character was into him really? I don't remember her being torn between the two of them. I think she was probably already questioning – I think she was more worldly and more attracted to a genuine person. Because she was an outsider; why the heck was she even at this school? [Laughs] This famous tennis player running around, what the heck was I doing there? My sense was she was popping in and wasn't going to fall for him anyway. That's what I remember. And that when the character meets Screech, I think she immediately recognized the character as someone she'd want to hang out with.

For sure. It would've been great to see Linda around for more than one episode. There was such warmth there, and the show could feel so bitter. Then Screech could've been happy for more than five minutes.

[Laughs] I love that! I never thought about that. Darn it, why weren't you in the producers' room? I think that's a great idea. That should've happened. Darn it! [Laughs] Oh my gosh, that's fascinating. I have to admit I wasn't a big TV watcher; I never have been. I still am not. I would have a couple shows that I would watch here and there. I was only allowed an hour of TV when I was growing up, so I had to choose if it was going to be "Brady Bunch" or "I Love Lucy" or something else. It was very limited. I grew up in the theater and opera, and I was on the road a lot with my parents growing up, so I had more of a gypsy theater life. So I know the Zack character obviously was this whatever guy, but I didn't grow up having a connection to the character or any of them really. I just knew they were famous … A lot of people have said, "You should go back to acting," and for a long time there was just no desire. Too exhausted, too many other things going on, and I didn't miss it. Sometimes, now that life is a little different, I think I would have fun. I don't want to say I'm a different person, but I have evolved, and I have a feeling I would have a lot of new information and knowledge and life experience, and some of it not so great, but I would find that interesting to bring that [into acting]. I might punch Zack in the face this time, actually. [Laughs] What's funny is I did a show years later, not even that much later, and I played – wait a minute, who did I play? We did a movie of the week together, where he was a real asshole. It's called "She Cried No," and I guess ["Saved by the Bell"] was over and he floundered a bit where you stereotype one character. [The movie] was about college rape basically, and he was the bad guy.

Did you get to punch him in the face in that movie?

No, I didn't actually have any direct scenes with him. There were six leads or whatever, so there were a couple storylines going on. The girl that he allegedly raped, I was her RA or the senior on the floor of the college dorm or whatever, and I was dating her brother. So I was in more family scenes as opposed to scenes with him. I was not in the frat house, shall we say. Just one scene, yeah, but.

Maybe this is an absurd connection, but in terms of Linda being a tennis star and you becoming a jelly star, I feel like tennis and fancy, high-end jelly have the same level of approachable sophistication. I totally think that trajectory checks out.

[Laughs] I love it. "Approachable sophistication." I have needed a tagline for my jellies for the last eight years. [Laughs] Maybe that's what it should be: approachable sophistication. That's very, very funny.

I would be remiss if I didn't ask if there were any stories about sharing working on "Saved by the Bell" with any of your cousins, aunts or otherwise? It's silly to think about, but I feel like I have to ask just in case.

It's literally not silly. It's funny you should say that; there are definitely a lot of successful people in my immediate family in the same business. And not to say anything negative, but what I was doing was really never discussed. [Laughs] I definitely was not at the top of anybody's … I remember my mother telling me – she's from St. Louis, and she was a big Broadway person – and she was like, "You know, Hillary, you're really big in St. Louis. With family in St. Louis." I was like, "It's OK, mom. I don't need to be a star." That was never the thing. I just wanted to work, and I was having a good time. All that being said, I look back and when we were younger, we were all around each other much more and I thought, "What a shame." It's awesome to be a part of this really neat family, but when I look back the negative of that is that everybody is always so busy and working all over the world all the time. As the kids get older, I don't want to say the family falls apart, but everybody's really busy; they're all over the place. So there's not a lot of hangout time. We did that a lot more when we were kids, and so there was more time to share things. But as we all developed careers, when we would get together there wasn't a lot of discussion about what everybody was doing. And I don't know if that's just because people felt like they didn't want to be – I don't know why it wasn't, but we had other things to talk about. Does that make sense? I see my Aunt Blythe a lot more over the years and we've had relaxed times, and we've discussed jobs and stuff. I played her in a movie of the week, so we've worked together a little bit more. But specifically for "Saved by the Bell," I don't think there was any conversation. That was just the way it is. I'm sure you didn't need that very long answer. [Laughs] My non-famous family in St. Louis, everybody [saw] everything I did and was always so sweet and so excited and so proud. That was awesome. It meant a lot to a lot of people from my high school who didn't even know I was an actress. Like, "Oh my god, that's Hillary!" Those were the people, and those were the fun things that people got excited about.

Frankie Como aka Coach Rizzo in "Slater's Friend"

Despite rarely emphasizing its peripheral students, "Saved by the Bell" had rather memorable teachers. From the comeback-heavy Mr. Tuttle to the hearing-impaired Miss Simpson to the effort-impaired Mr. Dewey, Bayside educators were given a surprising opportunity to establish themselves on screen, a surprise considering how much the main cast dominated every plotline and scene.

That memorability extends to Coach Rizzo (Frankie Como), whose defining trait (having an exaggerated Brooklyn accent while filling in as the speech teacher) became solidified in "Saved by the Bell" lore by speaking at the funeral of Slater's chameleon, Artie. (Coach Rizzo saw Artie, but, you know, they didn't converse.)

Como, who now works in real estate and property management, answered the following via email:

What do you remember about this episode? When you think about this experience, what stories come to mind?

Please bear in mind this was a loooong time ago. I do remember having fun shooting, and the kids were great. In between rehearsals throughout the week we would all read our lines as a different character of our own choosing just for laughs. The director did that regularly to keep the kids loose.

Do you remember your audition and what they were looking for in Coach Rizzo? Was there anything in particular that stood out, or that changed by the time the episode was shot?

Actually I had read for two other roles on "SBTB" earlier in the season [Editor's note: I replied to ask what those roles were, and Como said he didn't remember], and this being my third read I was cast. For Rizzo, the comedy was in the Brooklyn accent coming from someone teaching diction or speech. I do remember auditioning for casting director Robin Lippin (who knew I was from Brooklyn) and producer Peter Engel, and needless to say they were looking for funny. I made them laugh. End of story.

What was it like filming the funeral for Artie? How difficult was it for you or anyone else to take it seriously?

Hilarious. We had a blast shooting that scene. We all had such fun, and I made the kids laugh a lot during rehearsals, particularly Dustin. So you may even notice Screech on camera fighting back a laugh as I was talking and he was playing his organ. Then again it may have been while we were singing, but I remember trying to make him laugh during the shoot and seeing it on camera when the show aired.

How would you describe Zack's behavior in this episode? Not only does he lie several times and try to avoid responsibility, he has a life-size cutout of Kelly come down from his ceiling, which is pretty creepy.

Yes, creepy, but I hadn't really given it much thought over the years.

How do you assess the cultural influence of "Saved by the Bell"? Why do you think Zack has been such an enduring character despite often treating people so badly?

I didn't realize "SBTB" had cultural influence. However, many TV characters with less-than-desirable traits were lovable to audiences. Go figure.

When was the last time you watched this episode? Has anything changed about the way you perceive anything that happens in it? What did you see as being the joke of showing Coach Rizzo teaching speech class? Do you think the show was laughing with him or at him?

Haven't seen it in ages. As I mentioned earlier the comedy is in a speech teacher with a thick Brooklyn accent. It doesn't matter to me if they are laughing with him or at him; it was a kids' show, and I was hired to make kids laugh. My ego was not involved. If people were laughing, I did my job.

How, if at all, do you think Coach Rizzo would behave or speak differently if this episode were made today? Would he still call Kelly "Miss Dollface Kapowski"?

In this day and age, I think it would be inappropriate to call Kelly "Dollface."

How would you feel about someone seeing Coach Rizzo as a caricature/stereotype? Do you think he's an exaggeration of reality, or do you think he is reminiscent of anyone you've ever known (if so, please elaborate)?

Caricature or stereotype, it doesn't really matter to me, and frankly I am delighted that there is any discussion at all about a character I played over 30 years ago. I did indeed grow up in Brooklyn and knew many "Coach Rizzo" types, so I knew going into the audition that a thick Brooklyn accent would be funnier for a speech teacher. So I purposely thickened my accent to match many of the characters I grew up with when I read for the part. Years later they needed a Brooklyn type to play Big Al Gambino on "Saved by the Bell: The New Class," and I got a call and was on the set the next morning without auditioning at all.

If challenged, could you sing all the words to the song about Artie now without looking them up?

If challenged, I would fail miserably.

Have you ever presided over any other pet funerals? If so, what is the story behind that, and did you have deja vu back to this episode?

I have had to bury some pets over the years, but presiding over Artie's funeral was a once in a lifetime event. :)

Eva Loseth aka Princess Christina in the two-part "Palm Springs Weekend"

It would have been a remarkable twist in the "Saved by the Bell" trajectory if Slater, after meeting Princess Christina (Eva Loseth) of the fictional Lichtenburg, left his school and friends behind to become royalty.

Obviously that did not happen, but there is plenty of chemistry between Mario Lopez and Loseth ("Doogie Howser, M.D.") in these episodes as the characters navigate enormous differences in where they come from. The actress, who now works in real estate while dabbling in theater, shared stories about becoming a princess on screen – and identified that her "Saved by the Bell" role means that Meghan Markle isn't the only actress who has appeared on your TV as royalty, went to college in Illinois and also has a white father and a black mother who's a social worker.

"When Meghan Markle got married, all my friends were like making fun of me. Like, 'Oh, Eva, you missed your chance for Harry,'" Loseth said. "We have a lot of similarities."

How did you get involved with "Saved by the Bell"? It's your first credit on IMDb.

I auditioned for it. I had just finished with acting school at the American Academy of Dramatic Arts. At that time, it was in Pasadena; now it's in Hollywood. I had decided that I was going to start my acting career in Chicago in theater, but I was going to school out in California. So when I graduated from the American Academy of Dramatic Arts, they had a performance showcase at the end of the year, like a show that you do that you can invite industry people to. It just so happened that one of my classmates' father and mother were in the business. His mom was a casting director, and his father was Michael Gross, the dad from "Family Ties." They had come to see me in the last show that I was in and recommended me to a pretty big Hollywood agent at the time named Harry Gold. I think "Saved by the Bell" was my first professional television job in the union. My first screen debut. You have a couple auditions. So the first audition, and then you go back in. You have a second audition, which is a callback, and sometimes a third. I can't remember what it was. I got coaching from my friend's stepdad, which was Michael Gross from "Family Ties." I went over to his house, and he helped coach me on the audition. I worked on the accent and just being a princess and preparing. I worked really hard on it and ended up getting the job. [Laughs] Peter Engel, the executive producer, told me after I got on set that, "You did one thing, and I said, 'That's our girl; you've got the job.'" Something like that. He said, "Do you want to know what it was?" I said, "Yeah, what was it?" He said, "It's the way you curtsied." [Laughs] I was not in the unions, and they helped me get in the actor's union to be able to do the job. I don't know how it is now, but back then you had to join the union so you could work in television AFTRA: The American Federation of Television [and Radio] Artists union. There were two unions at that time: SAG and AFTRA. And "Saved by the Bell" shot on video, so they went under the bracket of television artists. So Peter helped me join that union, and [I] drove down to Palm Springs by myself from L.A. and shot the episodes in Palm Springs on location.

Do you remember in terms of the audition what they were looking for in Christina?

I remember they said after the first time that my accent was too authentic. And so they wanted it to be a little more bland, where you wouldn't know exactly what country she was from, but you knew she was from somewhere. So I played around with a couple different dialects in the callback session, and then there was one he just kept wanting me to do over and over again, and that ended up being the one that they used … I think I just experimented with a couple different ways to make it not specific. So you knew she was from somewhere and probably an Eastern European country, but you weren't really sure where.

Was the curtsy something you had practiced while preparing?

Yeah. I have had extensive classical training. One of my passions is classical theater, Shakespeare and Moliere. So I've had a lot of training at the American Academy of Dramatic Arts where I studied, and especially at Bradley University, where I studied theater. In theater I played some roles that had royalty in them, so that wasn't foreign to me in the theater world. But, yeah, I really spent a lot of time, and Michael Gross, when I was in the audition process, really helped me not just with tweaking different dialects that we wanted to try but also being a second eye for the physicality of what it's like to be a princess and the way you have to sit and that kind of stuff.

I wonder if I would know the difference between a good curtsy and a not-good curtsy.

[Laughs] Yeah! I don't think the script called for it; I feel like it was just something that I did. I can't remember, maybe it did. I think I just kind of [did] it. He said that it set me apart from the other actresses. He was really, really wonderful. He and the casting director, Robin Lippin, were really, really supportive of my work, and because it was my first professional television job, I was super excited. When I left the final callback, I didn't care if I got the job or not because I had such a good time auditioning, and I felt like I rocked it. I felt like I did a really, really good job, and if I get it, great, and if I don't, I feel really good about my work.

Something notable about the relationship between Slater and Christina is the class difference. He says she's caviar, and he's hot dogs. How common do you think those issues are in real relationships? We see it on screen all the time, including Nicholas Sparks movies.

I think it's a very, very common issue, and I think a lot of storylines in film and television and books address those class differences and cultural differences. I think although that was a long time ago, there's still – I'm sure people will continue to have those kinds of struggles in relationships when they have been socialized to certain customs. On the flip side, you see a lot of stories where they're able to overcome class differences and cultural differences, and those are the stories I like. [Laughs] When they're able to be from different parts of the world and be from different economic classes or cultural differences but love is able to override those differences.

What would have been the next steps for them? A long-distance relationship between Lichtenburg and California?

I was hoping so! I really wanted to come back. I remember there was a little talk. My agent said, "It's going to be two episodes right now, but you'll see. You never know what they decide." But a lot of times the writers have so many storylines going, you just never know what they're thinking. Yeah, I saw them trying to have a little bit of a long-distance relationship, seeing how that worked out. They definitely were attracted to each other. She was really attracted to him being this all-American, cute guy. Seemed like a new experience for her, meeting this kind of all-American guy that represented a lot of things that she probably hadn't been exposed to. I think there was part of their interaction that was refreshing for her to get out of her princess world and have a bit of normalcy.

If it came to that point, what kind of king do you think Slater would have been?

[Laughs] That's a good question. I feel like I would really need to watch the show to really be able to have an educated opinion on that. He'd be a fun king, probably. [Laughs] I would really need to think about that. I haven't seen the episode to be able to think in my head what kind of king he would be. If he would be a generous king or if he would be a king that would be very dictator-like. I don't remember Slater's character being that pushy, but he was definitely focused on sports and masculinity. [Laughs] I'd have to put some thought into that.

Whether because of Disney movies or other stories we encounter as kids, I think it's fair to say there are some girls who grow up wanting to be princesses. Were you one of those girls, and did it spark any personal memories when you were becoming a princess on TV?

No, I was excited about getting the role as a princess, but I didn't dress up as a kid in princess outfits. I never really spent a lot of energy or focus on that. I don't remember as a kid ever longing to be a princess. I didn't have all those clothes and stuff as a kid. I did want to be an ice skater when I was young, though, and I did have little ice-skating outfits. And I wanted to be an actress when I was young. So I did have a lot of different costumes. But I don't remember ever really being exposed to royalty or that kind of class system as a kid. I don't think it was ever part of my parents' vocabulary. Even though my father comes from a country [Norway] that has a prince and princess, I never really looked up to those roles in society as something I wanted to be. For some reason it was never interesting to me. Being an actress was much more interesting to me. I was never really a princess-type girl. It was tons of fun to do for an acting role, but in real life, I never dreamed of being a princess. [Laughs]

Why do you think it is such a big thing for some people growing up? It seems like it's more of a thing for girls and princesses than boys and princes.

I think a lot of people are socialized into that from their upbringing, schools, parents, and I think especially it's not so prevalent now in this rise of feminism as we struggle toward equality of the sexes. I think that kind of idea of taking care of having every whim at your disposal and having kind of a fairy-tale, storybook lifestyle, I think there are kids that get into that and are socialized into that and their parents may have fostered that when they were younger. My parents didn't. My parents were very working-class; I had this book "The Little Prince," but I don't remember any books about princesses. It was just something that my parents never believed in themselves, and they didn't want me to probably aspire to be a princess or have a fictional idea of what I was growing up to be.

And it sounds like if you had met Harry, since you're not interested in being royalty, you'd have said, "Thanks, but no thanks."

Exactly. He's not my type. I can't even imagine what she's had to go through. I could never do that. I love acting, and I love performing, but I'm a more private person, and I don't like a lot of that spotlight stuff. I like the social scene in Hollywood in doses. But that kind of life that they're having to lead with paparazzi following every second and all of the criticism, I could never take that. It would be too much for me.

Did you ever receive any letters because of these episodes, from kids who looked up to you for being on the show or from being royalty?

I did! Not a lot because I moved so many times and a lot went to the studio, and I don't know how that process goes. I got maybe a handful or something like that. And I get calls every now and then about it, but I had a handful. They were all very positive, but there were no little kids who believed I was a real princess or anything like that. It was just fan mail, wanting an autograph or something like that. But I didn't have any letters of any substance. When I was on "Doogie Howser, M.D.," when I worked on that show, I did get some pretty concerning letters from organizations because I was Doogie Howser's sidekick Vinnie's love interest, and on TV I took his virginity in that episode. And so it was a big, big deal. He lost his virginity; I shouldn't say I took it. He lost his virginity to me. So it a very, very big deal. There were some very conservative groups that were very, very upset that the show took a turn like that. So we did get some mail about that. But everything from "Saved by the Bell" was very nice. Mostly people just wanting to get my autograph and picture and stuff.

But the conservative groups didn't write, "Go back to Lichtenburg!"

No. [Laughs] I didn't get any mail like that at all.

Plus: A story about Lark Voorhies and Elizabeth Berkley

"I have very, very crazy, thick, curly hair that can be very wild and can be very difficult for a lot of stylists who haven't worked with African American hair before. So that's always been kind of an issue in my life. When I was younger with stylists who weren't familiar with how to do my hair. At the time, because I straighten my hair sometimes and I wear it curly sometimes, at the time that I was shooting it my hair was very, very similar to Elizabeth Berkley's. So when I got to the makeup chair, the stylists said they wanted to make sure that I didn't have the same hairstyle as her. I had worked really hard, I got up super early in the morning 1. To practice golf [Laughs], to get a golf lesson and 2. To get my hair really good so I didn't have to worry about somebody not knowing how to do my hair, and it would be really easy and good for them for the shoot. This is kind of a girl thing, but when I got there and she was like, "OK, well, we need to do something different with your hair so you and Elizabeth don't look the same." Because they always like to have people have a little different look, especially [since] she's the star of the show. So they started basically combing my curls out, and most black women know that when you comb thick, curly hair out it turns into this huge afro. So they started brushing my curls out, and my hair was starting to look crazy. So I was literally trying to be a really good sport, and this is my first job and I was just like, 'OK, I'm going to have to grin and bear it. I'm just going to look terrible on my first television show. I'm just going to look terrible.' And Lark came into the trailer and she's like, 'What's wrong? You look like you're about to cry.' [Laughs] And then she took me aside, and she had a zip-lock bag with all of her own hair products. And she said, 'This is your first time working in television. You're going to experience this as a black actress as you continue to work in television. And not every studio hires hairstylists that know how to do [African American] hair.' So she's like, 'I'm really good at doing my own hair, and I bring my own.' So she showed me her stuff, and Elizabeth came over and said some words to me right after that. Elizabeth and Lark were so kind and so sensitive to look out for me. As a guest actor, you just come in for one or two episodes, and you're gone. And they get these guest actors every episode, so they're constantly dealing with new people every time. They don't have to be nice to everybody. They've got their own [stuff]. They just went out of their way to be so kind and supportive to me. So I ended up seeing Elizabeth just kind of in town on a couple things. I worked on 'Quantum Leap,' which I think her husband at the time was the producer on. I ran into her after I worked on the show, and the couple times I ran into her was very, very nice. And Peter, the producer, invited me to the cast party at the end of the year, so I got to see everybody then. And Lark and I ended up playing best friends on an episode of 'Star Trek: Deep Space Nine' called 'Life Support' where she brings me on a blind date with this character Nog that goes terribly wrong. So we got a chance to work together again, which was just really nice because we had a little bonding during that episode. And Tiffany was very nice too; I just didn't have much interaction with her."

Sean Masterson aka Lt. Thompson in "Close Encounters of the Nerd Kind"

Sean Masterson has a remarkable comedy resume for someone that isn't a household name. He worked with people like Steve Carell and Mike Myers at Second City in Chicago, performed improv for a decade with Drew Carey ("Whose Line is It Anyway?" live shows) and created and co-wrote a web series featuring Kristen Wiig, Jeff Garlin and David Koechner. Now doing a mix of writing and real estate, he still performs improv as part of a group with Dan Castellaneta, better known as Homer Simpson.

Three decades ago, though, Masterson appeared in an early "Saved by the Bell" episode as a bumbling member of the Air Force's UFO investigation unit, who Zack and co. try to dupe into believing Screech is an alien to earn $10,000.

Masterson has these three stories queued up before I can even ask:

- "My episode had Screech with a monster mask on, and during the week I'd been hanging out and hearing the kids talk. The kids were 14, 15, going on 21. The language was very colorful. So when we were doing camera blocking, there comes the moment where Screech comes around the corner with the mask on and I'm supposed to think he's a real alien, and then he runs away from me. And we had this big, TV double-take. And I improvised during camera block, 'Don't worry, kids; an ugly son of a bitch like that can't get very far.' Everybody laughed and then got silent. It turns out the producer was a born-again Christian or had recently converted or something. The point is he didn't have a huge sense of humor. I got a call that night from my agent. He goes, 'He's really upset with you, the producer. If it wasn't shooting the next day, he would've fired you.' I said, 'Oh, OK.' The next morning, I went into his office and I said, 'I'm so sorry.' He said, 'You know, certainly I've heard that language before. But I think about the children.' I'm like, 'Have you hung with these kids at all? Because between the F word and MF word and really?' Of course, I just humble-hearted it and said, 'I'm so sorry, it just came out of me. I'm an improviser; I didn't know what I was doing.'"
- "Between scenes, the audience is made up of children, really small children sometimes. We're going from one set to the other and the cameras are there, and this little kid goes, 'Lt. Thompson! Lt. Thompson!' I go over and go,

'Yeah?' He goes, 'Can you play?' I go, 'I'm sorry, buddy, I'm shooting a show right now. I'm working.' He goes, 'OK …'

- "When we were doing bows, and I think the guest cast goes first and they move down to the series regulars, I was next to what's his name, Glossier or whatever, the blond kid. We're all getting nice golf claps, 'Here's this person who played this.' And then they go, 'Here's Zack.' And the place goes crazy. And he looks at me and goes, 'Yeah. That's right.' [Laughs] He gives me a side glance like, 'Yeah, I'm pretty big.' I was just like, 'Oh, yeah. I get it buddy. You're on top. I get it.' So those are my three little fond memories of that show. It was a lot of fun to do."

What followed touched on everything from the way "Saved by the Bell" addressed white male privilege to the impact of the things we watch as kids:

How would you describe Zack's behavior in this episode? I can't decide if it's one of his less-appalling schemes or felony fraud and awful.

It's funny, the whole premise of your book because I was describing to somebody how it's odd to even look at "Animal House" today because even the good guys are borderline rapists. They're borderline the bad guys. Any form of male scheme can be perceived as super negative. I think it's a typical kids' show plot to get us to the place where – to me, that moment with the mask and the Air Force guy is the reason the episode exists. When you've pushed your little thing to the point where the adults take notice and it could mean real trouble. So of course I had to use that line. [Laughs.] Because I haven't watched all the episodes, I don't have a huge perspective on his behavior, but it was par for the course. It's very odd when you realize that wasn't it the same producer that did the follow-up show "California Dreams"?

I believe so.

And that thing was girls in skimpy outfits. I had friends who actively watched that show because it was hot girls, and I think they were in high school at that point. And, like you're saying, the questionable morality of every episode, you add the extra layer that the producer had some sort of moralistic mission kind of makes it an odd thing. At the same time, a lot of Scorsese's movies all get a passing, beautiful grade from the Catholic council because all of his characters that do bad end up dead or in jail. So maybe that was the rationale behind it: "I'll let these kids do anything because ultimately they pay the price." I just thought it was hilarious. The reason a lot of actors did it in the early days was it was a Saturday morning sitcom, so no one's going to see it. You'll get some experience, it's a line on your resume. And the thing exploded; it became huge. It's really funny … Those kids were really relatable. They were very empathetic. Everybody but Zack. All he had was arrogance, and arrogant doesn't lend itself to being too empathetic.

To that end, how do you assess the cultural influence of "Saved by the Bell"?

I actually have a lot of respect and love for the show. It was so discounted; even my agent trying to get me to do it had to reassure me nobody would see it. I think when things hit cultural icon status it's because they're answering an unmet need or something we don't want to acknowledge. It touched on very special episodes without going down that path too often, which I think "Happy Days" did and became kind of [makes "zzz" sleeping noises], whereas "Laverne and Shirley" always kept it nice and stupid and fun. I think a show can get dragged down by trying to overreach too often. And I don't think it did that; it kept it bouncy and fun. It skewered white male privilege. You can kind of almost see it through that lens now. Zack is the poster child of thinking he's going to get away with everything for whatever reason, and he doesn't usually. It had a multi-racial cast, which wasn't par for the course really then. It is now, but it wasn't.

So when you say that about white male privilege, do you think that was intentional, or it's just through a current perspective?

No, actually I think things that are this simple of a show that hit this big a nerve aren't necessarily by design. Because every year 100 pilots are made, 18 shows get picked, blah blah blah. I was in a thing called "High School USA," which was a spinoff of a Michael J. Fox TV movie of the week that didn't go. They couldn't pull off what "Saved by the Bell" pulled off. That was a single-camera, live-action shoot. This was years before "Saved by the Bell," but it was the same thing. They couldn't keep the tone bouncy and fun with enough interesting faces and stories that are for girls, stories for boys. I don't think there was any master plan. It's one of those happy accidents. And writers start writing to the strengths of the cast. They get a sense of what the kids can do. I think the principal pulled some great work in that show. Was Don Barnhart the director or the actor?

Dennis Haskins was Mr. Belding.

Dennis Haskins, yeah. And I think he was great for that role. He didn't play down to it. He knew this was a big moment in his career, and he treated it as such. It's like once something's a hit everybody's like a genius; I've been on enough shows with really talented people that didn't go. They were just as smart. I think a lot of it is out of your control. I watched my "Friends episode" that I hadn't watched, and I never realized at the time what a great cast they were. How the casting was 50% of that show. I think the same is true of "Saved by the Bell." It was a really strong cast, and everybody could play their position well.

I guess part of what I think about is that "Saved by the Bell" was for kids, and the impressionable nature of viewers. Think about if the characters on "Friends" treated each other the way Zack treated everyone. They would have stopped being friends after a week.

Well, again, that's the white male privilege. Why is he the leader? Everything's positioned from his point of view. And things all work out on a certain level for Zack. They didn't so much attack white male privilege, but they certainly questioned it, and they certainly exposed the arrogance, and how many get-out-of-jail-free cards did he get? I don't think in the writers' room they were trying to pull back the onion on white male privilege, and white male privilege is what we call it now, but it's really about the mechanics of growing up, being cool and "Where do I fit in?" That whole show is about "Where do I fit in?" And everybody's always trying to figure out how to fit in. He's not; he's kind of been given Elvis status.

That's a really thought-provoking spin. I admittedly lament the degree to which he can make the same cruel mistakes repeatedly while everyone shrugs it off.

I think pretty people work on a different set of rules. I think there's a degree of shit behavior that people will put up with in the real world if she's beautiful or he's beautiful. And there was always an underlying thing of that. These kids were really attractive. They're TV kids. Screech wasn't. [makes sad trombone noise] Everybody else [felt like] they're going to be fine. My wife always says, when she sees something about somebody having a hard time and they're just gorgeous and they've got money, she's like, "You know what? I'm not going to worry about that person." I think that whole cast you don't worry about, but you do worry about Screech, who not surprisingly had the worst run of it, probably because he didn't have that to fall back on. I think the nice thing is for [Gosselaar] as his career and his life went on, they didn't hold the childhood success against him the way previous generations of producers did. He was allowed to grow up and get another job and be a man. Be an adult. But I think ultimately when we get back to "Saved by the Bell," it's pretty people with pretty problems, but there had to be enough relatable acting and relatable writing, even in the silliness, that kids cared. Because it really had a life span. They're talking about bringing it back again. There's a zillion Disney and Nickelodeon shows they're never going to bring back.

I wonder what most young viewers took away from the way the episodes played out. Was this teaching people about loyalty and hanging onto your crew in high school for better or worse? There are moments I look back on and think that impacted how I saw things.

That's the key to your book. That's the key to everything: That this had an impact on my life, and that's the value it had. And maybe it was good having a born-again guy as the producer who was looking for moments to mine. So much of kids' entertainment doesn't touch anything. Or they do it in such heavy-handed, "we're looking for an award here" moments. And sometimes it's "You don't want to do this because that's the result of that. That's what that leads to." I was born in '63, and the movies that most resonate with me, even to today, are from '73 and '74. Because that's when I went to the movies every weekend, and I saw everything. "Bang the Drum Slowly" resonates with me. You ever seen that?

I know of it, but I haven't seen it.

It's about two buddies, and it's a baseball movie, and one of 'em gets cancer and he knows he's going to die in a year. And he's kind of the Forrest Gump, dumb catcher, and that's De Niro playing that. And his buddy's basically trying to take care of him as he says goodbye to the world. I mean, I'm 10 years old and I'm watching this, and it never left me. It's my "Brian's Song." It's my "Holy shit. This is so inappropriate, but it's not because it gets you thinking." I think wherever you can get that, if you can get that from a TV show, not that heavy, but if you can get moral dilemmas questioning the consequences for your actions, the impact that your cruelty has on other people. I think the problem with "Saved by the Bell" – and I haven't watched them the way you have, but I would say from what you've said is Zack never took any of those lessons over from week to week. They reset the thing so we always had to go back to jerk so they could mine that again.

He never lost any friends; nothing was ever permanent.

There was never a cost for his cruelty. He just had to acknowledge it. But maybe acknowledging it was enough. Now they wouldn't do it that way. Now he'd learn, and someone in episode 10 would say, "Don't you remember that from episode 3?" Because now we tell continuing stories. Back then it was very clear you had to keep everything modular, that could work in syndication, that nothing touched anything because you never knew in what order they were going to show your shows. So the whole business model has changed.

So how much did your episode influence the degree to which you do or don't believe in UFOs?

Oh, it made me very skeptical. If I could be fooled by Screech in a mask, anyone could.

Derek Berry, co-founder of the Saved by the Max pop-up restaurant in Chicago and L.A.

When Derek Berry and his business partners initially planned to open Saved by the Max – a pop-up restaurant identical to the Max on "Saved by the Bell" – for a month in Chicago, demand was, um, considerable.

"It sold out in, honestly, like 30 seconds," Berry said. "We thought the site crashed and we weren't reading it correctly."

The spot obviously was an enormous hit in Chicago and likewise when it moved to L.A., where Saved by the Max enjoyed even more cast appearances as well as visits from celebrity fans (you may or may not have seen SBTM in an episode of "Keeping Up with the Kardashians"). Berry, who has also worked on pop-up restaurants tied to "Breaking Bad," "Beverly Hills, 90210" and "Good Burger" (with a Mooby's delivery pop-up during quarantine) and is planning a Saved by the Max return tied to the show's reboot, is a fountain of positivity, "Saved by the Bell" knowledge and remarkable stories from his time at the restaurant.

What do you remember about watching the show as a kid?

One of the first things that always sticks out to me when someone says the words "Saved by the Bell" is the crazy, over-the-top colors, nostalgia, the '90s. So whenever I think of the show I'm just like, "Happy times, finer times." The show genuinely made me happy. The characters and the level of cheese that happened, we look back at it now and we're like, "Oh my gosh! This is crazy." But at the time no one thought that way. It was like the best ever. So I think just how pure it was at the time and how it's held up. So even though it's cheesy now, everyone's like a diehard "Saved by the Bell" fan.

When you say it made you happy, why do you think it struck a chord with you?

It was Saturday morning, and you were younger and living this easy time in your life. And that's what I instantly go back to in my head when I watch it. I'm remembering those Saturday mornings. I'm remembering the storylines and what I thought of it when I was younger. I was super young and clueless looking back on it now. Like the "No Hope with Dope" episode, I had no idea. I thought it was, like, a cigarette. Just little things like that. It's so funny that it resonates years later in a different way. It makes me happy now because I laugh at how cheesy it is, but back then it made me happy because it was an awesome TV show for people of that age.

When it comes to Saved by the Max, where and when did this idea come from?

I was at a birthday party for a five-year-old, and the owner of Debonair Social Club in Chicago, who gave me my first job when I was doing nightclub stuff, was there, and he was asking me, because at that time I'd become a partner in Beauty Bar, which I still am, he was like, "How are things going over there?" And I was explaining to him the new business model we had and bookings and '90s and nostalgia. He was like, "That's awesome. If you ever wanted to do anything ..." His restaurant had closed a couple months prior and he was just about to open up something else, so there was like this gap. And I think in our eyes it was like, "Yeah, we'll do a nightclub night there" or something like that. But I went home that night and was just thinking, like, "Man, what could I do with a restaurant space? How could I pull that off?" And then I started thinking all the successful things we've done at Beauty Bar, and ever since we do our '90s night, which is going eight years deep at this point, we would do things like "Not Another Teen Movie" and "Scary Movie" or whatever, "Home Alone." But when we did "Saved by the Bell" ones, they were always the biggest. People would always come dressed as Zack Morris and have big, chunky phones. So I was like, "I wonder if there is a brand extension for the '90s night we're doing." We'd always wanted to do this thing called the Bayside Prom, and we were doing it at Concord, and I was working there at the time, and it just didn't shake out. And while we were like, "Man, we think this Bayside prom could work at the restaurant." "What if we just took it over and did a 'Saved by the Bell' restaurant?" And then from there it spitballed: "Oh, wait, the Max. Could we do this?" I didn't even at that point think into it much because I had been doing theme and trivia nights forever where we weren't trying to get licensed or anything like that. So I was just like, "I'll just post an event page up and gain some interest locally." And it ended up going viral. Getting picked up. I can't remember, it was RedEye or something. It hit the wire, and from there it blew up and it was just like, "Now it's real. It's happening."

So how do you actually set it up? How did you get in touch with NBC?

They actually got in touch with me. When I announced – the plan wasn't even as big as it turned out to be. It was just like, "Hey, we're going to do this thing; we've got some availability for a couple weeks. And we'll see what happens." And when it blew up, NBC ended up reaching out and saying, "Hey, normally with these kind of things we would [have reservations], but it seems like you guys are generally coming from a fan-driven place 1, and 2 it's really far down the road [in planning]. So instead of raining on a bunch of parades, why don't why we see if there's a way to work this out." So me and Zack [Eastman] hopped on a plane to L.A., went and met with NBC that Friday, said, "Yeah, we understand we shouldn't have done this, of course, it's not licensed. We didn't really think it would take off like it did." They were really understanding. They were just like, "Let us know that you can pull it off with the integrity we think this should be done." At that time, it was fairly new for them; they had never really licensed out something like this. They normally licensed T-shirts and merchandise. This is a real source of approval; we're going to see people under the NBC IP. So there was definitely a lot of getting to know each other, and once [we had approval and] we put it on sale, it had blown up. We originally talked to them about doing it for a month, and the month we put on sale sold out in, honestly, like 30 seconds. We thought the site crashed and we weren't reading it correctly. Because all the stock was gone. So we regrouped and were like, "This thing is a lot bigger than we thought" with NBC. "Can we do another six months so we can at least get everybody who wants to come?" So we released a couple extra months of stock, and those sold out instantaneously as well. So we were like, "Wow, this is pretty amazing. Where do we go from here?" To really take a step back and really plan out. It moved pretty fast because when I announced it, it had an opening date already. So there wasn't much time for NBC to really push back and say, "Yeah, we're going to need to do this and renderings and fly in for R&D food tasting," like all of our partnerships since then. That one was just like, "Can you pull it off? What's the idea? OK, go for it." And we did. But we announced it in mid-February or so, and we opened on June 1. So it was really fast turnover, but I wouldn't have had it any other way. I think if we had time to plan it, it wouldn't have happened the way that it did. The excitement of how fast it came together, and how unofficial it was at first, made it exciting. Going into some of these partnerships, you can come off as cookie-cutter. Your announcement piece, your branding, it's what's to be expected. When we were navigating that a little bit more at that time, and NBC has always been a great partner, so I'm not saying they haven't allowed us to do things. But since then I've worked with a bunch of other studios who have been more like, "It's gotta be A-B-C." With that first Saved by the Max stage, we were pumping out content that was super left field and really fan-driven. It wasn't a studio speaking; it was just me engaging like, "Do you guys remember this and that and Kevin the Robot? He's going to be here. 'I'm So Excited'? We have a drink named that." It was like for the fans, by the fans. That's why I think it blew up the way it did. People genuinely felt it. That excitement, for me, was just like, "I love the show. How can I get other people who love the show to be genuinely pulled into what's going to happen here?" It was people like me and you. We know those little banger moments: Becky the Duck and having a fake little duck there when you walk in. And leaking out photos in the early periods of it, doing things like that, where nowadays it's gotta be an official press rollout and it's gotta have exclusive photos lined up before you open. In that day, we were just leaking out all kinds of content. It just got people so excited. It was so fan-driven that everyone felt it.

So do you not need to pay NBC for anything?

No, we do. We eventually locked in a partnership. So when Saved by the Max happened, it was unofficial, we locked in a partnership, and we have a long-term partnership, them and us. We've done it in two markets officially with them and are planning some stuff for the reboot right now. We're a licensee, so we pay royalties to them. It's an unconventional model. I can't speak on what it is, but it's a lot different than your normal, "Hey, we have to have a couple hundred thousand dollars out front to do this." We're real partners. We go into it together, and we come out of it together. That's been important for everybody because we're all invested in different ways. For us, we're growing our company; it's a business model. For the studio, it's a major brand extension for a new show that's about to come out or nostalgic calendar play or something like that.

Is there something that was the hardest to do in terms of putting it together?

I think, honestly, just to recreate the Max the way we did; it was difficult. We had a room picked out, and then we just had to go, "OK, now we gotta work with it and make it look like the Max." People were entering through the actual door, and that was the real tricky part. "We need to put this room together that you walk in a different door, and that's a fake door, so how do we make it work?" It was working with designers, architects, figuring out the room you walked into and how to make it feel like the Max but [with a separate entrance] because no one ever entered through the big blue-and-pink doors. It was just a photo prop.

Is there an episode or episodes that stand out in your mind as being the best uses of the Max?

I definitely referred to "Save the Max" a lot when we were building. A lot of the shots in that one. I'm trying to think – when Slater did his famous dance in the tights. Because a lot of those episodes, it was fully stacked with furniture, but in those they had scooted a bunch of it away so we were able to see certain things like the floor layout, what the stairs looked like … and they were such great episodes in general that focus on the Max. And some of the angles we were getting, they were only in one episode ever. Like you could see this random angle and we're like, "Oh, man, that's great." Like "What video games are there in the corner?" And it was only like two episodes where we ever got close enough to actually pick out what video games were there and try to find those.

Were there ever any times in Chicago or L.A. where any people who came to the restaurant recreated something unexpected from the show?

Dude, like every night. I lost track. Every moment of the show ever was recreated, from the Jessie pill moment to full-on dance scenes. The Mario-Lopez-in-his-tights scene, it's on our Instagram, but a guy recreated it move for move. I put him on a photo app and lined them up, and it was identical. So there was just so much stuff that you're like, "Man, I can't believe people thought of that." Someone came as Artie the Lizard. Like came to dinner in a full lizard outfit and surprised his friends. No pop-up since then – and we've done about four or five since – have I ever seen people want to recreate or role play like that. There are people coming dressed as Heisenberg or Ed from "Good Burger," but they're not in character. I think with "Saved by the Bell," there were so many episodes that were very memorable and you could recreate them. You could do a Zack Attack outfit. Even down to the outfits, people would walk in and it would take me a second. Like, "Oh my god, that person's dressed up as Rod Belding, Mr. Belding's brother that was only on one episode."

And there were people coming in with the most deep-cut character recreations. It was literally every night. Since then, at the other pop-ups you hope one person comes dressed up as a character a night or a couple a week. It was every single night at Saved by the Max.

That must make it so fun every day to feel like, "I have no idea what's going to happen tonight."

Yeah. And the amount of celebrities that came in L.A. that booked their own reservations and loved the show – the Kardashians shot an episode here. They reached out to us and were like, "Hey, we heard about your restaurant." They loved the show. And then they just came out and shot an episode a week later. So for us it was like, "Who's going to show up here? What random person that you didn't even think liked 'Saved by the Bell' was diehard and shows up?" And everybody came in L.A. It was people who are so much more famous than any of the characters, it's astounding. I kind of laugh. So Chrissy Teigen came in, and she has gone on to be so much more famous than all of these characters on "Saved by the Bell," it was like if Mr. Belding walked in right now would she be weirded out or would she be like, "That's so cool"? Because she was a diehard "Saved by the Bell" fan. It's just so crazy. Between everything in L.A. happening here, it was really fun, and you'd have to love working here. We would give them "Saved by the Bell" quizzes monthly to make sure they were up to date on their knowledge of the show so they could help sell the experience and make it a full-on experience for the guests.

It seems like there was a wide variety of cast appearances as well. Is there a story that stands out in your mind of one of those being the most memorable? I'm sure audience reactions were varied depending on the person.

I think the way that Mario did it was awesome. When he came in, he put a bunch of hidden cameras in the room and then just came in for service, ordered dinner and sat there eating dinner when we opened doors. People were coming in there and literally losing their shit. It was insane. To me the unexpected factor when those happen are the coolest. And the times Mario came in Chicago and in L.A. were unexpected. I knew, but we didn't tell anybody in the staff, so when he came in it was a lot. The day that Mario came was actually two hours after the Kardashians left. I remember we were like, "What else can seriously happen today? We should just close the doors. Nothing else can happen." The most random characters: Mr. Dewey, Rod Belding, they would get the same attention that Mario Lopez would get when he was here. They are treasured characters, and my mind was blown. We would have Moose and Ox and Nerdstrom. I created "Saved by the Bell" day randomly in August a couple years ago. I was just like, "Hey, this day that the show premiered, we're going to call it national 'Saved by the Bell' day." We were open at that time, and we got a bunch of characters to come in and we did a signing and photos and Lisa Turtle came, Belding, [Max], and it was amazing. And everyone was as excited to see – Melanie Morris, there was a line to meet her. And you're like, she's been off the air for 20, 30 years at this point, but people did not care. And to me it just shows how much that show excites people and that they even remember those characters and they want to take time out of their day and come reminisce with some of these people that haven't been working for decades.

When it comes to any of the celebrity guests, do you remember anything memorable someone said about what the show meant to them?

I think there was a clip on the Kardashians – it's on my Instagram – but where Khloe Kardashian said this is like her dream come true to be able to eat at the Max. That was a pretty big co-sign, not for us but for the brand and as far as people being excited. That one sticks out. We've had other random people who were really, really supportive about Saved by the Max and continue to be to this day even while we're closed and working on what's next. Lauren Lapkus, Paul Scheer, some of those comedians out in L.A. who are really big into nostalgia and '90s and stuff have been super supportive, come in multiple times, brought their friends in, reached out to us like, "Hey, what's going on, what's next, how can we help?" But as far as the big ones, Khloe Kardashian, just obviously because who she is, is pretty big.

So how do you assess Zack's behavior, and if you had to guess how many times he lied throughout the series, what would you say?

[Laughs] That's a good question. Man, what's funny is Dashiell's stuff ["Zack Morris is Trash"] proves how bad of a human sometimes Zack was, right? I'm thinking how many episodes was there. 45?

45 lies total is your guess?

I'm trying to remember how many episodes there was. I guess that'd be low because there's multiple episodes of lies. So maybe 210.

The total for all of Zack's episodes and movies is 329, and the book does a statistical analysis of his behavior season to season, how he treated women, how the show treated Jessie and more.

I can't wait to read it, man. This is going to be fucking awesome!

Thanks so much. So why do you think Zack is so enduring despite having episode after episode where he deceives family and friends for his own benefit?

I think that time in TV, it was [what] a lot of people were looking for. Like the naughty dude who's still kind of a good guy and prevailed at the end and came out with a positive message. Like when he didn't want to date the overweight girl in the episode and the positive light on it. He made himself lovable by the end of every episode. We probably can look back statistically at TV shows, like why did people like Al Bundy? He was a total dick, but we all loved him, and he was this awesome, funny character. And by the end of every episode, he would say something that would make him endearing, and I think that's like Zack's M.O. He did some bad stuff that people probably could relate to, so it didn't make him too hateable, but by the end of the episode he was apologizing and there was a positive message, so you were viewing him as you parted ways with the episode in that positive light.

Do you remember any time you watched as a kid or more recently when you reacted to it any differently and didn't feel that way? Like you thought, "Man, he sucks"?

I love Zack Morris so much and I probably watched it so many times that it'd be hard for me to view an episode differently. Yeah, there are some things that definitely in time you're just like, "Man, that's complete cultural appropriation, what the fuck. I can't believe that was written." But I don't know that I'm looking at Zack's character in that as much as I'm like, "Damn, that's crazy the writers went there at that time." I guess, no, I never really viewed Zack differently, but I guess I look at certain episodes now, I'm watching with my kids, for example, and something will happen and I'll be like, "Ahh." So maybe in that sense, but overall I still really love the character, and I think it's amazing we're pointing out how bad he is, yet he continues to be loved.

Do you have a favorite episode?

I've always loved the Zack Attack episode. I just love how it was shot. I always watched those "Behind the Music" growing up, and it was just funny to see something shot a little bit differently than a normal "Saved by the Bell" episode but to have them involved in it. It was just memorable. The songs to this day, those are bangers. Everyone knows them. And it was on one episode. People just remember those; it's crazy. They play in the restaurant, and everyone knows every single word.

Like 100 people singing to "Did We Ever Have a Chance?" in unison?

Yeah. Like six days a week, every three or four hours. It's crazy. That and "Friends Forever." I had one of my friends cut a bunch of stuff, like the "Snow White and the Seven Dorks" rap that Jessie did. When that comes on in the restaurant, people know it. I'm like, "How do you know that? That's insane." It just shows that people continue to this day to either quote it or rewatch it. And it stays relevant because of that.

Dashiell Driscoll, creator of "Zack Morris is Trash" and writer for the "Saved by the Bell" reboot

To the surprise of no one, Dashiell Driscoll really knows his "Saved by the Bell." When the creator/writer/director/narrator of Funny or Die's massively popular series "Zack Morris is Trash" mentions the "Teen Line" episode and I talk about Zack not kissing the trio of girls who fall outside his comfort zone (Melissa, Wendy and Laura), he hesitates for a moment and notes that, in fact, Zack coerces a kiss on the cheek from Laura but doesn't kiss her himself.

There's no denying that Driscoll paved the way for analysis on Zack Morris' terrible behavior, and remarkably "Zack Morris is Trash" and a spec script he posted (in which "Saved by the Bell" characters engage in a hilarious, "Seinfeld"-esque contest) led to Driscoll being hired as a writer on the new "SBTB" reboot. He contractually can't say anything about that, but he does indicate that he won't be making any "Zack Morris is Trash" episodes about the "Saved by the Bell" universe beyond Zack and Kelly's wedding.

When I prompt him to guess how many lies Zack had throughout the series, he asks if I'm counting the movies and college, and then estimates between 400 and 500.

"Well, by 'Price of Right' rules, I lost," he said. "Maybe I'm including things I suspect he lied about and not outright falsehoods. He very regularly uses lying as a language to get around responsibilities. Not the best lesson."

I read an interview where you talked about catching the show in reruns and your perspective changing when you watched it later, not remembering seeing it the way you did the second time around. What do you remember thinking and feeling the first time? What were the ideas and images that planted themselves when you watched it as a kid?

I guess I kind of associated it with Saturday morning cartoons, which is when it was on. As a kid that was my first insight into high school, I think. That was the first TV show I saw where there were people in high school. I thought it was a fun, zany adventure every week. The images I can remember, things that stood out in my mind were definitely the pink borders for the fantasy sequences and the over-the-top costumes and premises. They did a good job – the show's creators said, which I'm sure you've read all this stuff, that they had to compete with Saturday morning cartoons, so they made everything super vibrant and super big 'cause the counterprograming was animation. Yeah, that definitely stood out. I saw it as a really young kid, and in high school I would come home and it would be on this – it may have been in the cable numbers, but I think it was actually L.A. public access. There was a channel called KDOC, and they would rerun two episodes every day after school, and I would watch that as I did homework. I was not too much of a critical viewer at the time. That was light nostalgia for a thing I had just watched six or seven years ago.

To what extent do you think you or young viewers as a whole thought Zack was cool while watching it the first time around?

100%. I would say I definitely thought he was cool. Again using the term critical, to the non-critical viewer I think he was absolutely presented as cool. Not doing your homework is cool, and having fun … he's presented as very cool because his responsibilities are so low and [any problems] he seems to just skirt right past. Parents can't touch him, he always gets to do the fun thing, he always, always has some girlfriend of some kind in every single episode. He is a cool guy, and I would say the vast majority of viewers I would guess perceived him as cool.

When I look at everything he ever did, some things that stand out are in "Mystery Weekend" his friends don't blink an eye at the idea he could be a murderer. In "The Election" episode, he essentially is Trump. When you look at the bulk of the series, does anything stand out in your mind of him being the worst of the worst?

I mean, a lot of it, the truth of the show, which "Zack Morris is Trash" ignores for comedic effect, is Zack was the worst to teach kids lessons. He tried to learn things by the end, even though there wasn't a whole lot of continuity between what he learned and how he behaved the next week, but the one episode that started me making "Zack Morris is Trash" was the wheelchair episode. The way he handles meeting a human being who is in a wheelchair for 22 minutes is pretty jarring. Even if the lesson he's trying to learn at the end is about acceptance and everyone is equal regardless of how they were born or what they're dealing with, the way he talks to this poor girl in a wheelchair for the duration of the episode is absolutely shameful. [Laughs] I think probably the worst thing he's done is the bathing suit calendar. Because all those girls are underage and the creepy photographer shows up who wants to take Kelly to France, who thank god is on the level. But that situation could've gone south a million different ways. And the fact that those calendars are out, I'm sure a lot of not-nice photographers got their hands on them. And that's probably the worst thing he did in the series.

Yeah, Greg Kean, who played the photographer, said the character should've left as soon as he learned the photos were taken against their will. That said, what lesson

do you think the show actually provided? As you said, there was no continuity, and Zack did the same terrible thing over and over.

It provided the wrong one. [Laughs] The lesson it provided was if you're handsome and blond and charismatic and this archetypal, good-looking American man, you can kind of do whatever you want. [Laughs] You mentioned the murder mystery episode; [that] you can pretty much get away with murder in this country, which is certainly not a good lesson. Even if parts of it are evidently rooted in a pretty grim reality, and that's unfortunate. But this show was competing with cartoons, and I'm not sure at the time anyone was sitting and saying, "This could be a real milestone piece of entertainment for like a decade that people would look to aesthetically and tonally." "Saved by the Bell" gets referenced so many ways in so many different things, I'm not sure everyone had their eyes on how this will look and feel 20 years down the road or 30 years down the road. But that feels like the lesson it gave, which is certainly not a great one. And there were other lessons too in smaller things. Jessie was way ahead of her time, and a lot of her activism that gets played for laughs is pretty spot-on with a lot of the progressive cultural climate for the past 10 years. And Jessie kind of got the last laugh in all of that. There were nerds that were portrayed on "Saved by the Bell" as being like nebbish side characters and Screech the ultimate lackey. Nerds seem to be doing OK for the last, honestly, for the last 30 years. "Saved by the Bell" was a little off on some things. It was a mixed bag.

Do you think any of the toxic masculinity, white male privilege stuff was intentional and making a valid commentary? Or only after society has made small steps are we looking at it that way, and the show was not intending that?

There was definitely some intentions. The way that Jessie is regularly calling out Slater and to a lesser extent Zack, the kind of womanizing … there's a real effort there to say this is the way it should be. But then Zack and Slater just have the louder voices in the room on all those jokes. Their counterpoint is always louder than her point. I'm struggling to think of an example where they really get put in their place for more than 15 minutes. [Laughs] I'm not sure that it happens. But it might, and I might be missing it.

The show's aggression toward Jessie goes up consistently, to the point that in the last high school season, out of her 16 episodes, in 11 of them people are treating her badly. So you're right that she's sometimes a great voice for what's right, but it was also clear how often the show was like, "You said your piece; get out of here."

Pretty much. That's interesting to know it goes up as the years go on. They kind of crawl into their grooves as characters.

Do you remember a time you went looking for something in your writing process and found, "Oh, wait, he's not being terrible"?

The first season of "Zack Morris is Trash," which came together – I guess it would be like driving a train while you put the tracks in front of it would be a good metaphor because I didn't know as I was making the first one, I thought maybe this could be more. But as soon as it hit it was like, "There needs to be another one in a week." As that was happening, it just so happened to be during the fall, and I could see the holidays on the horizon as the Fridays went on. So I knew we were going to hit Thanksgiving and I knew Halloween was in there and Christmas was the end date, and I was hoping the murder mystery weekend could be the Halloween episode. Because that's the one I really remember as a kid. For some reason, the ones that stood out episode-wise were that one and the Malibu Sands Beach Club episodes. Maybe because they were different literally, so it was easier for them to stand out. But when I went back and watched the murder mystery one – and I've done it a few times, and maybe it will be in a "Zack Morris is Trash" episode, I don't know; not all of them quite fit the formula – he didn't seem to be that bad. You're right; his friends do suspect he could be a murderer, but the way he handles an actual murder happening seems to be, "Let's pack the bags and get out of here." I was actually surprised, especially when I was that deep in the research the first season of saying "How far does this all go?" that amidst a murder he actually buttons up and drops it a little bit.

Are you able to explain how your involvement in the reboot came about?

Sure, I think I can speak a little bit sparingly here. Yes, I was contacted by Tracey Wigfield ["30 Rock"], who is the showrunner, and she had seen some of the videos by the suggestion of Mark-Paul Gosselaar. So Mark-Paul Gosselaar had told her about these videos, and we had an interview and she read the spec script I wrote, and it was very surreal that this whole thing that I'd just kind of been doing to do and because I love doing them and people love the videos got me a job writing on a scripted sitcom. That was a tremendous career jump and a tremendous culmination of all that stuff. And as soon as it was done – I was in the middle of making season 5 at the time, I was four episodes in, and I had to call Funny or Die and say, "This sounds crazy, but I have to stop working today because I start a new job on Monday on the 'Saved by the Bell' reboot." And they were all very happy and very understanding. And I said, "As soon as I'm done, I'll make the last six." It felt very surreal to put down the pen so to speak on the reboot and go home and just pick up [Laughs] right exactly where I left off and be in my apartment yelling into a microphone about Zack Morris' antics in 1991.

Between "Zack Morris is Trash" and "A Very Special Episode," you do such a good job getting at the truth of what's going on in these episodes and having fun with nostalgia with new perspective. I think about growing up watching "Full House" and "Saved by the Bell" and believing they were valuable, but now the idea that the family-friendly TV of our youth is horrible can be a cognitive disconnect. Does it ever seem weird as you're going through all this? It's like the sci-fi movie where everything I ever knew was a lie.

Yeah, the weirdest one for me is actually one I never saw or liked or had any interaction with, and that's "7th Heaven." I had never seen a "7th Heaven" episode before, and when I was in the middle of "A Very Special Episode," which I started because "Zack Morris is Trash" was a hit and I knew there was a finite number I could make – there's only so many in the series – and the idea was kind of to branch out. And I was like, "Now people will be watching. I'll reach 'Fresh Prince' fans and 'Family Matters' fans and 'Boy Meets World' fans." And I learned pretty quickly, "Oh, this is just my perspective on TV. I'm just revisiting my TGIF lineup." And a friend of mine named Anthony Troli, who also used to work at Funny or Die with me on the social team, he said, "You gotta see '7th Heaven'; it's the craziest one of these things. And not only is it the craziest one, but every episode is a special episode, and every episode they're trying to teach kids something, and the way they do it is just insanity." And he sent me a link to the episode where Shiri Appleby is in a street gang. Shiri Appleby is like a 97-pound Jewish girl; she is not a hardened criminal. And in her bedroom, she has nunchucks and pills and knives, and it's hilarious. The idea that this is what she's holding onto for her safety or others' is, honestly, incredible. I could not believe "7th Heaven" was a real show and could not believe it went on for 200 episodes and that they would deal this punishment to people even in real life. If you step out of line on the show, you were met with the harshest consequences. Jessica Biel, I think, did a racy photoshoot for Maxim or FHM; she did it, as I understand, to rebel against her squeaky-clean image on the show, and she was kicked off the show. [Laughs] They got rid of her; they sent her to a boarding school or something. The show had this moral compass that was so deranged, and then you find out years later the actor that played the dad had these horrific sexual abuse allegations with children. So that was, "OK, not only is the universe in this show absolutely off the wall nuts and it went on for 200 episodes, but the human beings who were involved in the production were way off. This is a really weird, weird thing that a lot of people for lack of a better word took for gospel." I know a lot of people who grew up in religious households, and "7th Heaven" was one of the shows they could watch because it had the seal of approval so to speak. So that is the craziest one.

But when I go back and see "Full House" and Stephanie, maybe she smoked cigarettes and learned cigarettes are bad, or "Family Matters" and Steve gets too drunk and falls off a roof, it feels silly, and I know the intentions are often in the right place. Even the Mr. Belvedere episode, which is in season one of "A Very Special Episode," it's the big finish finale where there's a kid who gets AIDS. He has AIDS from a blood transfusion, which is a real thing that is happening in the 1980s. And "Mr. Belvedere," they were trying to teach a serious thing. They handled it very poorly. There's a laugh track, and it's not done well.

The heart is usually in the right place in a lot of these episodes. The execution is just absolutely dogshit in retrospect. [Laughs] But at the end of the day I think what is funny to me is no one was, as far as I know – maybe there was some morality police at the network – these shows were all just trying to make entertainment, and occasionally they'd say, "Well, now it's time for a serious one." And that's funny to me too, that they were trying to inject this moral high ground tone into show business. Why? Why do we have to do this serious one? Why do we have to tackle addiction? Because kids are watching, I guess? Because the network said we need to? I don't know; I wasn't in the room at the time. But that tension is funny. And then because there's no real continuity, next week they just go back to someone lost their pet cat in a tree or something. It goes back to right where we were in sitcom land. That yo-yo is very funny to me.

Yeah, the idea that now that viewers have seen them do an obstacle course to pretend they're in the army, what people need to see is them crashing into a telephone pole.

Yeah, correct. In "Saved by the Bell" terms, absolutely. I think there's the season two finale of "Special Episode," I've tried to build to the craziest, but like Punky Brewster sees the Challenger spaceship exploding, which was a thing that happened and a thing a lot of kids had to sit in classrooms and see. I understand the network's interest in saying, "Let's make a thing kids will understand and help them," but looking back on it all, it just feels very odd.

In terms of the way we reevaluate things, art is subjective to people's own personal experience. But in the world we live in now, in terms of discussions of toxic masculinity and white male privilege, if someone's watching "Saved by the Bell" now and having that same twinkly, innocent view of it that we had when we saw it as kids, is that borderline irresponsible at this point? Or is that a silly thing to perceive about a kids' show?

I think everything [Laughs] – pretty much everything ages poorly. I think it's not limited to "Saved by the Bell." You can go back and watch a lot of movies from the '80s and a lot of movies from the '90s and even a lot of movies from 10-plus years ago that the jokes and the way they handled issues and the way those things are portrayed has really, really changed in society and in people's hearts and minds. I wouldn't say it's irresponsible to be naive on viewing, especially depending on your age, but it certainly helps to have some context. And it's a good thing that things change. It's a good thing that the media from 30 years ago feels dated, and it's a good thing that the media from 50 and 60 years ago feels even more dated. Not just in the cameras they use and the clothes they're wearing but in the attitudes and the way people are treated and the lessons that need to get learned and how people learn them. So I wouldn't say it's irresponsible to not have the critical lens on, but I would say it's kind of hard to watch old TV and not [recognize] the values being shifted and the tones being shifted. And I would say that is certainly a good thing. An even better thing would be if we all didn't learn everything we know from television. [Laughs] I don't quite have the answer on that one. I certainly learned a lot, for better or worse, from TV and movies. It's great that things have come so far, and it's such a relatively short amount of time that these things feel on a lesser end of the spectrum silly and on a higher end of the spectrum just straight-up irresponsible.

You're right; people have talked about how something like "American Pie" hasn't aged well. But being in the moment, people would probably look at current

material and say, "Everything now is fine; we've come a long way." Do you feel like in your mind it's a guarantee that when 10, 20, 30 years go on, that's the cycle of things being dated, or things have changed enough that if someone in 30 years tries to look at something from now and do their own version of "Zack Morris is Trash" with something else, is it possible they might have less material to work from?

Well, it's hard to say how TV and movies will look down the road, but I'm confident saying everything we do now will look stupid through the lens of time. And that's across the board. So do your best day by day. Even now watching TV and movies, just due to the current state of the world, I see people gathering in large groups [Laughs] on a TV show that takes place last year and I think, "Whoa, whoa, whoa, they should really not be in that park or at that concert right now." There's a world we could live in where we'll look back at TV shows 30 years from now and kids will be asking, "What is that thing people are doing with their hands when they slap? Isn't that what you're not supposed –?" "Yeah, it's called a high-five; people used to do them all the time." Who knows what the future holds, but I'm confident every single thing we do will look dumb. Certainly way down the road, but maybe as soon as five minutes from now.

Acknowledgements

First, I have to thank my wife, Dana Pais, for supporting me throughout this project, from the start of the outrageous idea and as I watched episode after episode, often marveling at new perspective on the material. I'm so lucky to have a wonderful partner who is on board for ongoing writing efforts like this.

To my son, Theo, who was not yet two when this book started being written but who I hope will one day engage in its style of critical thinking and enjoy processing its lessons. So proud of you and thankful for you always, big guy.

To my sister, Lauren, who read the entire manuscript and provided great feedback about aspects to emphasize and areas that were particularly sharp. Thank you for always batting around ideas about entertainment, even when they don't involve paper towels and the Mallory Gallery.

To my parents, Shel and Faye, who have always supported my writing and my fondness for thinking about material in strongly opinionated, time-consuming ways. Thank you for being spectacular allies and guides.

To everyone who spoke with me for the book – Ed Alonzo, Susan Beaubian, Derek Berry, Jennifer Blanc-Biehn, Edward Blatchford, Blake Boyd, Larry Cedar, Frankie Como, Hillary Danner, Dashiell Driscoll, Troy Fromin, Eddie Garcia, Andras Jones, Greg Kean, Eva Loseth, Sean Masterson, George McDaniel, Stephen Mendel, Patrick Thomas O'Brien, Melody Rogers, Julie St. Claire, Anne Tremko, Nancy Valen and Dion Zamora – thank you for your generosity and openness.

To Trent Koland, for his work on the cover, and Sean Ely, for his work on the book's trailer. Thank you both for your patience and talent.

And to the many people who responded positively to the concept and provided feedback on the writing and other ideas (or helped in other kind, impactful ways) – particularly Brett Schacher, Mike DePilla, Michelle Sweeney, Marc Peckler, Erin Showerman, Mike Posternack, Alex Dowd, Monica Eng and Steve Young – thank you for your time, insight and support.

About the Author

Matt Pais spent 11 years as the movie critic and music editor for the Chicago Tribune's RedEye, reviewing more than 2,000 movies and interviewing Will Ferrell, Brie Larson, LeBron James, Kacey Musgraves, Justin Timberlake and hundreds more celebrities. He released his debut collection of fiction, "This Won't Take Long: 100 Very Short Stories of Dangerous Relationships, Impaired Presidents, Frustrating Jobs and More," in 2019. In his current work at MDRT, he has won numerous Excel Awards (in the podcast and blog categories) and covered topics including cybersecurity, elder financial abuse, and what to say and not say to people who are grieving. He has been a member of the Chicago Film Critics Association since 2006. He majored in journalism at the University of Illinois at Urbana-Champaign and won a William Randolph Hearst Foundation Feature Writing Award in 2005. He now lives in Chicago with his wife and son and, no matter how many times he sees it, still worries that Bryant's throw to end Game 7 will sail over Rizzo's head. Follow him @mattpais and mattpais.com.

CPSIA information can be obtained
at www.ICGtesting.com
Printed in the USA
LVHW110902150820
662970LV00022B/114

9 781735 25040